Two River Farm and

The Cry of the Jackal

Preface

If you are a man or woman; who has ever had to look after another man's child. Thank you.

You have done a great service for humanity. No reward, no amount of gratitude can ever be enough compensation; for it must be something you give freely and willingly; without expectation of gratitude or reward.

Foreword

The names of some of the places and characters in this novel have been discombobulated to protect the individual identities of the characters.

If you share a name with any character in this book; it is purely coincidental and is not meant to be you. No responsibility will be accepted by the author for any offence caused by any such remote coincidental occurrences.

Finally; I dedicate this book to Childhood; the toughest of all human endeavours. It is a wonder how anyone ever makes it, through it.

Chapter 1 Who Am I

Who am I. What am I. Quite frankly; I don't know; in fact I don't think I've ever figured that out. But; to try and answer that question; let me take you many years back in time to 1974; to the place where I was born; "Two River Farm".

A shadow passed overhead. The mamba tilted its head skywards and its eyes immediately spotted the danger. In a blink of an eye; it had lowered itself and disappeared in the long dry elephant grass.

Overhead; the sky sounded like it had been cracked open. I had heard that noise once before; it was the sound of a Martial eagle diving at supersonic speed. In a heartbeat, the mighty bird landed with a thud; no more than a stone throw away from where I stood. It took one look at me, its eye big and crystal yellow blinked in a very strange way. Feathers around the neck flared out, and with one fluid motion, it lowered its head into the long grass for a second, then leaped into the air spreading and beating its wings hard; the body of a dead snake dangling limply from one of its talons.

For a while; I remained motionless, unable to comprehend what had just happened. In the stand-off with the black mamba; my whole life had flashed past my eyes. First the snake had struck me on the forehead; with the force of a small hammer injecting its burning lethal venom deep under the skin, then satisfied that the poison would do its work; it had vanished in the long grass.

I had staggered forward, rapidly losing sight as the venom worked its way into my eyes and brain. Barely able to see, I had staggered across the river and finally, the venom had reached my heart; my heart had stopped beating and I had dropped dead.

A few hours later as sunset fell and it had started to get dark; my grandmother had noticed that I had not got back home from school. She had sent Steven; one of our farm workers to look for me. Somehow; Steven had known exactly where to look and he had found me laying on the pebbles on the riverbank, facedown; my lifeless body turned jet black by the mamba's venom.

He had picked my body up and carried it in both arms; walking slowly without displaying any emotion and unperturbed by the weight of my body. I saw him carry my body right past Auntie Lizzy's kitchen hut.

By then; the sun was setting and streams of light rays streaked past giving a fiery red glow to everything. I saw Violet running down screaming the moment she saw what Steven was carrying; her light-brown skin glowing like fire in the evening sun. She was my cousin, very pretty and fascinating.

When Gogo; my grand mother heard Violet screaming; she had looked up and upon seeing my limp lifeless body in Steven's arms; she had sunk to the ground, and sat on the sand in the yard throwing dust over herself, catatonic, wailing uncontrollably.

"My grandson, what am I going to do; what will I tell your father. What am I going to say to him?".

Gogo; loved my sister and I deeply. She tried to protect us in any way she could. If anything ever happened to either one of us; she would have been heart broken. She always said to us.

"When you father decided to go to England without her; your mother left you two with me".

Your mother said, "There you go; Madube, take your son's children. I'm leaving!".

Just like that, my mother had had left and never came back. They told me I was three years old when she left. I could not remember her face; I couldn't even remember ever having a mother.

Even as I lay lifeless in Steven's arms; I felt sorry for Gogo. I had let her down, dying like that; in such a mundane way, with no-one around to explain what had happened. That was so painful; how could I have done that to her.

As the eagle flew away and became a spec in the sky; I slowly regained my consciousness back from the deathly reverie. I was surprised; how in what was only a few minutes; maybe even just a few seconds; I had seen my death in my head, as if it had really happened.

Death, isn't really painful at all. When you really know you are about to die; you accept your fate with courage; it's the ones that get left behind that you really feel sorry for.

As I started walking; I realised that, at the same time my life was flushing by; my brain had spoken to the snake, I already knew, that I could not blink or move a muscle; because the snake would see any movement as a threat and would strike; so only my mind spoke. My eyes never blinked; as I stared into its beady little black eyes and a hellish black mouth; dripping wet fangs as sharp as elephant tree thorns.

"Mr Mamba Sir"; my brain said.

"I'm only a little boy, I have no quarrel with you, let me go home to my sheep and cattle. I promise I will never come this way again. I don't really want to die; I want to see my father one day".

The mamba had opened its mouth; real wide and hissed back, as if it had heard my thoughts. Its mouth was jet black, velvety shiny and smooth like a brand new toy.

"Don't worry; little boy, you won't feel a thing; it will be quick and painless"; a rugged old voice had rung out in my ears.

"No please!", my mind said.

"I promise to God, I will never be rude again, I will never complain about work and I'll never complain about having to look after sheep and cattle ever again. Just let me go home. Please!".

A shadow had passed overhead and a real miracle had happened.

Instinctively, I started walking, my mind totally absorbed by what had just happened.

As walked, I wondered; what was the purpose of dying, you live all these years, seven years struggling through life and all sorts of hardships and then you get bitten by a snake and in a few hours you're dead; gone forever, never again to see the sunrise, play football or see the face of a pretty girl. It didn't make sense, you could live all these years and be gone in a flash. What was the point of that. Why keep me alive for so long and then take me away in a flash

I took surviving the encounter with the mamba as a sign, that no matter what, I would live to fulfil my purpose in life.

The path veered closer to the river. The grass was green and soft beneath my bare feet. I watched every step. This was just the sort of grass a mamba enjoyed slithering about it in; waiting for the next victim to wonder within striking distance. More often than not; I relied on my six sense, an internal antenna that warned me of impending danger; but after an experience like that I decided to take extra care.

Soon I came across the Sibanda's river garden, with its black alluvial soil freshly turned over and a few patches of cabbages, onions and Chomolia vegetables. Here, the river forked into two streams; one heading leftish and the other making a rightish turn and continued towards our farm and toward the dam. I crossed the river by a low point that also served as bridge on a dirt road that led to the Sibanda's homestead. A clear stream of water gently trickled past the boulders dotted across the river to enable the crossing when the water level was higher.

I avoided going near the mermaid pools further to the right of the river on my own. My cousin John, had given them that name because the water there was dark; almost black and very deep. The water in them never went down all year round; even in the driest of seasons. As kids, we had always imagined if there really were such things as mermaids; this would be their home.

The mermaids; called 'Njuzi' in Shona; were legendary human like creatures that leaved in really deep waters just like these. They were supposed to have extraordinary powers and if they found a child of my age; they would kidnap it and keep him for many years until he emerged from captivity as fully grown man endowed with great healing powers.

I didn't mind becoming a great healer; but the thought of living under water put me right off the idea. No matter how smart the mermaids were; I just couldn't figure out how they would be able make someone be able to live and breathe under water. I hated the darkness and the cold; so this was a big no no for me and I kept my distance from the pools.

I followed the left branch of the river heading west, and in a short while crossed the barbed wire fence of our farm. Creatures leaped or flew off at the sound of my feet approaching in the long dry grass. Sometimes a ground bird flew off; almost a touching distance from me. Birds were my favourite animals. We were forever trying to catch or kill them in anyway possible so we could roast and eat them; but such was their wiliness that years had gone by without my ever managing to kill one.

 Further up; the river all but disappeared, it became a wide splash area of perfect white sand. During the school holidays we would sometimes come here to play in the sand whilst the animals grazed nearby; but I was in no mood to play that afternoon; so I carried on walking barely glancing at the Muzeze tree spread out on the bank of the river where it made a turn left; at almost a right angle. The Muzeze tree was almost in season. Its long pods matched its long thin leaves, making it impossible to see the pods until late winter when they had matured and dried. Only then did they turn brown and become easy to distinguish from the leaves and easier spot and pick out and enjoy the bitter sweet flesh in the dried up pods.

I crossed the the paddock fence again onto the dirt road that ran alongside the irrigated field. I had made it home alive.

Gogo was exactly where I had imagined she would be; sat on a reed mat outside the kitchen in the shade weaving a reed mat to sell. I threw myself into her arms and said; "Hello Gogo!".

She hugged me and said, you must be hungry, "There is a pot of mixed nuts in the kitchen and some sour milk juice. Go and help yourself".

Sour milk juice was the bitter watery mix left over after the 'amasi', the sour milk was separated out. Mixed with a couple teaspoons of sugar it acquired a beautiful stale; bitter sweet delicious flavour; that quenched thirst and filled the belly as well. Sometimes, the sour milk juice would contain so much sour milk it would practically be sour milk; very runny sour milk. With a bit of sugar this was practically a meal, a very delicious fulfilling meal.

Chapter 2 Afrikanda

I do not know why; but every now and again I would do things that no normal kid would do for no particular reason at all. Just a mad impulse to do it; like the day of my encounter with the black mamba; I had decided; instead of walking the four or five miles home along the road with all the other boys from school I would take a short cut across the thick forest and follow the river all the way back to our farm on my own.

This was the forest was wild country where; at night we would hear hyenas and jackals howling through the night. There had even been a story of the Tariro river lion going round. It said that every so often, a rogue lone old lion would pick a drunkard walking back from a shebeen in the middle of the night and devour him . Nobody, knew for sure if this really had ever happened; there had never been a body found half eaten or anything like that. Certainly we had never heard the lion roar at any time. On the hand though; the hyenas laughter from this area; lulled us to sleep every night. The hyena's made a noise that sounded like they were saying "Who are we". They would go something like 'Who're wee, who're wee'; and we'd go 'You're stupid hyenas, shut up we're trying to sleep'. Who're wee! Who're wee! If you say it fast enough, that's exactly the sound of a hyena calling its gang of friends in the middle of the night.

I don't know why I took that risk that afternoon; but I guess, it must be because since the age of four or five I had spent all those years before starting school at the age of seven wondering around every bit of our farm herding sheep with my cousins and most of the time own my own.

I had come across so many snakes and wild animals I had become practically fearless.

My favourite time however was always the school holidays when Uncle Ben and his family came back from town to spend the holidays on the farm. The farm had been left to him and his brothers by our grandfather who had died; decades before I was born.

Five or six families had lived on the farm once; but in time some of the brothers including my father had left the farm and made their homes elsewhere. By the time I was born, only two brothers lived on the farm; uncle Bill and Uncle Ben. Uncle Ben worked in town and only came back to the farm during the school holidays; but uncle Bill lived on the farm the whole time.

During the school holidays the farm was a hub of activity; full of people. Life was perfect and simple. The boys had a simple task; to look after the animals; and the girls helped around the home with the cooking, washing dishes and collecting firewood.

One morning during the school holidays we had decided to take the cattle to the paddock to graze them on the lush valley grass that grew all the way along the southern river. Two rivers ran through our farm; a northern river with the dam and a southern one the main paddock and a pool that we particularly loved swimming in completely naked. The rivers flowed east towards the my school, Fort Milton School and joined on the Sibanda's farm near where I had crossed the river after my encounter with the black mamba.

That morning there was a small army of boys as all the families of the five brothers had come home on holidays for Christmas and to help in the fields.

We drove the cattle to the paddock; but right from the outset the animals had their own plans. Led by the head cow called, Manzuma they headed for the top corner of the paddock. Four farms met at this corner; separated by a main road that ran all the way to Fort Milton School in one direction and all the way to Selukwe in the other. On one side was the Sogwala and Maposa farms and on the other side were the Shumba's and our farm.

Distracted by a quick dip in the Nzwire tree pool we had forgotten about the cattle. The Nzwire tree pool was a pool on the southern river paddock; that filled up with clean clear water in the rainy season and was the perfect depth for swimming and playing in. It was the pool where I had learned to swim in the traditional way; many years back. To teach us how to swim; an experienced swimmer like my cousin Mandla, would trick us into getting on their back and then he would swim to middle of the pool and drop us off his back leaving us there to sink or swim. Somehow; no-one had ever drowned. You just did what everybody else did, kick the feet hard and paddle hard with the hands like a dog and always made it back to the edge of the river. Once over that initial fear; swimming was a doddle.

Only when we had played in the water for so long that we had cooled down so much we were shivering with cold did we realise that the cattle had gone. We hurried out of the water and put our clothes back on. A low bellowing in the distance; however told us exactly where the cattle had gone. We ran up towards the corner of the paddock as fast as we could. We could tell from the type of bellowing the bull was making that something was about to happen. As we got near the top of the paddock we could see that Afrikanda; our bull had somehow breached the fence and was charging up and down the Maposa's fence looking for a way onto their farm to pick a fight with the Maposa's bull on the other side of the fence.

Much to our surprise the entire Maposa clan of seven or eight boys was there. A whole gang of the Shumba boys were also just arriving on the scene. Everyone could see the unfolding scene. It was every boys dream; to watch a good bull fight. Sometimes; although our parents did not allow it; after going to the cattle dip various groups of boys would bring their bulls together to start just such a fight. This fight was happening spontaneously and, I guessed it was no-one's fault; it could not be blamed on anyone.

Across; the other side of the Maposa's fence the Maposa's bull; called Ngorima was posing for Afrikanda our bull; showing off his size; tilting his head down to show off his sharp pointed and perfectly symmetrical horns. Immediately; I could see a significant mismatch. Ngorima was a huge brown bull, built like like a wild buffalo. Every last inch of him was pure muscle; big tall, wide and strong.

Afrikanda on the other hand was a tall slender jet black bull; agile and athletic; every inch just as muscular, only not as wide and not as imposing as Ngorima. If this was a race, Afrikanda would easily have won it, I thought to myself; but this was going to be a fight, not a race. It was more like pairing a heavy weight boxer with a middle weight fighter. So long as the middle weight fighter could dodge the fists from the heavy weight, he would be fine; but if only one punch found him; it would be curtains for him.

By the time the older boys assessed the situation; the excitement for the bull fight was already fever peach. Words were exchanged between the older boys and they broke apart and went back to their groups. The Shumba boys group immediately sided with the Maposa camp. Who could blame them? Ngorima was so big and fierce and was the obvious favourite.

The Maposa boys started cheering their bull; "Ngorima!, Ngorima!"; they cheered.

"Come on Ngorima!". The Shumba boys joined the chorus on the side of the Maposas.

"Ngorima!, Ngorima!"; they cheered.

Ngorima responded. He moved his head this way and that way, displaying his sharp horns. He started throwing back some earth with one of his front legs.

Afrikanda stopped pacing, right beside Ngorima, mirroring Ngorima's every move.

"Come on Afrikanda!"; we cheered seeing how eager our bull was to do battle.

The two bulls sized each other up, displaying their strengths as if to say, "I'm bigger and stronger than you".

Suddenly and without warning Ngorima turned towards the fence and as if; by some choreographed move; the two animals locked horns across the barbed wire fence. Horns crashed and popped like two giant logs banging together.

There was pandemonium in the small crowd, "Come on Ngorima!"; they screamed.

"Come on Afrikanda!"; louder and louder we shouted as the bulls battled each other.

The bulls pushed and shoved each other, crashing and banging their heads up and down the fence. They reached a fence post and without stopping; snapped it in two like a twig. The fence tumbled to the ground.

Now; the animals were facing each other on open ground. Ngorima pushed Afrikanda right on to the dirt road where we stood. We had to take a few steps back to avoid being trampled underfoot the tonnes of beef muscle.

Afrikanda fought back; pushing Ngorima right back to the fence. We cheered loudly; "Come on Afrikanda!".

Round and round, backwards and forwards they went until they were foaming at the mouths; thick white form which soon turned red from the blood dripping down the the animals faces; from small surface cuts caused by the barbed wire. Crash bang, crash bang, the bulls pushed each other. Horns locking and heads banging like a concert of axes chopping wood.

Afrikanda tried to get round Ngorima's defence and plant a horn into his neck; but Ngorima; for such a huge animal was incredibly nimble. He matched every move Afrikanda made with the same lightning speed. He countered Afrikanda's move by doing exactly the opposite. Instead of trying to defend his flank he simply lunged forward and down burying horn between Afrikanda's front leg and neck and with a mighty head jerk lifted Afrikanda's front clean off the ground.

Afrikanda bellowed in agony and turned to run away. He had his back to Ngorima; but without running off; hesitated then switched back and faced Ngorima. Ngorima performed what I could only call; a victory salute. His head tilted down; wrinkling his neck like a an open curtain.

Afrikanda wasn't impressed with this move. He rushed forward and the two bulls locked horns again. This time Ngorima showed no hesitation. He was like a master choreographer. He tossed Afrikanda's head to the right. Afrikanda locked horns again and Ngorima simply tossed his head to the left. Then he charged burying both sharp horns into Afrikanda's shoulder blade.

My cousin, Daniel started crying. "He will be killed he cried!".

"Boys, boys what are you doing?"; came the unmistakable authoritative booming voice of Mr Shumba, roaring like a lion.

"You're fighting the bulls. Don't you know these animals could kill each other?".

"You; Fidelity"; he said, shouting at the eldest of his sons there.

"I'm ashamed of you; you should know better than to encourage something like this. As for you; Bhebhe and Maphosa"; he said addressing Mandla my eldest cousin and Charles, the eldest of the Maposa boys.

"I will be talking to your parents about this. Stop these animals at once!"

He was right of course. I had never imagined a bullfight could turn out like that until I saw that fight. By the time we looked back at the animals, Afrikanda was halfway back towards our farm limping and bleeding from his wounds. Ngorima; bleeding from his own small wounds stepped over the broken fence and marched gallantly towards his herd.

Afrikanda joined the rest of the herd; but soon they walked off to graze elsewhere. He spent the rest of the day standing listlessly in one spot; his energy depleted from the fight. We decided it would be best to let him be to rest and recuperate and left him to graze on his own. I could tell by the look on the big boys' faces; they were worried he might even die and they didn't really want to watch that happen.

We were all; both ashamed, at not only, of letting the fight happen; but also at losing it as well. The Shumba and Maposa boys would be talking about this victory for years to come. It was complete humiliation. To top it all up; we had the spectre of Mr Shumba reporting us to uncle Ben about the bull fight to contend with, sooner or later.

I wondered how long it would be before Mr Shumba went to spoke to uncle Ben. I was not too afraid of the punishment that would follow; because usually whenever we did something bad as a group, we got told off but; never got canned. It was a lot harder to whip eight boys than it was to hit one. Still; it was something hanging over our heads and enough to knock some of the fun out of the day.

It's a shame no man can stop time; because it would have been nice to stop time that day so we didn't have to go home and face the adults. Sooner or later though; your stomach get's so hungry; the sun beats hard on your head and you know you have to get back home for lunch.

Lunch's during summer holidays were always glorious feasts. There was always meat; fresh vegetables and always enough to go around so that after lunch my belly was always so full and it stretched out like a pregnant woman's belly; and even hurt quite a bit sometimes; just from being too full.

That day was no different. There was sadza with meat with that delicious sauce that comes from the meat itself; cooked with finely chopped tomatoes and onions. There were was the obligatory handful of Chomolia. By the time I had eaten a couple of mouthfuls; I had totally forgotten about the bullfight.

The kitchen was loud and lively with many conversations starting and stopping and new one starting up again. There were easily twenty or more people in in that hut that afternoon. The older men sat on small chairs; the women and children sat on the floor, tightly around the room. The fire in the middle of the kitchen floor, having done its job of cooking the meal, was now just dying ambers covered in white and grey ashes.

Each person had their own plate of sadza, meat and vegetables. The plate either rested on crossed legs and feet or was the floor. We ate with the bare right hand; taking a lump of sadza; shaping it into a small ball and dipping it into the sauce, and then picking up a small bit of the Chomolia leaves finely chopped and fried in rapeseed oil or sunflower oil and lightly salted. All the while saving the meat till the end. Nothing in the world was more delicious and more satisfying. The food was so good; it washed away any pain and any worries instantly.

Then out of the blue; uncle Ben suddenly announced; rather loudly; over the voices of everyone in the kitchen.

 "Oh, Oh!; I nearly forgot, we are here enjoying lunch. Have the boys got back from their bull fight, yet?"

We looked at each other. I nearly choked on a mouthful sadza and I could; see John had swallowed a whole chunk of meat without chewing it and was in a lot of pain.

I couldn't believe that word about the bull fight had already got round and we were the only ones who didn't know it. All the men looked at Uncle Ben.

"My God no, Uncle Percy said suddenly sounding serious, I forgot too, do you want me to go and fetch them!".

Everyone; was watching our stunned faces and burst out laughing. Uncle Percy and uncle Sizwe laughed so hard, they nearly fell off their chairs.

Mandla and Jabulani even managed to chuckle a little. I had a feeling, Uncle Ben knew we had learned our lesson and nothing more was ever mentioned about the bull fight again. We had escaped without a scratch.

Chapter 3 The Crocodile

The year I started school; grade one at Fort Milton School. I quickly realised that most of the time, life at school was quite separate from life at home. The two didn't mix. When you left for school you completely forgot about home and the same when you left school; you completely forgot about school. However; occasionally the two lives collided in ways that made you wish you had never been born.

By July or August the dry season was well underway. The skies above were permanently blue; broken only by a few specs of wispy clouds scattered here and there; in the eternal blue sky. Sometimes you had to search the skies to find even a single wispy cloud.

Often I looked up at the sky and wondered why it was blue and where all the stars went during the day. I even strained really hard one day; to figure out if I tried really hard would it be possible to see a star during the day. I thought may be one day if I tried hard enough; I could be the first person to see one during the day; and everyone would be amazed and say 'what a remarkable boy I was'. It never happened. It amazed me endlessly, how at night there were so many stars in the sky it felt like; if you could stretch your arm high enough; you could simply collect a handful of stars and stick them in your pocket. What fun that would have been.

I quickly settled on the idea that during the day the sun was just too bright for the stars to be seen. After all it did not take much to see the moon as a white cloud-like spec during the day, and yet at night; it shown enough, to light up the night sky. I parked the consternation with the puzzle of the disappearing stars for something to figure out when I was older. I could not really ask the adults; because you couldn't really speak to adults. You could only speak to them when spoken to and never the other way round.

The sun beat down hard, particularly in the afternoons when walking the four or five miles back from school. Cicadas and crickets made a cacophony of noise; the hotter it got the louder they sang. They were so well camouflaged that you could look at the spot where the noise was coming from and never be able to see the cicada. That noise was deafening; I often wondered what they were so mad about. As you approached, the spot the din was coming from; the noise would suddenly stop and as you walked past the mad symphony would startup again.

It was not too long after my encounter with the mamba; that one afternoon; after running around and playing football and overheating under the burning sun; a group of us first graders decided to go and cool down with a swim in the river after school. Sure enough when the bell rung a whole bunch of us descended towards the river, past the School tuck shop. Most of the boys in the group came from the reserves; south of the river, called Tariro; the same river that upstream ran through our farm. The other boys came from the farms in the north of our farm. There was an electric excitement in the air all around as we marched eagerly towards the river.

"Can you swim Shaba"?; Bruce asked Shaba, in the sort of voice that said I bet you can't swim. Shaba gave me a nervous glance. I knew that he couldn't swim.

I didn't like Bruce very much. His parents lived and worked in Harare township in; Salisbury (present day

Harare). All he ever talked about was the wonderful exploits he had done in the big city; during the school holidays. Half the time it did not make any sense to any of us rural boys; because we had never been to a big city. He had his own rules and liked to play rough; like kicking and punching, sometimes playfully, sometimes not so well meaning. That day he had not bothered to wear the school uniform. Instead he was wearing a brand new matching yellow safari shirt and shorts. Very nice, very smart; but it was not the school uniform.

I had the distinct feeling that if, I had tried to wear anything like that to school I would have been sent straight to the headmaster's office, or straight back home. It amazed me how some kids could get away with anything whilst others would be punished for even the minutest of infractions. Simbarashe whom we called Simba for short; the most gentle and innocuous boy I had ever met and a group of other boys from the reserves knew of a deep murky pool along the river where they were sure they had seen a crocodile.

We were all very excited. We had never seen a real crocodile before and we were very eager to see what it really looked like. Confident in our numbers we descended to the river. I had never been to this side of the river before and had no idea rivers could get that wide. The river was so wide at this point I was amazed that the same river could be so different from one place to the next. In one place it was so wide; with beaches of clean red sand it looked like it had been freshly swept with a broom. The river's sandy beaches were broken up by so many boulders sticking out of the riverbed; some flat; some quite tall; most as smooth and shiny as glass.

The riverbed was mostly dry except for a few deep pools with very dark water. One such pool was nestled behind a big boulders. Its water was an ominously dark. It looked too deep to risk going in. Piye stood on the boulder, threw some rocks in the water to see if anything moved. There was no crocodile in that pool. A much larger; but flatter boulder, glassy smooth in places from years of water erosion, emerged from the water and formed a nice natural platform for us to take off our uniforms and leave them there; whilst we swam; completely naked.

Soon enough some of the boys had the idea to climb back up the huge boulder on the river bank, then jump into the water. To me; it seemed like a completely insane thing to do; but once the first boy, the most daring of us all, Bruce had jumped in making a huge splash we figured out that jumping in was not going to kill us; so we all followed suit. We all had so much fun jumping off the boulder into the water and completely forgot about the crocodile we had come to see.

We played and splashed around for a long time; racing each other the short distance from the edge of the sand to the boulder. We all knew only two kinds of strokes, paddling underwater; eyes closed and what we called 'Bangu', which involved paddling with both hands like a dog whilst kicking the feet alternately, thus propelling oneself forward. This was a slow and a very exhausting way to swim and you couldn't keep it up for very long. We chased each other in the water to our hearts content.

After so long in the water we were shivering cold and took to sitting on the large flat hot black rock to warm up. Once warmed up; we were back in the water having a wild time.

Before long we were daring each other to jump from an even higher rock at the edge of the riverbank. Since the water was black and it was impossible to see the bottom of the rock pool; you had no idea; when you jumped in how far you would go down before reaching the bottom; or worse, whether there was a rock just beneath the surface of the water, so that when you jumped in, you could hit a rock really hard; bruising a leg or arm rather badly. I had experienced such a thing a few times in the rivers on the farm and I wasn't about to be the first to jump in.

However; there was no shortage of takers; there was always somebody trying to prove themselves the bravest of us all. Three or four boys lined up to be the first to jump in. Once again Bruce went first; then Phil went in and hit the water at almost the same time followed closely by Simba. They all disappeared under the water for a few seconds and emerged a short distance from where they had jumped in. They were laughing excitedly and splashing water into each other's faces. That was the signal that we needed and we all followed; jumping in from the new height and making huge splashes like cattle at a cattle dip.

The great height of the new boulder, a bit more scary, pumped us full of adrenalin and we played with renewed vigour. I couldn't remember when I had last had so much fun.

Bruce; the town boy got up on the rock and announced that he was going to dive in; head first.

I had no idea what he was talking about. I thought that he was just going to kind of drop himself into the water head first like someone falling down. Instead he lifted his arms up in the air and leapt up and forward like a bird taking flight and splashed cleanly into the water with his hands touching the water first disappearing under the surface and emerging a whole distance across the rock pool to the sand on the other side. I had never seen anyone do something so crazy in my life. Even; as much as I didn't like the boy; it was a beautiful thing to see. However; I couldn't help thinking that, if he had hit a rock under the water during that dive; he would have cracked his skull wide open.

I glanced up and saw a group of older boys from our school, watching us play in the water as they walked by. I didn't pay much attention to them and they seemed to be in quite a hurry. We carried on playing for a while.

"Crocodile, Get out of the water, get out of the water!"; Shaba screamed. Shaba had been playing by the edge of the pool the whole time.

"Get out of the water!".

He was gesticulating madly; pointing at something in the water some distance from where we were standing. One by one we passed down the message and hurried out of the water and stood on the rock. Just further on, in the pool was a large reptile heading in our direction. It left a trail of ripples behind it. Then, when it saw us it headed for the opposite bank and hauled itself out of the water onto a large dark boulder.

We started laughing. That was not a crocodile; but a large monitor lizard. The largest I had ever seen; but it was definitely not a crocodile. He made his way onto our boulder, and settled to sleep paying us no attention; whatsoever. This was his territory and he was king.

"That's one big crocodile, Phil joked!". Every one laughed.

Out of the water a gentle breeze was making us shiver with cold, teeth chattering even though it was a hot summer's day. Our naked skinny brown bodies covered in goose bumps like a plucked chicken. We decided to call it a day. We hurriedly put our uniforms back on and went our separate ways. By the time I got home the sun had already gone down.

"Where have you been?"; asked Uncle Bill.

"We had football practice!", I lied.

Even; I surprised myself with how quick and good my response was; even though it was a complete lie. I had come up with it on the spot; on my own.

Chapter 4 The Lost Shorts

The universe speaks, a distant whisper fainter that a mouse tiptoeing across the edge of a wall; a little nudge here, a little tag there; its language is shrouded in mystery; its daggers forever poised, pointed and sharp; its march unstoppable and when it touches you, the results are certain, final and unforgettable.

Nothing could have prepared me for the events that followed our little visit to the river to find that crocodile and cool down with a swim. I got to school early as usual; as I loved school very much; especially in the summer months when the weather was nice and hot.

The walk to school, barefoot; in the summer was painless and quite enjoyable even; unlike in the winter months when the ground was frozen and the feet froze too. Walking on the sharp stones by Tariro river, with feet frozen hard was like walking on sharp nails. In the winter months round May and June; overnight the temperature dropped so low that the surface of water left in a bucket outside froze solid. The morning due on the grass was frozen solid so that he grass looked like it was covered by a white sheet of ice. When the morning sun rose, it made the icicles sparkle like diamonds; shimmering with all the colours of the rainbow. It was beautiful; but impossible to appreciate; because we were so cold the whole time. The thin jerseys if you were lucky enough to have one; offered little protection. By the time; we got to school hands and feet were frozen hard; and it took the whole morning to thaw.

I was excited about seeing my friends and talking about our exploits the previous day. When I got to school; the mood amongst my friends was sombre. Most of the boys had already arrived and were gathered in little groups talking quietly. I could tell from a distance that something wasn't quite right. I didn't have to wait too long to find out what was wrong.

"Bruce lost his shorts yesterday; he couldn't find his shorts after the swim"; Shaba announced to me, the moment he saw me; his voice shaky and nervous. Shaba was the smallest guy in the class who also found all subjects really difficult; but he was a good and trustworthy friend.

"What do you mean; he couldn't find his shorts?"; I asked incredulously.

"How did he get home?"; I asked.

"He walked all the way home; wearing, just his shirt!"; Shaba explained looking quite serious.

I chuckled joyfully, as I imagined Bruce turning up in his village; everyone sitting outside roasting maize on the evening fires outside; seeing him arrive home; half naked like a small toddler and bursting out laughing at him.

"Where is he?"; I asked.

"He is not coming in today; his aunt and uncle came in to speak to the headmaster this morning. They wanted to know what had happened to his shorts; because they were not cheap old shorts. They said that they were not going to buy new shorts for him because someone purposefully took his shorts"

"You boys are in big trouble!"; said one of the older boys I had seen walk past us whilst we were swimming.

By now Piye had arrived. He was called Pearson; but we pronounced it Piyesoni, and Piye for short. He too was a very good friend of mine.

"So what happened to Bruce's' shorts; we asked him"; as if he had all the answers.

Piye was the cleverest boy, in the class a good friend of ours and everyone turned to him for answers to tough questions.

"Someone must have taken them; obviously", Piye replied.

"But who?"; we asked.

"We all left at the same time and there was no one else there!"; Phil retorted.

We all looked at each other searching each other's eyes for answers, for clues; but there were none to be found.

Even though I thought it might have been one of the older boys; I saw walking past; I didn't say anything, because I couldn't see how they could have sneaked by and stole a pair of shorts.

The shorts could have been blown off the the rock by the wind into the water; but that seemed unlikely. Why just his shorts and nobody else's. We had all been swimming butt naked, and left our uniforms in a pile on the rock. The rock was a pretty wide with plenty of room so it would have required a really strong wind to move the clothes which we would have noticed. So; what had happened to those shorts?.

Simon; who was the tallest guy in the class; but the gentlest of boys, always with a smile on his face all the time and was forever telling jokes said.

"I think the crocodile liked those yellow shorts so much; he took them and he's probably wearing them right now, sunning himself on that big old rock."

We all laughed nervously, for we knew how much trouble we were all in, if those shorts were not recovered. The very fact that the relatives of that wayward boy had confronted the Headmaster about the shorts, meant only one thing. Big Trouble.

It was a real mystery; that only those particular shorts and not any of our shorts had disappeared. My mind was working overtime trying to solve the problem; that for a moment I totally forgot about the bigger imminent danger. The bell rang and it was time for the morning assembly.

Once assembly started; I totally forgot about the lost shorts; until at the end of assembly; the headmaster announced that, some boys had taken themselves off to the river to swim the previous day, without permission and without telling anyone.

One of the boy's shorts had been stolen. The boy had to walk all the way home half naked, with his thing dangling in the open like a baboon.

The whole school burst out laughing; except for our little band of swimmers; our hearts in our mouth with fear and panic. Nothing was more frightening than the headmaster; at this point I would have happily taken the bite from the black mamba all those weeks back.

The headmaster; Mr Ncube continued.

"I want you all, to know that, such behaviour will be not be tolerated here at Fort Milton School. Those boys will be punished, severely. Those boys put themselves in grave danger. Going off swimming in open water on their own. They could have drowned, could have been washed away by a flood or taken by a wild animal. No-one; and absolutely no-one is allowed to go swimming after school, before school, or any other time for that matter!"

When the headmaster said this; I felt as if I had been punched in the stomach by a gorilla. My whole body was trembling with fear. I knew we were in big trouble; very big trouble.

"The following boys remain here after assembly when everyone leaves!"; the headmaster announced.

He started calling out the names of everyone that was at the swimming party. My name was called out last. By now I was close to throwing up from fear. My legs felt like jelly; I was paralysed with fear. The headmaster whispered something to the deputy, Mr Mbele; and the deputy whispered something to a couple of male teachers and they whispered to a couple more male teachers. The headmaster then marched off to his office.

With everyone else gone to their classrooms; our small band of intrepid swimmers felt so small; isolated and vulnerable. I had never felt so lonely whilst in a group of other people as I did that morning. I felt small; insignificant; like a tiny ant about to be squashed by tractor tyre.

"You boys; get under that tree and lineup in a single file"; the deputy headmaster who was a big giant of a man; fat and tall; dark as the night; but with a friendly face and easy going manner ordered; pointing at the bell tree; his voice booming like a bull with a megaphone.

I didn't dislike or fear him; because he was the father of the prettiest girl in my class. Her name was Precious and she was like a princess. A beautiful dark princess, tall, slender and graceful like a secretary bird. Her eyes were pure white crystals with pure jet black pearls for pupils. Her skin was soft and smooth, dark and lovely.

When I had started school a few months earlier, I had made a new friend, called Frank promise me that he would not try to ask her out before I did. If she said no to me then he was welcome to have her! The pact had worked; but months later I had still not mastered enough courage to talk to her.

So no; I did not think that, that man with such a beautiful daughter was going to hurt us in anyway shape or form. The worst he was going to do was say; you boys were very naughty; but make sure you don't do it again; now go back to your classes.

We started walking towards the tree, as instructed.

"Run you little scoundrels!"; commanded one of the teacher that had been nicknamed, Mr Big Head; on account of his unusually big round head.

So, we ran as he had ordered.

Three or four other teachers had remained behind, to help the deputy with meeting out the punishment. The teachers approached the tree; slowly and leisurely; chatting amongst themselves. They looked so relaxed as if they were going for a morning stroll.

"You boys like swimming, yes!"

Mr Big Head asked with a wicked smile on his face.

No-one answered.

You what's your name he said pointing at the biggest boy in our group, one of my best friends called Simon.

He must have thought because Simon was the biggest; he was our ring leader.

The ring leader was in fact Piye; one of the smallest guys in the group.

"My name is Simon; Sir".

Simon replied timidly, his eyes looking down at the ground.

You never looked at an adult in the eyes or even the face when they were talking to you. You always cast your eyes on the floor and only spoke when you were spoken to as a sign of respect.

"Right Simon. You like swimming, ha!", said Mr Big Head.

"Six lashes each, that ought to teach you a lesson. From the wall around the bell tree; each teacher picked up a long stick. The sticks had been hidden behind the wall the whole time.

Mr Big Head picked up a stick nearly the size of a baseball bat. I nearly fainted when I saw it. It was multicoloured, painted with patterns on a python. It looked like something you would use to kill an animal with and not to cane a small child with.

"So who told you to go swimming yesterday?"; Mr Big Head asked again.

"No one sir", Simon answered timidly for such a big boy. Even though he was only in grade one he was almost the same height as Mr Big Head; who was a very short man by any measuring stick.

"So why did you do it?"; Mr Big Head retorted.

There was no answer.

"Turn around, stand still. Hold you arms forward!". He ordered.

Mr Big Head stood behind Simon, great big stick; as thick as the handle of a baseball bat in one hand and dragging it in the dust on the ground.

"I said, stand still!", he shouted working himself up.

He took a great big swing, lifting the stick high up in the air and brought it down hard on Simon's buttocks.

Simon screamed in agony, and brought his hands down with palms facing back to protect his bottom.

"Move your hands away or I will break your fingers; Move your hands", Mr Big Head ordered.

"I said move your hands away!"; he shouted again.

Whack, the stick went as it landed on Simon's buttocks.

Again and again, the poor boy was pulverised, all the while screaming and pleading with the teacher to stop.

"I won't do it again!", Simon cried, tears streaming down his face and clear bogeys dripping out of his nose uncontrollably.

"That's right you won't do it again!"; Mr Big Head exclaimed.

Whack. "Move you hands away!". Whack.

After six or seven of those monstrous whacks; Mr Big Head order Simon to stand to one side.

The other teachers had much thinner sticks, proper whipping sticks. Next to be whipped by smaller more humane stick was Piye; then all the teachers joined in the carnage.

Piye didn't; cry or complain. He just stood there; quietly received his punishment and once done was ordered to stand next to Simon. He stood there with his arms folded looking angry rather than upset.

By now my fear had subsided somewhat; even though I was facing quite a beating. The whole thing seemed ridiculous. It didn't make sense to me to punish us for someone losing their shorts. We went swimming all the time at home on the farm, what did it matter that we went swimming after school. Besides no-one had ever told us this was not allowed. In any case I thought to myself, even as I was not rich, it was just a pair of shorts that had been lost, surely he could just buy another pair, why make such a big deal about it.

Mr Big Head was enjoying himself, working himself to a frenzy. Sweat was dripping from has big forehead.

"Who took the shorts; which one of you mongrels; which one of you ugly brutes took the shorts?"; he kept shouting as he trounced the next victim.

No answer. Just screams, of please Sir, stop; I didn't do it.

"No one will own up, ha! You will each get six lashes more; until you talk; I'm telling you!"; announced Mr Big Head.

No one owned up and surprisingly no-one pointed a finger at anyone else.

It seemed that the disappearance of the shorts was really a mystery. No-one really knew what had happened to them; otherwise after all that beating; they would have owned up if they new something.

"You there!, bend down." The deputy head teacher ordered Philip, cane in hand and gave him six flashes, really hard. Then he moved on to the next boy. The boys screamed in agony clutching their buttocks in pain. The canes went up high, in unison, and came down hard on the boys' back and buttocks. It looked to me like the teachers didn't much care where on the back the canes landed.

"Get your hands off or I'll break your fingers!"; they ordered as each kid instinctively covered their rear end with the palms of their hands to protect themselves from the severe beating.

I was sure that when it was my turn I was going to be unlucky enough to get Mr Big Head. Since I was very skinny and even my butt did not have as much cushioning as the other boys'; I was quite certain he was going to break my bones. I was terrified that he would break the bones in my butt and there would be noway to fix them. Bones in the legs or arms; could easily be fixed by tying a splinter around the break; but bones in the butt; I could not see how they could be fixed and I really did not want to be crippled for life.

Once they finished with a group and ordered the kids to wait next to the boys already done. The boys were crying in agony. The next three or four were ordered to bend down, and the beating started again.

"Take your hands off your buttock, okay!"; the teachers ordered.

Smack, smack the whips went. The screams were loud, eight or nine boys screaming altogether made quite a lot of noise.

Then I saw, my chance. In the chaos when the teachers finished with the that group, as the boys that had just been beaten scurried to join the now large group of the ones that had already received their punishment; I followed closely behind them clutching my buttocks and screaming as if I had just been whipped myself. I had no trouble turning on the tears; because with all that beating going on I was already nearly in tears anyway.

I nearly got away with it; but one of the teachers pulled me back.

"He hasn't been done!", he said holding my arm so tightly it hurt. Two teachers stopped the beating and looked at me. My eyes were streaming with tears; real tears; not from pain; but from fear and I was fully clutching my buttocks and I was kicking my legs up and down imitating the boys who had just been beaten.

I screamed louder and screamed; "No; it really hurts". The rouse worked.

"Ah, let him go uttered the deputy", in dismay; probably at my scorn little figure. The teacher who had caught me; tutted; let go of me and quickly moved on to the next unlucky victim. I joined the group that had been done and continued to put on the act; just like the other boys.

When all the boys were finished Mr Big Head; shouted

 "Be quiet all of you; or I will give you six more lashes each!".

With that, the crying turned into muffled sniffles. Then he said.

"I hope you boys have learned your lesson. Let me never catch you going swimming, ever again. Do you hear me?"

Silence.

"I said, do you hear me?"

There was muffled, response of "Yes sir" from those of us all, who could manage to speak through the pain.

"Now go to your classes, and let me never catch you misbehaving again!"

We ran back to our classroom. The lesson and had not started as Mrs Maputo had not actually arrived. I could see some of the boys were having a hard time sitting down. The pain on on their butts must have been unbearable. I smiled slightly on the inside; because it had been a close shave; but I had escaped unscathed. I dared not mention my rouse to anyone, not even to myself.

For some strange reason we never saw Bruce again. Some said that his parents had taken him out of Fort Milton School, so he could go to school in Harare township in Salisbury. I guessed they were so upset about the colossal loss of their son's shorts; that they had decided to take him out of school altogether. The shorts never turned up. No one ever mentioned swimming again, and soon Bruce was just a distant memory. Life went on; but once every so often, I couldn't help wondering why, a pair of pants had caused so much trouble.

The first term of grade one went by pretty quickly. In that short space of time I had learned to read write recite the alphabet, count to any number I wanted.

Thanks to Piye who had expertly explained that numbers were very easy. He had said for any number, you can always think of one larger than that number, and you can go on forever like that. Then he had explained; how the tens, hundreds, thousands and millions worked. When you really think about it; he had said; numbers were very simple. He had also explained addition and subtraction to me before the teacher had. He was clever beyond belief.

Most importantly, I had learned that I loved to learn. I loved school. But; if learning was fun break time was even better. How glorious those twenty minutes between 10:00 and 10:20 am was. It was pure magic.

The break time bell went off and classes poured out into the open. It was a time to explore, get together and play with friends. We headed straight for the playground besides the old Jacaranda tree right next to the first grade classroom. Next to the Jacaranda tree was a small patch of grass with a seesaw and some other dangerous looking climbing frames; right next to a deep hole in the ground that was used for dumping rubbish. It had a permanent plume of white smoke drifting from the middle of it. Something always seemed to burning in that hole.

We played on the seesaw oblivious of the choking smoke drifting through the air; sometimes four, five boys on either side of the seesaw going as hard as we could until there were only two boys left; one on either inside. The two then battled it out until one fell off and the one left was declared the winner.

From the edge of the playground an orchard of guava trees stretched out north for over an acre; crossing the road that ran through the school. The school orchard was strictly forbidden to all pupils and punishment for any infraction was very severe. I later learned that when the guavas were ripe; we were made to climb the trees and pick the ripe fruits. These were then bagged and sent off to be sold at the market.

The school consisted of two main buildings opposite each other, offset; so that the top building to the west started about halfway opposite the bottom building to the east. They were separated by a wide forum of super fine sand and dust, in the middle of which was a small tree; that looked as old as time itself. Its short thick trunk was knotted, rugged and twisted like an old mans torso. One low dead branch from which the school bell hung poked out like an old man's arm pointing at something in the distant past as if to say; look here boys; I've seen things that will make a grown man cry. This is the spot where we had received our punishment for Bruce's lost pair of shorts. If that tree could talk; what stories it would be able to tell.

This seesaw creaked and squealed with the weight of seven or eight kids on it; but each time one side touched the ground and the other side reached the top a kid would come flying off and land on the grass with a thud; but suffering no injury making us laugh out hysterically with joy. This caused even more kids to lose their grip and fall off the seesaw.

It seemed like we had only been playing for a few minutes and the school bell would go off again, telling us to go back to our classrooms. There was only one class per year with about thirty seven to forty five pupils in each class.

Each break time was always different. I never figured out how some kids always knew what was going on in school. It was as if they permanently had their ears to the ground, listening for whisper of news; however slight and they would then pass it down the grape vine to the rest of us.

One break time Piye announced that someone was selling 'cent cools' in school. We ran out to the yard to find out what the excitement was all about and sure enough; there was a whole group of kids crowded around a man dressed in a blue uniform and a bright red cap. The kids were all clamouring. "Me, me, me!."

Already some kids were dispersing; one holding a small plastic bag the length of a small half ruler, filled with a brightly coloured drink. Some plastic tubes were blue, some green; some orange, and some raspberry. Every kid with the bright coloured drink was being pursued by his close friends. Three girls who I recognised as Patricia, Diana and Vimbai were sharing one. One would take a sip and then pass it to the other, then back to the first. They looked like they were having the time of their lives.

"Does anyone have any money?"; asked Shaba.

Even though I knew that I had no money, I judiciously checked my pockets. Needless to say I didn't find any money. Luckily enough; somehow, Frank in our little group had a penny and bought a blue cent cool and shared it with us just like the girls had been doing.

The taste was amazing, one sip hit the back of my head as if something had exploded in my brain. My vision became sharper, my hearing perfect. I was immediately euphoric. It was literally the best thing that I had ever tasted.

"How much are they?"; asked Phil.

"They are one cent, that's why they call cent cools", explained Piye.

For the first time in my life, I understood what money was for. I dreamt of tasting another cent cool. I would do anything to get my hands on one a cent so I could get myself one of those brightly coloured cent cools. I imagined how wonderful it would be to find five cents on the ground somewhere; I would use it to try all the different colours starting with the green one. Despite the name; they didn't really cool you down, they were just very delicious.

I loved school more than anything in the world. It was a place I could have so much fun with so many friends; a place where everything was well organised and there were rules for everything. It made complete sense to me; when you should come to school, what you should wear, they even lined us up at assembly and checked if we were clean and had brushed our teeth. So on the way to school, we would always stop by a bush somewhere along the way, break off a small twig, chew the end until it was nice and fluffy, then use it to brush the teeth and toss it in the thick grass when done. School was a place with order, and I liked order.

However; even with, all those rules; I soon found out things had a habit of going wrong and always catching us unawares. It was as if trouble was always waiting around the corner a little distance away; a little slip here and a little slip there, then bang; trouble.

One morning after break time we had just got back to the classroom, the teacher was busy marking our exercise books as she did every so often. The classroom quickly descended into a buzzy drone of background noise. I was busy drawing pictures in my art book when I happened to look up and and see Phil bothering Precious; who I was secretly besotted with. She was pushing him and telling him to go away. He kept going back laughing and doing more to annoy her.

Then he went behind leaned down resting his arms on her shoulders and whispering something in her ear. She turned around and pushed him away. He laughed joyously; went back to his sit; but by that time I was already halfway across the classroom and got to his desk as he was sitting down.

"What do you think you're doing?"; I asked and slapped him really hard on the cheek.

There was loud gasp from everyone in the class mixed with laughter and cheers from some. I walked back to my desk and sat down.

Precious and her friends looked at me; rather approvingly and laughed.

Phil's eyes were bloodshot red with anger. Only after I had sat down; did I realise what I had just done. The gravity of the situation was quite dire. Phil, was a big lad, much bigger than I was with a natural aggressive bone in his blood.

As I sat down back at might desk I had this deep sinking feeling I had gone a little bit too far and I had no idea what had possessed me to do such a thing. My heart was beating very hard. At the same time; I kind of felt pleased with myself. I had fought for someone I liked, and I felt that I had done the right thing.

No sooner had I sat down than Mrs Maputo called my name out loud and beckoned me to her table with her pointing finger. I stood up and marched up to her desk and stood in front of her.

She was the wife of the headmaster; and yet they didn't share the same surname. She was a plump woman of about the same age as many of my Aunties who were probably in their thirties at that time. Her size and figure reminded me of one of my many Aunties; but completely on the opposite spectrum of the skin tone. She was as light skinned as you could get without actually having no colour at all; I thought to myself as I glanced at her and looked at the floor, ready to be told off. Her face was smooth, and without a single blemish. Her bare legs were perfectly smooth and without even a single scar. This told me that she had lived an easy life; never having to work hard in the field under the burning hot sun.

Everything, about her screamed; a leisurely luxurious life. She sat behind the teachers table as if she was being held down by the very tight blue dress that she was wearing. The dress was open at the top so that her shoulders were bare. Around her neck she had a neckless with white balls that started larger in the middle and got smaller and smaller as the went up around her neck.

"Your aunt told me that you're a very naughty boy at home, Nkosi. Now; I can see why. I will have none of that in my class. Do you hear me?"

I nodded without looking up. I knew exactly which Aunt would have said that. I was a bit shocked because I had no idea that the two of them knew each other and had actually spoken about me. I realised that; if that was the case then I was as good as dead.

"Go and stand outside until you learn how to behave!"; she ordered.

I stood there for a second; not really understanding what she was telling me. I was thinking to myself. Was that some sort of punishment, to go and stand outside. Punishment was to be smacked or slapped or pinched; standing outside was nothing. So, I stood there wondering; well; what's the punishment!

"Go!"; she ordered again; pointing at the door and shoeing me with her hand as if I was some kind of a mangy dog.

"And, shut the door behind you!", she ordered.

So, I went outside like a wounded puppy with; a tail between its legs. As soon as I shut the classroom door behind; I was overcome by how lonely and isolated I felt. It was like being severed from my friends. I felt like my whole life was collapsing around me; like the whole world was moving forward without me. It was a deeply uncomfortable feeling, one that I had fought for years whilst following those sheep around; day in day out, before I was old enough to start school.

I looked left and right and there was not a single soul in sight. The sun was shining and there was not a single cloud in the sky as usual. There was an eerie silence, not even the birds were singing; nothing was moving, not even the leaves on the lone old bell tree. Hundreds and hundreds of children in their classrooms learning, so they could one day become doctors, teachers, pilots or nurses and here I was; stuck outside and not allowed to do the same. I was terrified, the isolation was unbearable.

Was this the end, I had made to grade one and now I was being excluded from class after a few months. My whole world had come crashing down, and I wanted to get back in. I decided to knock and get back in and tell her I had learned my lesson. First I knocked gently, no answer, then

I knocked a bit louder, no answer, then I pounded on the door. I heard rapid footsteps from inside approaching the door. I waited. The door swung open, Mrs Maputo stood in the middle of the door with one hand on the door knob; and the other on her waist.

She looked livid. Her face had literally gone red.

"What are you doing?"

"Come here you naughty boy!".

She grabbed me by one ear and frog marched me back to her table.

"Hold out your hand"; she ordered.

I did as she ordered.

She took out short fat stick from a draw in the table. I knew what was coming and I withdrew my hand.

"Hold out your hand, I said!"; she ordered demonstrating with her left hand.

I held out my left hand with the palm facing upwards.

She lifted the short stick up and brought it down hard on my hand really hard. It stung like the devil.

One, two, three, four, five, six the stick came down as she mouthed the numbers with her lips.

"Now go and and sit down. If you ever misbehave in my class again, I will send you to the headmasters office. Wait till you Aunt hears about this!".

Distraught and my pride hurt; I sat down sobbing like a baby; but I didn't care what the other children thought; I was just glad to be back in the classroom and vowed to never get on the wrong side of Mrs Maputo again.

Mrs Maputo lived up to her promise and soon word got home that I had tried to smash the door in and nearly broken it. All lies of course; but I didn't my mind as long as I could stay in school.

Besides; I had long got used to Aunt Ruth spreading lies about me. For a few brief seconds my mind drifted to the picture of my aunt and uncle back on the farm. With her it was a love hate relationship; but he was relentless. My first memory of his sadistic cruelty was taking me to the kraal one day to milk the cows. It had rained all night and the cattle had churned the cattle kraal ground into a putrid black squelchy quagmire of mud and cow dung and cattle urine.

He had ordered me to go into that murky mess; bare foot and drive one of the milk cows out so it could be milked outside on the nice green grass. I had climbed over the kraal and stood on a dry patch on the side looking at the pool of smelly, murky cow dung and mud. There were all sorts of bugs and worms I had never seen in my life before, crawling about and swimming in that quagmire. I could see hundreds of tracks left by the bugs as they skimmed the muddy surface and dived below the surface. I could see worms as thick as my thumb with long thin tails crawling on and in the mess.

There were worms as long as a ruler swimming about, there were round worms, flat worms, segmented worms, smooth worms, there were bugs with hard shells and bugs with soft skin. There were all kinds of bugs in there. You could see bubbles of air welling up and sticking out where a bug was underneath breathing. You could see streaks left by the bugs where they had crawled across the murky cow dung.

I had been quite sure that the moment I stepped in that mess; those bugs would simply converge towards me; burrow into my feet and crawl all the way up the veins of my legs into my body and eventually my heart and brain and I would be dead by the end of the day.

"Get in"; he had ordered whilst he and Steven, one of the farm workers stood watching me from the edge of the kraal outside. I had noticed that he was wearing a thick black raincoat and green gumboots, all impervious to water and bugs and yet he was sending me in there; barefoot to die.

"I shook my head, no!". I had said; sure that the moment I stepped in that muck all the bugs would converge upon my feet and feast on my legs.

"I will come in there and beat you to a pulp; get it", he had shouted, whacking the side of the kraal with a cattle whip.

The sound of the whip whacking the side of the kraal had been enough to make me take my first step in the muck.

It was gross. The mud was warm and I could feel things on and around my feet and legs half way to the knees. Squelch, squelch the mud went; getting between the toes right up to the middle of my sheen. I drove Manzuma, one of the milk cows out and got out as soon as she was out, only to have to repeat it again for the next cow, Mganu; but on this occasion something had buried its teeth into my foot and I had screamed in agony.

When eventually, I limped back across the river and I had washed my feet and checked the bite. I had been relieved to find out it was only a thick elephant thorn buried in my foot and broken underneath the surface and not a bite from one of those creatures. Removing the thorn was quite easy, I just used another thorn taken from a thorn tree to dig out the broken thorn from my foot. The relief was immediate. It was so strange how something so tiny as the sharp end of a thorn; broken not even too deep in the foot would be so uncomfortable and make it impossible to walk on that foot until it was taken out.

They say it never rains but it pours; the very next day about exactly the same time disaster struck again. It was break time and we had gone outside to play and having a wonderful time as usual; expecting nothing to go wrong.

We been running around the Jacaranda tree when I bent down to pick up a shiny button that someone had dropped, when from nowhere someone buried their foot in my backside and I landed on my face in the dirt. I cut my lip and it hurt like mad. There was laughter all around. The boys from the reserves were cheering Bruce for a well executed kick. He was lapping it all up. I got up and my eyes locked on him nestled amongst his friends.

I lost all control; my anger was unbounded. I ran towards him at high-speed and at the last second I've flicked my foot forwards and drove it straight into his stomach. He was thrown back and landed on his bottom. He clutched his stomach and rolled over in agony. His friends from the reserves looked at him on the floor and looked back at me with mouths wide open. I guess they hadn't expected that response from me.

It was my turn. There were cheers for me all around from my friends. I knew what it felt like to be kicked in the stomach; if done right, it hurt like hell. When the pain subsided Bruce got up; dusted himself; angry and ready to kill me.

Fight, fight fight!; everyone cheered.

I was surprised by how clearly I was thinking. In my mind's eye I could see exactly what he was going to do next and I could see exactly what I was going to do in response. I surprised myself because I wasn't at all scared. Not even a bit.

He came at me just as I had predicted and tried to punch me in the face. I moved my head to the side and his fist went flying past. I aimed for his nose; because I knew if I made him bleed; that would be game over for him and the fight would be over.

I sent my fist forward as hard as I could. I missed his nose; but my fist landed on his lips and split his bottom lip open and it started bleeding.

The bell went. He wiped his mouth and looked at his hand turned his head to the side and spat out red foamy red spit.

I will kill you, he said backing away slowly. His words did not match his actions and I hoped he had got the message and would not bother me again. We all started walking back to the classroom.

As I walked back to the classroom and the adrenalin started to subside; I realised the gravity of my situation. From being virtually friends with everyone, I had made many enemies in two days. Bruce was taller and bigger than I was. Physically he was a better species in every way. He was a semi town boy who came from a well-to-do family even though they lived in the reserves.

I didn't like him very much anyway; because he was always a bragging about something or other, especially all of his exploits in Harare. He talked about fighting a lot and beating up other kids in Harare. I never understood why he had to beat up anybody; nor how anybody had time to go around beating up anyone else. I spent all my time working on the farm either following the sheep and the cattle or working all day long in the fields. I had no idea what kind of life he had or was living up there in Harare.

Even though; the fight had ended with me landing a nice punch; I felt that I had been lucky; saved by the bell as it were. If the flight had gone on for much longer I wasn't sure what would have happened. Even after receiving a bloody mouth, he was still threatening. Most kids would have run away crying; but not this boy. He was still threatening to kill me; so I expected trouble in future.

Bruce threatened me a couple of times after that; but for some reason it never quite developed into a fight. We kept a respectable distance from each other and never got into any disputes. By the time we got to the swimming incident the past had been long buried and we were almost friends again.

Two horrible incidents out of nowhere and then nothing. I often asked myself where trouble came from; where it was made and when did it choose to show itself and why. Trouble like a wily monster, hid in the shadows growing fatter and fatter; bolder and bolder. After a while when it had fattened up on your forgetfulness and all the good time you were having; it struck mercilessly; and when it did, it seemed like the world was coming to an end for you. Then all of a sudden; as quickly as it had appeared, it would again vanish into the shadows. I soon learned that you could not avoid trouble; try as hard as you might, it always came for you, the only thing you could do was wait and hope that hope that when it showed up it didn't kill you.

So it was at last we came to the end of the term. One morning Mrs Maputo told us that the next day there would be tests. There would be an English test, a Maths followed lastly by a Shona test.

There had been gasps from some of the kids in the class.

What is a test; I asked Piye, who sat next to me and was the cleverest boy in the class and seemed to have an answer to everything.

He explained that in a test the teacher writes questions on the board and we had to answer the questions correctly without asking anyone or looking for the answers in a book.

I blinked a couple of times as I tried to understand what he was talking about.

"Questions, questions about what"; I asked; I had never come across the idea of a test before.

"Questions about everything we have learned so far this term"; Piye explained.

Oh, I see, I replied, a little bit deflated. I didn't see what the fuss was all about.

This doesn't seem so bad I thought to myself. It seemed a bit pointless; as of course if you ask me about something I've learned already, then I would definitely be able to answer it correctly. It would make more sense to ask me about something I had never, seen before and see what my answer would be then teach me it; so that I know what I didn't know before. That to me made far more sense; but what did I know. I was only seven.

The next day; when we got back to class from recess the whole blackboard was covered in questions from one to thirty. It was the English test.

Mrs Maputo explained that we had to answer the questions in one hour; no talking or looking at the answers in the book.

Then she ordered us to start.

I was about half the way through the questions when Piye raised his hand up and declared that he had finished.

"Very good Pearson!", said Mrs Maputo smiling graciously; she walked up to him and collected his exercise book.

When I realised that Piye had finished so quickly and the gracious response he had received from Mrs Maputo. I tried to answer the questions more quickly so that I could finish next; but before I could even answer the next question Precious; the deputy head's daughter had raised her hand and proudly announced that she'd finished.

My heart started racing as I got really annoyed at being beaten in the race to finish. So I started racing through the questions reading as fast as I could. But; four or five more kids finished before I got to the last question. I was positively infuriated with myself; I had always been very sure of myself; but when five or six kids finished that test before I did it made me question my abilities and that made me very uncomfortable.

Finished; I raised my hand. Mrs Maputo walked towards me, her red high hill shoes going knock, knock, knock on the hard shiny cement floor of the classroom. I swear I could see a slight smile on her face. Was she pleased; because I had finished early; I wondered. Aware that any intransigencies in her class were really dangerous; I had buckled down and done everything I could to; if not win her favour at least not do anything to annoy her.

So what now that I finished the test. I sat there twiddling my thumbs playing with the pencil with nothing else to do. You couldn't leave the room or talk; because that would have disturbed the other children.

After a while Mrs Maputo, announced.

"You have 10 minutes to finish, 10 minutes!"; she repeated.

I looked around and there was panic among some faces. I could good see Shaba one of my friends was still looking at the starting edge of the board. Which meant that he had not done the middle or the last part of the board. With ten minutes left he had no chance of ever finishing.

"Five minutes until the end of the test, five minutes, finish up", yelled Mrs Maputo

"Time up. Put your pencils down, no more writing. If you carry on writing, I will deduct a mark from your final score".

Mrs Maputo went around collecting all the exercise books from everyone and immediately started marking them. We were allowed to talk. She went into her on world; ticking, crossing and writing in the exercise books. I had a sense; that she wasn't so bad after all.

Piye leaned over and asked me what I put down for one of the questions which had been the hardest question in the test. I told him what I put down and he immediately said that I was wrong and to check the text book.

He grinned happily. He seemed very pleased with himself that he had got the answer right and I had got it wrong.

The penny dropped and I realised something. I realised that these tests weren't just there for fun; or to please the teacher. They were some sort of competition between the pupils to see who was the best.

He was smiling because with my answer wrong he had won and I had lost. I realised something else; he had asked me; because he saw me as competition. For the first time; although I had always considered Piye as a friend I felt a sudden desire to punch him on the nose.

I was angry with myself for getting the question wrong. The moment I realised what was at stake; I wanted to do better than him and wipe his smug smile off his face; but I realised this was a tall order. He was the smartest boy in the class. Up until then the only competition that mattered to me was; whether I could win a fight if challenged by someone. I had always thought that we went to school to learn so we could get good jobs when we grew up, I had not realised it was a big competition as well.

For three days in a row, at around the same time we had a different test. We had English, followed by Maths then lastly Shona. Then it was all over.

The last day of the team arrived soon after the tests. Instead of recess we all had to go to assembly outside; not in the usual place; but just sit on the grass under the jacaranda trees by the see-saw. The whole school sat under the jacaranda trees. We were spread all the way to the edge of the orchard. The older pupils had been asked to put a row of chairs in front, from the class rooms for the teachers.

The teachers sat in front of us on the chairs whilst we all sat on the ground. The sun was warm and comfortable. I could smell the smoke from the burning pit; but it didn't bother me anymore. The Headmaster stood up and gave a resounding speech. He said most of all he had been impressed with the cleanliness of the school.

Then he said I'll pass you over to the deputy headmaster to announce the end of term results.

"Mr Mbele, please". The head master said turning to the deputy.

The deputy head Mr Mbele, stood up.

"Thank you headmaster. I will start with grade sevens. I will announce the position for each pupil in grade seven starting with the last place"; Mr Mbele said, his booming voice loud and clear for everyone to hear.

He started by saying, in last place number thirty seven and called out a name all the way till number four.

Then he said, "for the next three people when I call out your name come up here and collect your certificate".

In position three, position two, in position one. Two big boys and a tall girl stood up and approached Mr Mbele who shook their hands and gave them each a certificate. They looked so proud and stood in front of us holding their certificates with a red stamp on them.

Then Mr Mbele announced the grade six results, the grade five, four, three, two and finally my grade; grade one. In the last position number forty three. My heart was by now in my mouth. I still hadn't realised until then that the tests had been important on an apocalyptic scale.

Number twenty seven and so on Mr Mbele carried on calling out names.

My name had not been called by position ten, nor by position five. By now, my heart was pounding so hard I could hear it in my ears. My whole body was trembling as if gripped by some sort of fright; but I was not frightened. I had no idea what to call this new feeling.

"When I call out the names of the next three, please come up here and collect your certificates"; Mr Mbele announced.

"In third position, Precious Mbele".

It was the name of his beautiful daughter, he looked up proudly as Precious stood up and started walking up towards him, with a big proud smile on her face.

"In second position, Nkosiyetu Bhebhe".

"In first position Pearson Mombeshora".

I forgot to get up until; Piye kicked me on his way to collect his certificate and I followed him, shaking like a leaf.

As I walked up I caught Mrs Maputo's eye. She was smiling proudly. My heart was beating like drum in my chest. Mr Mbele shook my hand and handed me the certificate. I held it up as the rest of the school clapped. I could feel the hairs at the back of my head standing. I was so happy I wasn't a dum kid. Maybe, just maybe with a bit of luck, I was going to be able to make something out of my miserable life.

Mr Mbele was a big man. He had a big smile on his face and his eyes never left Precious; neither did mine. He had a big benign face which explained to me why Precious was always so happy. Precious was dark like her father; but pretty beyond belief. He lifted her up proudly and put her down again.

"Well done, Puree"; he said to his daughter with beaming smile on his face.

Then he looked at me and said.

"Well done; Bhebhe"; using my last name as a sign of respect. The fact that he; used my family name made me like him instantly. He shook my hand again.

Lastly it was Piye's turn. Piye was tiny, even shorter than I was and I wasn't one of the big guys. But what he lacked in height, he more than made up in brains. He was super smart.

Mr Mbele; announced that he was the only boy who had ever passed with full marks for everything, without a single wrong answer in all the years he had taught at Fort Milton school.

"Well done Pearson. For that we've decided to give him something special" ; he said and he handed him a tiny silver trophy.

"He will be a great ambassador for the school. Well done he, repeated", and started clapping his hands. The whole school joined him in congratulating Piye.

The head master stood up again and dismissed the school. "Go home and enjoy your holidays and come back next term, nice and refreshed"; he said.

The end of the term, the mood was both sombre and exciting at the same time.

For every good; there is evil lurking on the side. Some kids had a different agenda. Rumour had been circulating all morning that there would be a last school day reckoning. The last school day reckoning, I had heard Phil whispering to Enoch; another boy from the reserves that I tried to have as little to do with as possible; that they settled the score by beating up anyone who had ever bothered them during the term.

I was not in a mood for a fight, especially after what had just happened. I just wanted to get home as quickly as possible and tell everyone that I had come second in my class. I didn't take any chances and I found my cousin; John and we headed home together with the Shumba boys who lived next door farm.

John, had come first in his class; beating Elliot, the headmaster's son. He had done it so many times he didn't seem that much excited about it. We all found each other; quickly and walked home together reaching home in time for lunch.

When we got home everyone was outside, across the yard, just past the Uncle Ben's house; next to the sterile guava trees. I had no idea how they had known we'd be arriving then.

It was a bright afternoon, the sun was shining; but it was neither hot nor cold; it was just perfect. I was feeling very proud, even as a seven year old I knew that getting an education would be the single most important thing in my life, and now that I had found out I had a knack for it, I was eager to share the good news.

The family were waiting for us; excited to find out what we had come in our tests. To my pleasant surprise everyone's was so happy when I told them my success and showed them my certificate. Even Auntie Ruth, John's mum lifted me up threw me up in the air catching me and saying well done.

5 School Holidays

It was such a happy occasion arriving home with good results. For about an hour we were treated like heroes. We had a delicious lunch of sadza and sour milk and enjoyed all the conversations around the kitchen fire. Auntie Ruth; reminded us that the town people would be arriving the next day.

The arrival of the town people was the most exciting thing in our lives. Auntie Thembi had already arrived from town ahead of everyone. We Loved auntie Thembi. She was kind and and very gentle. She never said a bad word about anyone. She was the youngest of Gogo's seven children; four older brothers and two elder sisters. One of the sisters had died and and her grave was in a remote corner of the farm. The other sister was; the eldest was called Auntie Lizzy; followed by four brothers uncle Ben, uncle Bill, uncle Julius and my father Cornelius who had emigrated to England.

She alone was unmarried and was fast approaching the time when it would be difficult to get married because she would be considered too old. She didn't seem worried about that so no-one ever mentioned it. Anyway; we loved her just the way she was.

We didn't dwell on our successes for too long; because the same afternoon we were back on the farm looking after the sheep and the cattle. During the school holidays herding cattle and sheep was a full time occupation without a moments reprieve. By the end of the day, school was a distant memory.

We spent the rest of the afternoon at the top of the paddock by the Muzeze tree. The sheep and cattle where remarkably good. They did that sometimes; stay in one place grazing quietly, which gave us time to play and enjoy ourselves climbing trees; stalking and shooting at birds with our catapults.

We liked the Muzeze trees; this one was one of many dotted around the farm; but this one was the biggest. It was surrounded by thick bushes and other trees all compact within a very small space of no more than a hundred paces. The only problem was that John had once seen a snake there he thought was a black mamba; the most poisonous snake in the world as far as we were concerned.

When it came to snakes, we didn't take any chances. So before climbing any tree we would scan the whole area for any signs of snakes and only after making sure there were none did we climb up the tree. We played in the tree the whole afternoon; climbed up to the very top of it, where we could see all round the farm.

The next day we took the cattle and sheep out early; overwhelmed with excitement for the town people who would be arriving that day. For a brief moment my mind went back to school. I thought about Precious. I wondered what she would be doing right at that moment. Her pretty face rolled around my mind; her beautiful pearly black eyes and gentle smile. I chuckled with joy as a vision of her joking and laughing with her friends flashed through my mind.

"What are you laughing at?"; John asked.

"Nothing", I replied.

"We should stay close to the road today"; John suggested.

"So we can see the car arrive".

We took the animals to the paddock and we hung around the top half of the paddock whilst keeping half any eye on the animals and the other looking out for the car.

The previous night Auntie Ruth had said that she was convinced that the town people would arrive the next day. The town people always came home the day after school closed, she had said, sounding quite sure. Uncle Bill had nodded in agreement; looking into the fire as if some sort of spiritual guide was going to leap out of it and confirm the whole thing. The fire in the middle of floor; flickered gently, throwing long spindly shadows over the kitchen wall.

The flies had settled for the night; no longer buzzing around surfaces, flying all over the food. They rested on the walls waiting for the morning. A thin wisp of smoke rose to the top of the thatched roof of the kitchen from the fire. The whole thatched kitchen roof was covered with a thick black coating of soot from years of fire burning on the floor of the kitchen. Cob webs hanging from the thatch looked like beads of black pearls from years of smoke collecting in perfectly spaced globules like beads on a neckless.

There was no chimney so, the smoke rose to the top of the cone shaped thatch roof and then descended over the rest of the kitchen. When the fire had just been lit, the whole room was covered in a thick shroud of grey blue smoke; but once the fire was well under way, it burned without producing too much smoke.

The kitchen was the central hub of our lives. The women cooked there and we all ate there; talked and told stories there. It was the place where everything happened. That small room was home. All the other houses on the farm were just places where we went to sleep.

From time to time we would see house mice scurrying along the top of the wall of the kitchen, bobbing up and down the beams off the roof resting on the top of the kitchen wall. In the dim light from the fire it was difficult to see the mice; but during the day you could almost have a chat with them. The would poke their heads out; their beady little eyes would look around the kitchen as if to say hello then disappear again.

Once the fire started to die down Auntie Ruth; lit a paraffin lamp. This was a simple old tin can of floor polish or wax with a wick floating in the paraffin.

The naked flame of the lamp burned with a bright orange yellow colour and was topped by an ever thinning blade of black smoke that smelled diabolical. We all hated that paraffin lamp and tried to have it burning for as little time as possible. Even then, in the mornings; John would blow out black snort from his nose, from the black smoke of that lamp. We kind of figured out that the paraffin lamp was not very good for our health. Nothing that turned your lungs black like that could be good for you.

The day seemed to drag on very slowly. We waited and waited for the town people to arrive. Soon it was already lunchtime. We could tell it was launch time; because Mr Smith's aeroplane was flying high above us heading towards Selukwe. Mr Smith was a white man who had a very large farm twenty or thirty miles east of Fort Milton school. Although I knew it wasn't true; as far as I was concerned the world ended at the dip a few miles east of the school, beyond that; who knew what was there. They; said that his farm stretched all the way from the other side of the dip all the way to the edges of the town of Shaman; somewhere near Mozambique and that it had more than a hundred thousand cattle on it. I couldn't imagine having to follow a hundred thousand cattle around, so I didn't even try to think of it. At the most we only ever had about twenty cattle on the farm; and that seemed like a lot of cattle to me.

Mr Smith's cattle were legendary for their size and good health; all big and fat. They said that he used to ride around on his motorbike inspecting them. He was said to carry a whip called a sjambok which he would use to strike any man or beast that didn't get out of his way in time. The sjambok was a rubber and leather whip with sharp metal studs embedded in it, and was said to be able to slice a mans hand right off when wielded by a true "Bhunu"; a large white man from "Zansi", South Africa. The very thought of such a man struck terror in our little hearts and we were quite glad he didn't live anywhere near us. From up there in the sky in his little aeroplane; he could do us no harm.

His reputation was common knowledge; but more importantly for us; his plane was a very reliable clock which told us when it was time for lunch, when it was heading west towards Selukwe, and time to start thinking about bringing the cattle back in when it was heading back east towards his farm.

It wasn't until the mid afternoon that we finally; saw the car carrying the town people arrive; trailing clouds of dust behind it. It was the white Peugeot 404. Then; much to our surprise it was followed by another and then another car. Three cars in total. All the car roofs had carriers; fully laden with bags. They must have seen us in the distance; running towards the road; waving frantically as the cars hooted as they sped past without slowing down. A few seconds passed, and the dust settled quickly behind the cars. There was not even the slightest breeze in the air. I wondered what it would be like to run through that thick cloud of dust.

Would I be able to breathe; would all the dust get into my lungs; would I be able to jump and float on the dust; I wondered.

Without the slightest thought for the animals we dropped everything we were doing and raced back home after the cars.

By the time we got back to the house; everyone had already got off the car and were settled in the kitchen having lunch. The kitchen was full of people. There was so much joy in the air. Our normally quiet and slow life was suddenly transformed into a hum drum of activity by the arrival of so many town people.

Every one was delighted to see us; but we were even more delighted to seem them than they could ever imagine.

John; Nkosiyetu, my goodness; how you've both grown so much; exclaimed "Mamomdala" which means Big Mama. She was called Big Mama, because she was the wife of the eldest of all my uncles; Uncle Ben. Uncle Ben was Big Daddy; but everybody just called him Uncle Ben.

Mamomdala was practically the queen of all the mums and was loved and feared in equal measure. She was a super powerful woman; and her word was final. Mamomdala was a tall dark and larger than life lady in every respect. She was a primary school teacher; but to us she was the centre of our universe; and like everyone; I loved and feared her at the same time. I loved her; because she always brought nice things for us from town; like balloons and sweets and cooked the most amazing meals like 'mpoqoko' and 'mxlanga'. Mpoqoko was made with flour and mealie meal and was served with 'amasi', very delicious thick sour milk. One time she had made something Lindiwe called; pudding. It was the most delicious thing I had ever tasted in my life. It had been mid afternoon, on a very hot day and the rarest of things had happened; two girls from the house had come out all the way to the bush to find us boys out herding cattle and sheep and asked us to leave the cattle with them and go home and have some pudding. We had laughed until our sides split; at this. Girls; looking after cattle; who had ever heard of such a thing.

So we had decided to go in turns; half of us would go first then the other half next.

The pudding was a brown paste as smooth as mealie meal porridge; perhaps even smoother. Even though it had been a very hot day Mamomdala had somehow managed to get that brown paste; icy cold.

As soon as the teaspoon touched my lips; an electric sensation travelled from my tongue to the back of my head down my neck to every inch of my body. I had never tasted anything that made me feel like that before. I finished the brown paste served on the cup saucer and licked the saucer clean.

Big Mamma hugged us both at the same time and gave us is a peck on the cheek each; for doing so well at school.

I'm very proud of you; Big Mamma said; with a big benevolent smile on her face. She was the only person I ever saw give anyone a kiss. She was quite amazing.

There were so many people sitting in the kitchen; but a little shifting here and there; they made space for our tiny bottoms to sit down on the floor. It looked like the whole Bhebhe clan had descended on the farm that day.

Everyone was there, there was Uncle Bill, Uncle Ben, Uncle Harry, Uncle Julius, Auntie Ruth, Big Mamma, Auntie Thembi, Gogo Madube and three workers Steven, Jason and a new guy I later found out was called Eddie. Uncle Harry was step brother of my uncles and lived in Bulawayo with his two daughters Khethiwe and Zimazile.

There were so many cousins, Mandla, Jabulani, John, Joseph, Michael, Lindiwe, Nonthando, Zimazile, Khethiwe, Thandi, Zandile, my sister Nomalanga and many other little ones

There were three other people I did not recognise, a skinny dark boy who looked slightly younger than I was; a little boy whose complexion was so light, I nearly mistook him for a white person, until I noticed his black curly hair, not much different from our own. I had barely paid any attention to the other person until Uncle Ben introduced her.

This is Mamcane (Aunt) Sibongile; uncle Ben said pointing at a young woman sitting, cross-legged on the floor behind all the girl children. Everyone turned to look in her direction. She was stunningly beautiful with softest even features I heard ever seen. She was almost as light in complexion as the new boy. Her skin was perfect without a single, blemish or scratch on it. Uncle Ben explained that she had come all the way from Mbembesi and only spoke Xhosa.

She had big bright eyes; she looked at us and smiled broadly; without saying anything. She didn't need to; her angelic smile and and the twinkle in her eyes said it all.

I had never seen the kitchen this full of people before. The happiness and joy lifted up from the souls sitting on the kitchen floor and filled the room like a ray of sunshine. You could wave your hand about and feel it between the fingers of your hand. It filled our hearts and lungs like the air we breathed. Such unbounded joy in the delight of everyone coming together; sitting together on the floor and enjoying seeing one another; some for the first time, some after such a long while. I was buzzing with shear delight.

Uncle Ben, then turned to me and pointing at the dark boy sat next to John; said.

"Nkosiyetu; this is your brother Thabo; he lives in Bulawayo with his mother!"

The boy smiled and I smiled back. I immediately felt connected to him; as if we had known each other all our lives. I didn't even know I had a brother up until then; but before my mind wondered off trying to make calculations which it did as soon as it was presented with a question uncle Ben introduced the little light skinned boy.

"This is Dreyfus"; uncle Ben said, pointing at the boy sitting on the floor next to Jabulani.

The boy looked about a year or two younger than John and I was.

"Dreyfus can't hear or speak!"; uncle Ben explained; looking at John and I as if to make sure; we absolutely understood what he was saying.

John and I looked at it each other; completely perplexed. I could see that he was asking the same question in his head, that I was asking myself.

"What in god's name does he mean the boy can't hear or speak?".

I looked at the boy and saw that he had a perfectly formed mouth and two perfectly ordinary looking ears. He was a little bit on the pale side; but in all other respects; he looked quite normal; like there was no reason at all he would not be able to hear or speak.

We both stared at the boy, which made his skin change colour from a super light brown to bright red. He was very well dressed, in dark blue polo shirt with a red, black and white trim round the collar, a silver zip and matching Khaki shorts and brand new tennis shoes.

He looked positively pampered and looked like he had definitely never done a single days hard work in his life. I couldn't wait to get him outside alone with us; away from the adults to find out if he really couldn't talk. I wanted to shout out loud in his ear, I was pretty sure if I shouted loud enough he would be able to hear; because just looking at him there was no way of telling that there was anything wrong with his hearing or voice.

Curiosity getting the better of us; we rushed to finish lunch quickly as we were eager to get out and play.

Where there had only been two of us to look after the animals for so long. The animal team had swelled to eight or nine boys. We joined by our cousins from what we called the lower houses; Daniel; Moses and Joseph. Daniel and Moses where Aunt Lizzy's kids and Joseph was the son of the Aunt who had died about four years earlier. The three had arrived in the cars; that afternoon; but had not joined us for lunch. We headed out to the paddock to find the sheep and cattle which we had abandoned before lunch when we ran after the cars.

Even though we had barbed wire fence around the farm someone still had to always keep an eye on the animals. The cattle could break through the fence and devour crops in the field; ruining the next harvest. The sheep in particular could easily get across the fence and disappear on the neighbours farm making it very hard to find them. Of all, things I hated; the most was losing the sheep; because it always sent me into a crazy panic.

We got to where we had left the animals; but to our dismay they had disappeared.

"Where did you say you left the animals again"; asked Jabulani whom we called Jabu for short.

"Right there!", I replied pointing at the exact spot we had left them.

"Let's call them"; Joseph suggested.

John and I looked at each other and burst out laughing.

"They are sheep and cattle; they're not dogs, you can't just call them back!". I explained.

Joseph was a real town boy raised on the streets of the townships of Bulawayo. This was his first time on the farm. He had absolutely no idea how to look after farm animals. From his appearance I could tell he never had to do any physical labouring; he was clean and well dressed. His skin was fresh; he was tall and good looking . No village or farm boy looked like that. Most village and farm boys I knew were all half starved scrawny little things with skin wrapped so tight against spindly bones; we looked more like walking skeletons for the best part. I longed to look like one of those town boys with their clean clothes; nice shoes; easy going ways and their perfect smooth plump bodies.

However; we were better in other ways; none of the town boys could walk barefoot in the bush like we could. They all complained that the tough grass hurt their feet. It made me laugh.

Jabulani on the other hand we loved and admired immensely. He was both a town boy and a country boy; switching between the two roles effortlessly. He now took charge as he always did every single school holiday.

"Which way were they facing when you left?"; he asked.

"They were not facing any particular direction they were scattered about pretty much everywhere"; Explained John

He scanned the horizon for any sign of movement. Nothing. Losing the sheep was usually traumatic experience; if I had been own my own I would have been panicking by now. Somehow, when we were in a large group; the responsibility was shared and I didn't feel so panicked.

"Let's go and have a look"; I said. After years of looking after those animals, I knew I was the best shepherd there was and if the sheep were lost; I could find them. I always use the same methods whenever I lost the sheep. It involved walking up to the last place where I had seen them grazing; spitting on my open palm; striking the spit with two fingers and observing the direction most of the spit went. This was the direction the sheep had gone. To make the decision a bit more reliable, I would also crouch down and find tracks left by the hooves of the sheep. Combining the two bits of information helped me decide which direction to start walking, all the while following the tracks left here and there by the animals. If for whatever reason the two bits of information didn't correspond; I simply repeated the steps until I got the results I wanted. It worked perfectly because I always found the sheep in the end.

I did my spit test followed by checking the tracks on the ground. They were in perfect agreement.

"That way I said, the sheep went that way!". My spit test caused a lot of laughter; but no-one protested. I think because they knew that I lived with these animals day in and day out and kind of knew how to find them better than anyone else; even if the didn't believe in the spit detective work.

We followed the tracks, which kept disappearing in the long grass only to appear again on a short patch. After a short while tracking John who had keen eyesight spotted the specs of white blobs in the distance and said; "There they are!".

The sheep were grazing quite happily near the river. The cattle where a short distance further away; behind some thick bushes.

Once we had found the animals we could relax and play. Without delay; our attention immediately turned to Dreyfus.

"Guys; let's teach Dreyfus how to speak"; John suggested. Everyone took turns to try and get Dreyfus to say something. Sometimes he was able to say words like mama or papa; but however hard we tried he could never repeat a whole sentence. He could not even say "My name is Dreyfus". After what seemed like an eternity of trying; Mandla ordered us stop.

"Guys he is getting tired; he's never going to be able to speak". Mandla said. "Leave him alone boys!".

"So how do we talk to him then?", we asked.

Mandla explained that we had to use sign language and speak to him with our hands. I couldn't help getting that sinking feeling that we had failed. I had experienced that feeling once before when one of the sheep had given birth and rejected its lamb. We had done everything to try and get that sheep to feed its lamb; but to no avail. We had caught that ewe, held it down whilst someone else tried to get the lamb to feed. That had not worked. Eventually, the lamb had got too weak to even suckle and had succumbed to hunger and thirst and had died. None of us had thought of using a baby bottle to try and feed it with cows milk or even baby formula. The adults had said, just leave it. There is nothing you can do. It broke my heart to see such waste.

The cattle and sheep carried on grazing in the paddock whilst we talked and played. Eventually the sun began to set. It hung low in the sky above the western horizon, throwing long beads of golden rays across the paddock. Our shadows stretched out across the ground like tall slender black giants.

"Every body, look!" said John pointing at an old anthill".

"Oh my God. There is dog with puppies!"; exclaimed Joseph.

"That cannot be a dog!". Explained Jabu. "What's a dog with puppies doing all the way out here on its own?".

"It's too skinny to be a dog, and look at its tail"; Mandla said shaking his head in agreement with his brother.

From where I stood, it looked just like a dog and as far I was concerned it was a dog.

Everyone had an opinion what it might be until; a man's voice from behind us announced emphatically.

"That's not a dog; it's a jackal!".

It was Steven; one of the farm workers. He had come tell us to bring the cattle in and find out if anyone wanted to help with smashing the head of a cow that uncle Ben had brought home from town.

Naturally we all wanted to see this spectacle. This was the first time that uncle Ben had brought a head of a cow for dinner.

Steven explained that he was going to smash it on the big rock opposite the gum trees. The rock was a massive grey and white boulder; several meters long and a few meters wide that jutted out, about a meter or so high above ground.

We gather the sheep and the cattle and followed him to the big rock. They head of the cow was was huge. It filled the entire wheel burrow. The big boys; Mandla and Jabulani helped Steven lift the cow's head out of the wheelbarrow onto the rock.

Steven took a sledgehammer from the wheel burrow and immediately started pounding on the dead cow's head with it. Once the head was pulverised and nearly flattened; he took out a big knife from the wheelbarrow; sliced off the skin; he worked his way through the carcass expertly slicing chunks of meat and throwing them into a yellow bucket he had brought with him. He placed big bones to one side and when he had finished slicing chunks of meat; he smashed the big bones up collecting the now much smaller chunks, some with giant teeth into another plastic bucket.

Finally; he chopped the skin of the head into small chunks and tossed them to our dogs that had somehow followed the trail of blood dripping from the wheel burrow all the way to the rock and were waiting for just such a feast.

"Right boys, good job, I'm done here"; Steven announced, as he loaded the wheel burrow, with the buckets of meat and bones; the sledge hammer and the kitchen knife.

Go and lock up the cattle and sheep for the night and I'll see you at home; he said picking up the handles of the wheel burrow and marching of in his blue overalls and black gumboots.

I was very excited about the idea of eating meat that night. I couldn't remember the last time I had eaten meat. It probably had been during the term a few days after the previous school holidays; all those months ago.

By the time we locked up the animals in their enclosures for the night, the sun had already gone down and it was just beginning to get really dark. We double checked the sheep pen to make sure that a jackal or hyena could not get in or the sheep get out. Satisfied with our work, we headed home; crossing the river in the dark and up across the barbed wire fence of the paddock and we were back on the homestead.

Back home the women were busy cooking on two fires; one in the kitchen and another in the yard outside. Huge pots with three legs where bumbling on the fires. The smell of meat cooking wafted in the air. My stomach started rumbling.

The food was not ready yet; so instead we joined the girls playing dodgeball in the moon and firelight. It was like being back at school again; the noise the screaming so many children; all relatives; all friends it was wonderful. Hunger forgotten; dodgeball teams between the boys and girls were formed and we carried on playing until at last Auntie Ruth called everyone.

"Children; children!"; she called in the nicest gentlest voice that I had ever heard her speak. She was completely different person during school holidays; unusually nice and kind. She referred to me in the kindest terms of possible; whenever there were other people; but the moment those people were gone it was a completely different story.

Holidays were a reprieve and therapy from many hardships, from loneliness, a reprieve from poor food; but most of all a reprieve from the torment she and her husband uncle Bill subjected me whenever they felt like it. The two of them had it in for me in a big way.

That night the knives had been put away; and peace reigned. We all ran to the kitchen and sat down on the floor. To my immediate annoyance the kitchen floor had been freshly cleaned that afternoon. This was one of Auntie Ruth's specialities that I resented; because once as a kid it had ruined a new pair of shorts that I had received from my father in England. To clean the floor she would first sweep the floor; then take a mixture of cow dung and water mixed into a thick paste; then smear it thinly across the kitchen floor. This refreshed the kitchen floor, making it look as good as new. But; when you sat down on the floor on a patch that had not dried properly, that cow dung permanently dyed the shorts with a nasty brown mark that did not come out in the wash. That is what had happened to my nice pair of peach coloured shorts.

As I walked bare foot on the floor, I could tell the floor was not completely dry and there would be a lot of wet bums. Fortunately; I was not the only one who had figured that out and the women were laying down reed mats all around the kitchen floor for people to sit on.

Two bowls of water passed round one for the women and girls and another for the men and boys to wash our hands before dinner. The adults washed their hands first then the bowls were passed to the children starting with the eldest child to the youngest. By the time down the bowl reached us the water was black with dirt from all those hands that had washed before. I wondered if there was any point in washing my hands in that filthy water; but dared not question it and washed my hands regardless. Then a couple of the women went out and tossed the dirty water outside in the yard, and then refilled it with clean water ready for washing the hands after dinner. It was important to wash the hands because we ate with our bare fingers.

The dinner was served expertly by two or three women, helping each other. One, sitting down passed an empty plate, to another kneeling over a big pot, she filled the plate with a large blob of sadza; then passed it to the next woman kneeling over a pot of meat and sauce, and a pot of vegetables who then scooped just the right amount of meat and vegetables onto the plate; announced who the plate was for and passed it down to the next person available and on until it got to the right person.

How; those women figured out how much to put in each plate so that everyone had a fair share was mystery to me. On a bountiful night like that night, each plate had three of four small pieces of meat, instead of the usual one or two and plenty of sauce, the gravy from the meat, without which it would be impossible to taste or swallow the sadza.

Whilst the adults washed their hands first. The children were served first, starting with babies and youngest; for the simple fact that the small children were already screaming with hunger by the time dinner was served. It didn't matter which meal of the day it was, we were always so hungry; that no sooner had you got your plate than you started wolfing it down as if you had not seen food in days.

That night the meal was practically a feast. There was plenty to go around and every plate was heaped with sadza; vegetables and the meat from the head of a cow that we had helped smash on the boulder earlier that evening.

Biting into a piece of meat for the first time in many months was unbelievable. The softness of the meat; the flavours of the sauce and salt and pepper as it touched the tongue; there was nothing in the world like it. I could hear the sound of the universe buzzing at the back of my head the moment that beef touched my palate. I could feel my body tingling with contentedness as it started to absorb the good nourishment. Nothing could describe the enjoyment of eating good food surrounded by so many friends and relatives. There was so much laughter and joy; and for a while time stopped; there was no worry or care in my head; just sheer joy of being alive.

The food that night was a veritable feast. Everything from the cow's head had been consumed, apart from the brain which had been removed; washed off the meat and tossed to the dogs .

I made sure there was no tongue on my plate. I knew what the cows did with their tongues and I was determined not to eat it; no matter how much I missed meat. Sometimes the cows used it to lick each other; cleaning each other's back and sides with their tongues. Even worse than that; sometimes they used it to clean their nostrils; sticking their long tongue right into their nostrils and leaking bogeys out of them. I really didn't fancy eating something that had been inside a cow's nostrils.

Whilst I wasn't particularly thrilled about it; but didn't mind at all I did get a large piece of a cow's jaw complete with a set of teeth. The meat around the teeth was soft and tender and delicious. I sucked the marrow from the bone and the teeth. Slugs of tasty delicious bone marrow globules shot out of the bone and hit the back of my mouth and gently slipped down my throat. It was delicious beyond belief. I cleaned my plate and was totally full without any room in my stomach for another morsel of food. I finished the meal with a cup of water as did everyone else. The water must have been collected from the well that day; it was still cold and fresh and had a kind of delicious sweetness to it.

We stayed up late that night; listening to so many stories the adults were telling one another. Later on; as if we had not eaten enough food that night; a big wok of peanuts was placed on the fire. The peanuts were roasted over the hot fire then; when nearly ready Auntie Ruth dissolved a tablespoon full of salt in some water in a large cup and poured it over the peanuts. The water sizzled as it hit the wok. The water boiled off rapidly creating a huge plume of steam which rose like smoke up to the roof of the kitchen. Auntie Ruth mixed the peanuts up in the wok vigorously with a wooden spoon until all the water was gone. This left the nuts coated with a thin layer of salt.

The nuts were then transferred into two large wicker baskets which were passed around in opposite directions. As a basket went past everyone dipped their hand into it and grabbed a handful of peanuts and tossed them in their mouths. The peanuts were warm and delicious.

There was so much chatter and laughter; so many different conversations going I just had to pick one and listen. But sometimes one of the conversations; became a topic for the whole room. As deed when uncle Ben announced that he was going to build a new house at the top of the hill near the Shumba's farm. The house; he explained was to have six bedrooms; and two toilets inside the house.

Toilets inside the house!

"How can you have a toilet inside a house; Uncle Bill"; asked stunned.

It seemed I wasn't the only one; who didn't think that; this was possible.

"Toilet in the house brother!", uncle Bill exclaimed again. "How would that work. Do you dig a big hole in the house; the smell; the flies!"

Uncle Ben talked about flushing and water washing things away; but it made no sense to me whatsoever.

The house would have a bathroom as well; uncle Ben went on. He explained that the house was going to have running water piped directly from the dam straight to the house. This I understood because he had already built an irrigation system which pumped water from the dam to a giant tank half a mile from the dam. The house would be bigger and nicer than the Maposa's house; he added. This is all I needed to hear. A house that was bigger and nicer than the Maposa's; that was perfect. With a house like that; the whole of Fort Milton would talk about us. They would think we were rich and that would feel really good; wherever we went.

For no particular reason at all; John who was much braver than I was blurted out that we had seen a jackal with puppies that afternoon.

"Where did you see this jackal?"; uncle Bill asked with a concerned look on his face.

At the paddock we all answered.

All the men went quiet and started consulting one another in muted voices. If there are puppies that jackal will be very hungry it will hunt and kill the sheep. We must do something; I heard them say to each other.

"Right boys!"; uncle Ben started explaining.

"Here is what you need to do tomorrow. You need to go back where you saw the jackal; find its den and cover every entrance with rocks. That way this jackal will abandon the den and move away somewhere else. You understand!"

It was really late when we finally went to sleep. The next day a smaller group of us took the cattle and the sheep out for the day. As soon as we let the animals out; the cattle immediately headed for the big rock where Steven had smashed the head of a cow. They were walking really fast and even running; as if they were being driven there by an invisible cattle header. Something was drawing them to that rock.

It was a very strange behaviour that we had never seen before. Normally we had to drive the cattle forward with a whip to get them to go where we wanted them to go. We followed them to find out what had possessed them. When the cattle got to the big rock, they did something we had never seen before. They climbed on the big rock and started howling; making really strange noises and picking up the small bits of bone in their mouths from the smashed cow head from the previous night. They were sucking and turning over the bones in the mouths; almost as if they were cleaning the bones as they did not try to crush and swallow the bones. It was as if there were moaning the dead cow. It didn't make much sense to me; why were they upset about the cow that they didn't know. It had not even been a whole cow; just its head. It wasn't like that cow had been one of the family; but they seemed very upset about it no less.

Manzuma; who was the indisputable leader of the cattle was the noisiest of the lot. She was reticent light brown old cow; who I was quite sure spent all her waking hours plotting how best to annoy us. She was so old she was there before I was born. She would lead the other cows to young growing corn and devour it given half the chance. She got us into trouble for eating the maize and ruining harvests more times than I cared to count.

Hearing the noise, Harold; the old ox who was the gentlest of all cattle joined in. Harold was remarkably intelligent for an ox. He seemed to understand instructions like stop and walk. He had no fear of humans and allowed us to stroke his face; hold his horns. John had even discovered that if you scratched a certain part of his tail he lifted it up and did a cow pad right there and then. It was a silly thing to do; but it was great for a laugh and good for impressing the town boys who didn't know a lot about farm animals.

Once; we even attempted to ride on his back like a horse; unfortunately he didn't like that very much. He simply lowered his shoulder and neck down so that you slid down his back and neck and went over the horns over his head. We didn't really want to risk this for fear of being impaled on his horns on the way down so we quickly stopped trying to ride him. John who was the most curious and most daring of us all had been the first to try and had slid down the back of that ox right over the horns and amazingly; had landed on his feet without a scratch. But; even as daring as he was; he was sure he had been very lucky; and even he didn't dare to try it again.

Slowly we drove the cattle towards the paddock. Without even discussing it we were instinctively heading towards the jackals den. As usual during the school holidays; we got up early in the morning and took the cattle to the paddock to graze for a couple of hours. We stopped by the river and made sure that the cows drank lots of water. The theory was that after drinking some water and a couple hours of grazing the cows' udders would be full of milk to bursting point; so when we milked them later there would be tonnes more milk. This was all done, before we ourselves had a single morsel to eat.

Mandla was carrying a pick and John was carrying a shovel. Somehow; they had decided that we were going to dig up the den; get those puppies and secretly train them to live like dogs. They looked like dogs and if they lived with dogs from puppy, they would behave like dogs. That is what someone in our group had decided, but I didn't know who. The idea made perfect sense to me. If the puppies grew up with dogs and around people they would essentially become dogs.

Eventually we got to the den. The den had been dug into the side of an old termite mound. The hole was large enough for a small dog to crawl in.

"What do we do what if the jackal is still in there? What if it attacks us?"; John asked

I'll dig said Mandla, and you get ready to hit anything that comes out of that hole with the shovel.

We also had a couple of knobkerries and catapults and we stood at the ready to strike at any thing that came out of the hole. Mandla started digging from one side with a pick whilst John stood over the hole; shovel at the side ready to bash anything that came out of the hole.

After a bit of digging nothing came out. Jabu suggested smoking it out. This was the technique that we used quite often to try and smoke snakes out of a hole. It had never worked. I was sure that either the snake died in the hole or the fire or the smoke didn't bother them. Maybe smoke didn't bother snakes at all. But it might work with jackals. So we gathered up some dried up straw and heaped it up over and inside the mouth of the hole.

Has anyone got any matches. Fortunately; this was one of those necessary things we always carried around with us; in case we needed to make a fire to roast some maize or smoke a snake out of a hole. John lit the straw and it quickly threw a plume of white smoke in the air in the gentle breeze of the morning. I guess we were too busy watching the fire instead of thinking about why we had lit it; because in a blink of an eye, in a time that was too short to quantify, the jackal shot out of the hole and bounded across the river and disappeared in the long grass before anyone could even raise the shovel up in the air to strike it.

This was all we needed to know that there was something in that hole. This encouraged us to dig harder deeper. Eventually the pick head just went through the ground.

"Guys I think, I've got something"; Mandla announced excitedly.

We all gathered round the hole.

"Pass me the shovel"; ordered Mandla who was the eldest and was practically the law. He punched through the thin layer of soil with the shovel and there inside was a big round hole. And inside it were six tiny jackal puppies; lying on a bed of straw and tufts of fur. They looked just like dog puppies. We picked them up and stroked them.

We were so excited; we already had three dogs and now we would have six more. I couldn't wait for them to grow so we could take them hunting and I was sure they would still have enough of their wildness in them to be able to catch small impala for dinner. We would be able to eat meat all year round. Mandla sat at the edge of the hole resting his chest on the handle of the pick. He had a sad expression on his face. His young brother brother; Jabu noticing his sudden change in mood asked.

"Why the long face; Brother?"

"You do realise we can't take them home don't you".

Alarmed, we cried. "Why not?". "The puppies are ours; we found them and we'll keep them!".

"Did you not hear what dad said last night?"

"We have to get rid of them because; when they grow they will turn into wild animals and attack the sheep?"

Both John and I cried out; aware that when everyone had gone back to their wonderful lives in town, it would be our responsibility to take care of the puppies.

"No, they won't turn wild. We will train them and never leave them alone"; we protested

"Yes"; Mandla replied. "But; what happens when you're at school?".

"We have no choice; we have to destroy them!"; he insisted.

I looked at the puppies. I couldn't tell them apart from dog puppies. How these could turn into wild sheep killers beggared belief.

"Who will do it?"; Mandla asked.

No one volunteered.

"Okay then; I'll have to do it"; said Mandla frustrated with the lot of us. He climbed out of the hole.

"Put one down here!"; he ordered.

John reluctantly put one on the ground next to the hole.

Mandla lifted the shovel up and brought it down hard on the puppies neck. The puppy stopped moving. Then he shovelled the dead puppy back in the hole.

"Next!"; he ordered.

Like that all the jackal puppies were dispensed and thrown back in the hole. Finally the hole was covered with the soil from the mound.

That night the jackal could be head crying for its puppies all night!

The next evening there was silence.

We never saw another jackal on the farm and the jackal incident was never mentioned again.

Chapter 6 The Dip

With so many people the water from the well was used up very quickly so every few days the tractor and the trailer were loaded up with a few drums and buckets. We drove the tractor to the well filled up each drum and buckets with water from the well. This water was only used for drinking and washing hands pots and pans.

The water in the drums stayed cool and fresh for a few days. Using the tractor and drums was a lot better than filling the bucket with water then carrying it all the way to the kitchen on one's head. The water in bucket in the kitchen went off very quickly. The bucket was always stood on the large black iron stove in the kitchen. I had only ever seen that stove used once in all those years. In the heat of summer months the water quickly warmed up and because the bucket was always open it soon; also filled up with dust and dead insects.

Sometimes; when really thirsty after a whole day in the field without a drop of water; in the mad rush to drink some water and forgetting to check the contents of the bucket I dipped a cup in the bucket and quickly drained it down my throat. It wasn't until I felt cockroach's legs scratch my throat as I swallowed it whole; that I though damn, I should have checked first. Sometimes it was a fly or an ant; but regardless it was swallowed whole. There was not much one could do about it, so I tried not to think about it. Sometimes, I would get a stomach ache, and wonder if it was a bug I had swallowed in this way try to scratch its way out of my tummy; but then, no sooner had the pain come than it was gone again, so I didn't think the bugs ever did us any real harm.

"You boys should go and sleep soon!"; suggested; Uncle Bill one night a couple of hours after dinner. You have a busy day tomorrow; he said smiling wryly.

Someone suggested we should sleep at the cottage that night so we would not disturb everyone when; we got up early in the morning.

The cottage was a couple of hundred yards from the rest of the homestead compound. It was called the cottage because it had a flat roof of zinc metal sheets. The cottage was a large rectangular building with two separate rooms and two separate doors. It had really high walls and a flat steeply sloping roof. One of the very large rooms was used by the three workers as sleeping quarters and the other was used as a storage room.

We had never slept in the cottage before; so we were extremely excited about the idea. We all disappeared to collect our bits for the night. I collected my reed mat and my old blue tartan blanket that I had had for as long as I could remember. The whole group of us and three workers camped out for the night in the large room.

We cracked jokes and told stories all night; but no one and absolutely no-one mentioned the jackal puppies. But all I could see when I closed my eyes; were their little legs dangling in the air as they were slaughtered; their still life-less bodies in the hole before it was covered. I fell asleep.

The next morning we were woken up at the crack of dawn whilst it was still very dark. It was quite a shock to my system. Uncle Bill announced that we would be taking the cattle to the dip that morning. That explained why he had got us all in one place. We got up begrudgingly. Whilst we hated getting up so early; going to the dip was the most exciting event in the life of a cattle herder.

Hundreds and hundreds may be even thousands and thousands of cattle were driven from miles around on the same day to the dip.

We had to drive the cattle seven or eight miles to the dip in the dead of the morning in the dark all before breakfast; all without breakfast or even a drink of water. Once the cattle were dipped; we had to make the journey back; all on empty stomachs and without a drink. It was a fine test of endurance.

Going to the dip was a monumental task. It required lots of people and lots of eyes everywhere. If you didn't pay attention with all those other cows from other farms and from the reserves you could easily lose a cow or a calf. There were a lot of other things to consider; whether there were scores to settle with anyone, what weapons to carry and the obligatory home made cattle whips. Most important of all though was the opportunity to watch a bull fight or two.

I fumbled in the dark trying to find my catapult. It was gone. But for me the day could not have not started any worse. The loss of my catapult was devastating, and yet there was no time to dwell on it. We had to get up and get ready quickly. This would be a long day. We went across the river to the kraal whilst it was still pitch black.

Much to our surprise Jersey; the black and white cow that had hardly looked pregnant was nursing a calf in the morning. Jersey, was the new Friesland cow that had got us into trouble the previous year when she arrived fresh on the farm. She was as tame as a dog and had no fear of humans whatsoever. She produced copious amounts of milk even when she didn't have a calf. Uncle Ben had bought her from a white farmer in Gwelo. There had been a great fanfare when she arrived.

When she arrived she was a fat healthy cow; but a year down the road soon after she joined the rest of the cows like Manzuma she had become bony and scraggly from the poor diet of dry straw and nothing else.

We had all got into trouble for milking her without permission. We had milked her straight into our mouths; which involved squatting next to the cow close to the udder; then pulling on one teat straight into an open mouth. You could do that with her because she didn't kick you like any of the cows. You couldn't try that with Manzuma she would kick you in the head and knock you right out. The day after she had arrived, whilst in the paddock we had decided to try the new cows milk. We had taken it in turns to stoop beside her udder and milk one of the huge teats straight into a wide open mouth. The milk was copious, warm, creamy and sweet. I had never tasted milk like that before. Unfortunately for us; one of the workers had seen the whole thing and reported us to uncle Ben.

Uncle Ben was not happy with this at all and had decided that he would punish us. He called us in individually and questioned us. He wanted to know who had decided that it was okay to milk the cow straight into our mouths like that. It was a very strange situation; because we knew the answer; it had been a group decision. No-one person had said, "You know what guys each of you must drink from the cow today". It had been a kind of crowd decision. In any case, the whole thing was a charade, because we were not allowed answer back when questioned. So we each, went and said nothing; because giving the right answer would have been considered rude.

"John you've been called in"; Lindiwe said to John with a big smile on her face. The girls were having the time of their lives at our expense; watching each of us go in with a terrified look on our faces and come back either crying or really angry. John took the three steps up into Uncle Ben's house. The house was like Uncle Bills; but built on a much higher foundation several steps all of three or four steps above ground. I guess it must have been built after uncle Bill's house when they had realised that after the rains the yard was turned into a lake and the house with the low foundation would sometimes flood.

The door opened straight into the dining room which also served as a bedroom. A door on the right side in the opposite corner as you went into the dining room opened into uncle Ben's bedroom. This was a sacred room where no-one was normally allowed in; all year round. Both rooms had a hard dark blue concrete cement floor. We hated that floor; it was harder than a rock and was kept polished and shiny at all times . It didn't matter how carefully you walked on it; sooner or later your slipped on that shiny floor and nearly cracked your skull open. It hurt like the devil himself, and the pain lingered own for several minutes after the fall.

John had come back out visibly unscathed. He looked slightly bemused by the whole thing. Jabu had not even bothered turning up for questioning. When Mandla was called in, we could her arguments coming from the room, then he emerged visibly irritated. He didn't seem to have the fear that we all had of his father. We were all terrified of him; but Mandla didn't seem to care for him much. I could not imagine uttering one word to uncle Ben; let alone answer back.

When he had finished interrogating us, he had decided that he was going to cane us all.

Unfortunately for him; when word of his plans got round to auntie Lizzy, his big sister and the most powerful woman on the farm; even more powerful than Mamomdala; things changed. Aunt Lizzy; never said much. We never saw her much either. She hardly, ever came out of her house except very rarely. In three or four years of the time I could remember I had only ever seen her outside on a maximum of three occasions. She ruled from her bedroom and her word was final. She had instructed that the boys were not to be touched. She had explained that they spend all their lives looking after the animals and it was very little pleasure for them to enjoy a little bit of milk from the animals that they looked after so well. They were not to be punished for taking a little bit of milk from the cows when they were probably very hungry.

Uncle had definitely been overruled; because even Gogo was immovable. She had declared that if he even laid a finger on any child; she would pack her bags up and leave for one step sons; uncle Jack in Hartley. Gogo was the second wife of my grandfather; whom she married after his wife; Gogo's sister had died soon after their marriage and only two or three children had been conceived.

Aunt Lizzy and Gogo had saved us. I was very glad to have escaped that canning. Uncle Ben had a special belt that we called the snake; because it looked just like a snake; complete with scales. We lived in permanent fear of that belt being used on us. It had come close to being used on so many occasions when we had slipped up; but fortunately for us, he never quite did use it on us; but its very existence struck fear in us and might have helped to keep us in line most of the time.

Anyway getting back to Jersey the cow; we could not have asked for a better start to the day. The birth of a new animal was always an exciting thing; but of all things; the birth of a calf was the most exhilarating thing to happen to us. It meant a lot of things to us; it meant that we had one more cow in the herd and we would have plenty of milk for months to come. The weariness of getting up so early was quickly washed away by new excitement and energy.

With the birth of Thokazi; John had quickly found a name for the new addition to our herd. We were particularly excited about the first milk from the cow after birth. This milk was particularly rich tasty and traditionally was given to the boys who looked after the animals. This was so exciting; because the other two cows that were producing our only supply of milk had all but weaned their calves. So; before long there would have been no milk at all. I had no idea what we would've done then. With Jersey giving birth, we were once again going to be okay for a very long time.

Steven decided to stay behind and take care of milking Jersey; who now to stay behind with the new calf that could not be expected to walk seven miles to the dip. He quickly milked the other two cows; before they were taken to the dip, then we were on our way.

We headed for the only gate on the south side of the farm, which was at the top of the paddock near the nut elephant tree. So we had to drive the cattle in the opposite direction to get to the gate, going out of the way and then double back on ourselves and head towards Fort Milton School four or five miles away. After Milton school there was another three or four miles to walk before getting to the dip.

Once we were on the road a quick look at the ground checking for tracks; made us aware that many cattle had already passed through there. This told us that the Shumba and Maposa boys were already ahead of us. This was okay. We didn't want to catch them up. It was only after the animals had been dipped that things got really interesting.

Besides; we really didn't want Afrikanda and Ngorima to fight again. It was not because we were scared; we just didn't think that the the two bulls were a fair match.

On that score we were all in agreement; but the question still; remained. What bull to fight Afrikanda? Afrikanda himself seemed to have sensed something was in the wind. Every once in while he would bellow in response to the bellowing of other bulls in the distance. We encouraged him by shouting; come on Afrikanda.

He was like a big African warrior; ready to charge into battle. It looked like he wanted a fight as much as we did. He was built like a rock; all muscle slender with a shiny velvety black coat. His horns perfectly symmetrical with the shape of a semicircle. They were white except for the tips which were black and almost needle sharp. He kept his horns sharpened by regularly plunging them into termite mounds and against old tree stumps. He walked with a surefooted stride; his sinewy muscles rippling with every stride.

We all respected him so much; like an old grand master. I don't remember ever seeing anyone hit him with a whip or throw a stone at him to move him along.

When we got to Tariro river the cattle stopped to drink and waded in the water. The cows moved their giant lips across the surface of the water sucking in the water as if they had giant straws in their mouths. They seemed to be aware that we were in a bit of a hurry; because they drank on the move; slowly creeping forwards as they hoovered the water up.

Manzuma was in the lead as usual, with Harold bringing up the rear. We crossed the river and soon we were going past the School store to our left. Soon after that we were crossing the rock rabbit hills. A great expanse of hills which was topped by large square boulders, like large cubes placed there by giants at the beginning of time; a long time ago. The boulders were hidden from site by a thick forest of acacia trees whose leaves were guarded by thick needle sharp thorns.

This was black mamba territory. Even though hundreds of cattle had passed this way and any snakes loitering about would have been trampled we still proceeded across the hills with care. A bite from a mamba was certain death. We watched every step, the side of the paths and branches above us.

The rock rabbit was a favourite meal of the black mamba, its name in Shona 'rova mbira' means killer of the rock rabbit. So; wherever you saw a rock rabbit, you could be sure that there was a black mamba lurking nearby somewhere. The rock rabbit hills suddenly opened up and descended into a valley bordered by a thick forest on each side; in the middle of which run a track that had been carved out by so many years of cattle trampling this way to the dip.

The sun was now emerging from its dreamy sleep overnight; streaming its a long warm beady red morning light across the valley. Mornings never seized to amaze me. Each morning a brand new day, never before seen by another human being who had gone before us, and I was there alive to see it. It made me feel proud to be alive, as if it was some sort of achievement. As much as I wanted to know what would happen that day, there was no way of telling. I could only hope it would be a good day. Most of the time it was a perfectly ordinary day; but sometimes extraordinary things happened. Seeing the sunrise was the best way to appreciate the new day and whatever it promised to bring.

Our cattle driving skills were suddenly called into action as we had to keep a gap between the cattle ahead of us; the cattle coming back from the dip and cattle coming up from behind us. The cattle in front kicked up vast clouds of dust which glowed orange in the morning sunlight. Mixed with the warm breath from the cows and a swarm of bugs; a hazy blanket appeared to sit atop the cattle ahead of us.

It was quite a spectacle.

The noise of whips being cracked; the whistling; the cattle calling filled the air like a thick fog. We were now just a couple miles from the dip. We drove our cattle close to the the group ahead of us; but keeping the cattle in a tight group just far enough so that they did not mix with the group in front.

The queue of cattle was moving at a remarkably steady pace. Our cattle were amazingly well-behaved. There seemed to know to stay in their only little group. Slowly; slowly we edged forwards.

Suddenly we saw it, a giant bull as tall as Ngorima; but with more than double the amount of muscles. It was the weirdest thing I had ever seen in my seven years in existence. The big brown bull had no horns.

John shouted, "Naked bull!"; pointing at it.

We laughed so hard our sides could have split right open. Without horns it was as if the bull was completely naked, like some giant big fat man had simply taken his clothes off and decided to run around naked. His big fat muscles made him look like some sort of caricature of an animal.

Afrikanda spotted him; he stopped and bellowed and dug the ground with one front leg getting ready to charge the naked bull. The other bull stopped and bellowed as well. He looked ridiculous.

A rather smartly dressed group of boys were driving the herd of cattle with that bull back from the dip.

To my utter surprise; Mandla shouted out loud at the smartly dressed boys, in a very mocking voice.

"Can your bull fight?"

"You wanna find out, my bull will totally kill your bull!"; the older of the boys in the other group jeered back.

"We all burst out laughing again". Some; how we could not imagine a bull without horns being able to fight a bull with horns. How was he going to fight without horns? It would be like two boxers; one with arms and one without; a forgone conclusion.

"Whats he gonna do, lick him to death?", yelled Mandla back in response.

The laughter that followed was infectious, I laughed till to my sides hurt, the others were doubled over holding the sides of the legs paralysed with laughter. Lick him to death. Like a dog. That was funny.

Bit by bit we pushed forwards towards the dip. At last it was our turn. We drove our cattle into an enclosure. Mandla handed over a brown card and seventy five cents to one of the young man sitting on the enclosure fence; supervising the dipping.

"You boys can go and watch the cattle dip; but make sure you stand well back. You don't want to get splashed in the eyes. The dip will blind you; completely blind!"; the young man ordered.

He was wearing an old; but nice black polo shirt which in those days we called a skipper, and a pair of red trousers. He was wearing sun glasses with a shiny wire frame, he had perfectly regular features; a big Afro; perfect white teeth and skin as dark as his shirt. On his left wrist; he had many multicoloured bangles and one of those watches with a leather strap that also covered the watch. I figured his job paid him quite well, although it wasn't something I would ever want to do.

We ran up to the other end of the dip. It was a long narrow deep pool of dirty brown stinking water lined on each side by a wooden fence. The pool was about one fat cow wide and maybe five or six cows long. The enclosure was triangular shaped, narrowing towards the dip to funnel the cows towards the dip.

Another young men went behind the cows and shoed them in with the aid of a manufactured whip, not one of the home made ones like our ones; that we made from the bark of young musasa trees. The whip had a tuft of fine white hair and cracked as loudly as our home made ones. I could see its advantage immediately. With our home made ones, we had to keep them wet to keep them flexible.

There was something very odd about the two young men. They seemed to be having the time of their lives. I didn't see what was there to enjoy so much about shoeing cattle into the dip all day long. I was quite certain, this would never be the job for me when I grew up.

We watched the cows from the other end of the dip. Manzuma was in front. She got to the edge of the pool and made as if she was going to take off like an aeroplane, she leaped into the air and landed almost halfway down the pool, with an almighty splash. She was followed quickly by another cow, then another.

When Afrikanda jumped in; it might have been the end of the world. He created a wave, that reached over the the edge of the pool and spread across the cobbled encousure. His splash reached us even as we stood yards from the splash zone. Some of the stinking brown splash, landed on my leg. It stung like a bee. I wiped it off quickly with the palm of my hand. It dried up quickly and the pain subsided.

On the side of the dip was yet another man. An old man this time; whom when he smiled had; but one single tooth in his mouth. He stood by the side of the dip; with a long pole in in his hand; that he used to push the heads of the animals under the water so that every inch of their skin was covered with some dip, to kill all the ticks.

The man pushed the animals heads under the surface of the murky water like an automaton. Going from one cow to the next, as they swam past him. It was funny to watch. He was wearing plastic overalls and goggles that covered almost his entire face. The man pushed a head down with the tip of his pole and wiped the dip off the side of his face with the other hand.

The cows amazed me; because even the small calves could swim and no one had ever taught them how to swim. I had been worried about the calves as their heads disappeared under water I thought that they would surely drown; but to my surprise; up their little heads popped out again swimming vigorously. Sometimes the smaller calves managed to turn right round and face the wrong direction; where upon the man with the pole pushed and poked them again in the right direction with his long pole.

Next; I was worried that the calves wouldn't be able to swim the whole length of the pool. To my surprise again; they swam the whole length with ease. It was very strange; they could just swim and no-one had ever taught them how to.

As the cattle came out of the dip; they climbed some steps onto another triangular holding enclosure. The dip was dripping onto the cobbled floor of the enclosure which was slightly sloped back towards that dip, so that the run-off flowed straight back into the pool. Once all the animals from the same group had finished dipping, the enclosure gate was opened and it was time to drive the cattle back home.

That was it, just like that; we were done.

In no time at all, we were back on our way home. The sun was already fairly high in the sky. It looked like it was going to be a hot day, not a single cloud in the sky.

More groups of cattle were arriving as we were leaving the dip. The cattle were kicking so much dust the whole place look like a herd of buffalo had just charged past there. The deafening noise of bulls bellowing and young man whistling the cattle drive call and shouting endlessly; sounded like the whole world had descended into that one place.

There were boys chasing after calves that were too frightened to go into the enclosure. One boy had his arms locked around a calf's neck whilst another had the tail and was pushing the calf towards the dip enclosure. We left along the same path following the returning lane of cattle, back towards the rock rabbit hills. All around us bulls were bellowing; raring to fight; but permitting a fight that close to the dip would have been a disaster. All we were concerned with at that point was to make sure that our cattle stayed together; lest they got mixed up with other people's animals and we lost a cow or calf.

By the time we got back to the rock rabbit hills, the groups of cattle coming and going had become thinner and thiner as groups dispersed in all directions from whence they came. From here on; if there was any group interested in a bull fight; they would be waiting around for an opportunity to challenge any passers by.

We crossed the rock rabbit hills heading back towards Fort Milton school and the school store. After the hills there were paths splitting off; going left or right every so often like the tributaries of a long skinny river.

I could hear boys whistling whilst driving their cattle back home; but there was no-one in site. I wondered where so many people we had seen earlier, had gone all of sudden. It did surprise me much though. Many times whilst looking after sheep; we would get distracted whilst playing a bit, maybe climbing a tree or stalking a bird with catapults for a few minutes and by the time we looked up, the sheep were nowhere to be seen. A few minutes was all they need to completely vanish. With everyone gone, disappointment was beginning to sink in. It looked like there was not going to be a bullfight that morning.

But to our surprise when we got to the school store; a whole bunch of boys had gathered into clearing behind the store. They had been waiting for us. It was a group of the Shumba boys and a whole bunch of others. I recognised the boy Mandla had challenged.

"Do you want to fight your bull?"; Tatenda one of the Shumba boys asked.

This made us all laugh

"What bull?; you don't have bull; Tatenda!". The Shumba boys did not have a bull on their farm. I could never understand that.

"Not my bull you dummy, that bull!", he said pointing in the direction of thick acacia bushes a couple of hundred yards away.

From where we stood we could not see any bull. There were several cattle spread out in the distance; but there was no bull among them.

One of the boys Mandla had challenged made the most complex whistle I had ever heard anyone make. Then; as if this was some sort of signal it had been waiting for; a bull emerged from behind a mass of acacia bushes. It was the hornless bull we had seen on the way to the dip. Except for the missing horns; it was an amazing animal; big, thick and fierce. If I had ever seen a rhino; I would've said it looked as big and strong as rhino. Pound for pound it looked twice the weight and breadth of Afrikanda. It was a deep brown colour and looked in superb condition.

How did the bulls get so big and fat surviving on the same meagre potions of dried straw that the rest of the cattle were eating, it was a mystery to me.

The bull was perfect in every way except for the fact that he was missing a fine pair of horns. Without horns; he looked like a creature from some far off lands no-one had ever heard of. We all exchanged glances. I could see some doubt creep up in Mandla's eyes. John was mumbling something incoherently; quite unlike him as he was usually so full of confidence. Maybe we had underestimated the size of that animal and Afrikanda was going to be killed. Only Jabu stood firm and pointed out that as big as the bull was; he had no horns, so what damage could he do. Poke Afrikanda with his ears!.

However; even then a lot was at stake; because there were boys from all over the place; the farms; the reserves; everywhere. Defeat would mean humiliation for us; losing to a hornless bull, whoever heard of such a thing?. I was thinking to myself, if we lost, it would probably mean humiliation for the rest of our school days and possibly for the rest of our lives. Life is an eternity when you are young.

As soon as the bull emerged from where he had been hiding and saw Afrikanda, he started bellowing and digging the ground with one of his front legs in preparation for a fight. He posed; length wise; showing his immense size. Then he posed front wise and then turned again to display the opposite side. He lowered his head slowly as if bowing in praise of the gods; for making him so big and strong and for giving him a chance to fight a puny little bull like Afrikanda.

Afrikanda wasn't in the slightest bit perturbed by all the posturing. As soon as he heard the bellowing and saw the hornless bull; he seemed to know that his moment had arrived. It was as if he had been expecting this all day long.

He left the herd hand raced towards the hornless bull. The hornless bull turned to face Afrikanda; all the while turning his head this way and that way and kicking up dirt with one of hist front legs. There was nothing unusual about this except the next thing that happened.

Usually bulls locked horns a couple of times; clashing the horns together; making a lot of noise, testing each other's strengths. Before going into a full fledged battle. Sometimes they would even circle each other like a couple dancing; stopping to lock horns again and again until they were ready to do full battle.

The brown bull didn't have any horns and what he did next was quite unexpected. Quite suddenly and unexpectedly he launched himself forward head lifting and coming down in the middle of Afrikanda's head with a loud clang.

Afrikanda caught by surprise; his legs turned into jelly and he almost passed out. But even before his limp body could drop to the ground the brown bull surged forwards; placing his head under the front legs of our bull; and jerking it up so hard that Afrikanda was lifted clean off the ground came crashing down on his back like a rug doll. I felt the ground shake under my bare foot as the poor bull fell on his back, his horns coming down and hitting the ground last.

This happened so quickly we did not even have time to think; besides; there was nothing we could have done to save him. Time stopped moving, all I could hear was the heavy sound of the brown bull breathing hard as it lunged forward for the kill. I was gripped by an immense fear that I was seeing our bull being killed right in front of our eyes.

Nobody moved nor uttered a word. Not even the other boys were celebrating certain victory. It had all happened too quickly for the mind to follow. The brown bull continued pounding Afrikanda whilst he was on the ground. He rolled Afrikanda along like a rug doll.

Finally, the older boy that Mandla had challenged chuckled and had a wide smile on his face.

"I'm sure he's dead"; he announced nonchalantly. By now all the other boys were cheering loudly. It was complete pandemonium. They were shouting.

"Go Zeus. Kill him Zeus. Finish him Zeus!".

Zeus as we now knew him by his name; literally rolled Afrikanda along like a ball and back onto his feet. Much to my surprise; the absolute impossible had happened; Afrikanda was still alive. Zeus was as much surprised to see him back up as we were and hesitated for a second.

That was all Afrikanda needed to gain back his confidence. Zeus lunged forward again, trying to hammer Afrikanda with his head; but that technique was old news. This time Afrikanda was ready. He simply tilted his head slightly presenting a sharp horn. Zeus was not expecting the sharp horn lunged straight into it ripping a gash on his forehead. Blood started pouring out.

Afrikanda had had years of fighting Sekuru; our big old ram which had head butted every single one of the boys who unwittingly got too close to the sheep. He had terrorised us until one day he had head butted Daniel so much and caused him so much fright that uncle Ben had decided enough was enough; it was time for him to go.

The meat from that ram had kept us going for months and his skin was now a very nice rug used to sit on; on the kitchen floor.

For some reason; every so often Afrikanda and Sekuru would just annoy each other; and spend an entire afternoon fighting.

Afrikanda had found his strength; however hard the brown bull tried he could not get past needle sharp horns. Zeus was bleeding from a couple of deep cuts one directly over his eye so blood was dripping over his eye. Afrikanda grew confident, he jabbed and stabbed Zeus with his sharp horns.

Now it was our turn to celebrate. We were screaming.

"Go Afrikanda. Come on Afrikanda!".

Zeus tried to turn tail and run; but that was a big mistake. At that very point Afrikanda lunged forward and buried both horns straight into his neck. Zeus bellowed in agony and fled the battle ground as fast as his big fat legs could go. Afrikanda gave a cursory chase and then stopped; bellowing loudly and kicking back dirt with one of his front legs.

There was pandemonium like l had never seen before; we were screaming jumping; hugging each other; throwing arms up in the air and even crying. I had never experienced such joy in my whole life. We had put a stamp in history, made our mark. We could now go and conquer the rest of the world.

It was already lunchtime by the time we got the cattle back to the paddock on our farm. Naturally uncle Bill was not very happy. The sheep had been left in their pen all morning. The big boys Mandla and Jabu didn't really pay him too much attention; so nothing came of that.

As if the day could not get any better; the girls had cooked the first milk porridge; the milk taken from the cow straight after giving birth to a calf. No-one had eaten it because; traditionally the first milk porridge was given to the cattle boys. Most of the boys tried a little bit but didn't like the taste; it was either too rich or had funny smell to them.

So a small number of us ended up with huge bowls of first milk porridge to ourselves. The porridge mixed with a bit of sugar and a tiny bit of salt tasted divine. I had no idea why anyone would not like it. I was quite sure it even tasted better than the pudding that Big Mamma had made once; all those years back. I could feel myself getting revitalised as I consumed spoonful after spoonful; it's goodness slowly seeping into my veins and restoring my strength after that brutal morning.

Not long after that feast lunch was served. We still had the the meat from the head of a cow. My stomach had never been this full before; to the point where it actually hurt.The day kept on getting better. After lunch uncle Ben gave a little speech.

"Boys you did very well with the cattle today, taking them to the dip and bringing them all back without a hitch. Well done!".

We looked at one another and smiled. If he only knew how close it came to being the mother of all disasters; he would not be saying what he'd just said.

Then from behind his back he produced a small plastic bag and handed it to Mandla. Mandla promptly opened it and took out the most amazing thing from it. It was a black and white leather football; just like the one they had at school. We literally screamed with joy and if any of the boys was still eating they stopped as we all ran outside to try out the new ball before uncle could even explain how it worked.

Mandla explained that inside the bag was something else called a bladder. He had to push the bladder into the mouth of the ball leaving just the bladder spout. Then he had to do up the two strings that looked like shoe laces and pull them tight. Once that was done we could pump the ball with a bicycle or car tyre pump; bend the spout over and tie it up tightly so that no air could escape, then push the spout in the small gap left for the shoe lace. Finally tie up the shoe lace and push it down under the lips so that it was flash with the edges of the leather. This was all easier said than done.

Mandla made tremendously effort to get the ball pumped and ready to play with. The most difficult part was threading the string through the holes over mouth of the football and then tying them together so that the string was flash with the leather of the football. Once done; we had a go at kicking the ball back and forth between us all in the yard.

Jabu suggested that we should arrange a match between us and the Shumba and Maposa boys.

First we had to build a football ground. We knew exactly where to build it. In the paddock was a piece of land about the size of a football ground with perfectly mown grass where the sheep had been grazing and it looked like the grass had been cut by a machine. The land was perfectly flat and level east to west; north to south it slopped gently south down towards the river. Apart from that, it was perfect ground for playing football.

All we had to do; was to mark the perimeter of the football ground and all the lines for the centre and the goal. To mark the lines we just cleared the grass with a hoe. For the goal posts we dug some holes in the ground and placed poles cut from gum trees. The football ground was ready. It looked pretty good. We arranged for the game to start a couple of hours before sunset when it started to cool down and when the animals didn't normally wonder too far off.

I have no idea how word got to all the tall boys across two farms; but at the arranged time boys seemed to arrive from everywhere. Much to our surprise; even the adults dropped their chores and came to play with the new football. Uncle Bill self elected himself as the referee. We split ourselves into two teams. As usual the Shumba boys joined the Maposa boys. We had a strong team including some adults and a couple of the farm workers. However; the Shumba and Maposa boys were all quite tall; whereas, apart from Joseph and Steven everyone else on our side was short in comparison.

Uncle Bill blew the whistle to start the game. A few minutes into the game Mandla scored a goal. A few minutes later Jabu; who was the best footballer both at home and at school; dodged past a whole group of Shumba boys; running uphill and hit a fiery shot past the goal keeper who simply stood aside. We were two nil up after no more than twenty minutes.

About halfway in the game we swapped sides; this time were playing downhill towards the river. The running was easier and the scoring easy. We made short work of the Maposa and Shumba boys that evening. The light started fading away. The whistle blew; the game was over. We had won; 5-2, against all odds. The Shumba boys were ungracious in defeat and wanted to leave immediately and so we let them go. We invited the Maposa boys to stay for dinner as we still had loads of meat left from the cow's head.

After locking up the animals for the night we walked back home in the twilight and played outside in the warm evening breeze. Somebody had the bright idea to play volleyball against the girls. Whilst dinner was being prepared we quickly rigged a volleyball net by tying strips of cloth over the washing line. It seemed everyone; even the girls wanted to play with the new ball.

Betty and Joy; the two house girls joined the girls side. Betty and Joy were two sides of the same coin. Both tall; slender and beautiful. Betty was light in complexion; and Joy was dark as one could get; but both were stunningly beautiful. They came a long way from one of the villages in the reserves. We had walked to their village once when I was even younger, maybe four of five years old and had to be carried on someone's shoulders some of the way.

On the way the girls had noticed a short tree totally infested by thousands and thousands of big fat black caterpillars. The girls had screamed 'Maximbi!' so excited at the sight of the bugs; and ran off the path to start collecting the bugs and filled two baskets they had been carrying. They had explained that these were the most delicious delicacy they had ever eaten. They would dry them out in the sun; then cook them in peanut butter. None of us could believe anyone could eat these bugs. I could not believe that such beautiful girls could eat something like that.

When we got to their village I had been quite sure we had reached the end of the world. After being offered a drink of 'maheu'; a brew made from left over sadza; mashed by hand and mixed with water and a bit of sugar and left to ferment for a day or two. A couple of swigs of that had been amazingly refreshing and satisfying. I had sat down watching a couple of vicious looking dogs; with large yellow canines. They growled viciously if anyone tried approach them. They snapped at flies buzzing around their heads; occasionally catching one between their gnarly teeth. Then we had retraced our footsteps; and got back in the dark navigating only by moonlight.

Our new Auntie; Sibongile had also joined the girls team. She was an Aunt; but she was only fifteen or sixteen years old. The girls didn't stand a chance against us; but they put up a good fight. They did however; do something amazing. In order to stop their short skirts from flashing whenever they jumped up to hit the ball they tucked their skirts inside bottom bit of their underwear so that they looked like they were wearing shorts. They looked amazing.

Dinner once again was a feast. There was sadza; potatoes; sweet potatoes; pumpkins vegetables and more meat from the head of the cow. There was plenty enough to go around and after a cup of water my belly was completely full.

Soon after dinner the Maposa boys decided to leave. Jabu decided it would be a good idea to walk them all the way back to their house. I think because we had had such a good day together; he just didn't want the day to ever end. Uncle Ben suggested we take his big silver torch. It was his prized possession. He never ordinarily let anyone touch that torch and here he was offering it to Mandla.

We set off in the dark. It was a warm night; moonless and dark so it was really handy having the torch. We reached the place where Ngorima had fought and nearly killed

Afrikanda when Garikai, one of the Maposa boys started screaming in agony.

"I've been bitten, something is bitten me!"; he was screaming.

"What was it, was it a snake?"; we were all asking him.

"Shine the light over here please; Mandla"; one of the Maposa brothers begged.

Mandla shined the torch just in time to see a large scorpion scurry into the long grass on the side of the dirt road.

"Oh my god; it's a huge scorpion. Is he gonna die?"; John asked.

We were less than half a mile from the Maposa house; so whilst a couple of the boys ran to the house as fast as they could to warn their parents; we walked slowly with the now hobbling Garikai; who was sobbing uncontrollably; because he thought he was going to die. We delivered him at his house. Fortunately the Maposa's were quite rich and had a car to take him to the hospital that very night. We turned round for the long track back home.

Chapter 7 Giri

It did not take very long for the football to be ruined. We played it every afternoon in the yard and every evening in our new football ground. The white and black paint started coming off the ball; exposing the grey leather underneath. In the evenings it turned into a volleyball that was played with the girls. At weekends; especially on Saturdays; when we didn't have to do any farm work apart from go to church, get back and look after the animals we played volleyball the whole afternoon as long as someone was keeping an eye on the animals.

Sooner or later the seams of the ball; started to tear and the hexagons started to come away and the orange soft bladder underneath started to pop through. We tried to patch the ball up by pushing a small piece of cloth inside The hole and this worked for a little while; but soon a thorn or anything sharp would go through the thin skin into the bladder. Once there was a hole in the bladder, even the tiniest of holes, the ball deflated and was rendered completely useless. We started patching the ladder until the repair Kit ran out.

Eventually, the ball was too far gone and we went back to making our own balls, by filling a plastic back with scrunched up newspapers and old rags and kicking that around. This was not much fun for the town boys; and nobody came to play.

One morning quite out the blue, Mandla came up with a game he called Giri that he said he played in town. This was by far this craziest game I had ever seen. It was some sort of variation of baseball that we used to play from time to time. The rules were the same as for baseball;

but giri was not played with a ball. Instead the batter had a bat with a flat surface like a normal two by two plank. To bat the batter would start by striking a short stick sharpened at both ends. By striking one side of the sharp stick with the edge of the bat the small stick jumped up from the ground spinning like crazy; then the batter would take a swing at it and launch as far as he could. The usual rules of baseball applied. All fielders had to try and catch that sharp stick whilst it flew through the air towards them like a speeding arrow.

Injuries to hands facies even any part of the body were common. I could see the madness of the game because once; I had tried to catch the short sharp stick flying threw the air and my hand had been impaled; with the stick almost going right through the hand. The pain had been unbearable; but the game went on amidst raucous laughter. It was madness.

Mandla loved this game and was extremely good at it. When he struck that stick it went whizzing by like a swarm of African killer bees. So we knew to stand well back and to duck when he was batting. But; one day, the gods abandoned us; he struck the stick perfectly; it took off whizzing through the air like a bullet. Daniel was standing too close and couldn't get out of the way quick enough. The sharp end of the short stick buried itself in his thigh. He screamed like a little girl; as Mandla tried to pull the giri out of his thigh. He couldn't as each time he tried Daniel screamed louder.

I took Jabulani's strength and cunning to get it out.

Jabu just went up to Daniel and said. "Look Daniel; snake behind you!"

Daniel went quiet for a moment and looked behind himself scanning the ground for a snake whereupon Jabu, bent down and quickly yanked the stick out of Joseph thigh. Blood streamed out of the wound. We sat Daniel down and poured sand over the wound from the road where we were playing. A technique we had seen Dreyfus use time and time again every time he stubbed his toe on a rock. The bleeding stopped immediately. Even though we all agreed that no one should mention this to the adults; that very lunch time word had already got out; and the adults knew everything that had happened.

Mandla got a dressing down from uncle Ben. This was the first time I had ever seen him getting told off for anything. Giri was banned. We were not allowed to ever play it again.

"What if you took someone's eye out?"; uncle had asked Mandla quite beside himself with anger. My sentiments exactly, I thought to myself. Whilst it was a real fun game to play; the thrill of managing to get out of the way as that sharp giri stick flew towards you was amazing. But regardless, I thought it was completely crazy and dangerous and I was quite happy never to play it again.

Holidays went by quickly; but the last few days of the holidays went even quicker. This had been the most exciting holiday I had ever had. As far as I could remember it was the only holiday where kids from the entire family clan ever came together, imbued us with knowledge of one another that would last us the rest of our lives.

One Sunday morning Uncle Ben announced that the town people were all going back that day. The whole morning was spent loading up the cars; washing getting ready for the journey. The mood was sombre. The sun didn't seem to shine so bright; the breeze wasn't so cool and the food didn't taste so delicious. For those of us staying behind it was heart breaking. Not knowing when and if we would ever see some of our cousins again. It would be months before we saw the town people again.

The only comforting thing was that aunt Sibongile was staying back. She had won the hearts of everyone on the farm. Her warm and happy go lucky personality filled the atmosphere and made us feel like every day was going to be a good day. We loved her accent and the mistakes she made when trying to speak Shona with a Xhosa accent. She didn't care; she loved everything and everyone.

At fifteen or sixteen she was already an amazing cook, and her job was to stay back and help Auntie Ruth with all the chores whilst repeating grade seven which she had failed a couple of times already.

Chapter 8 The Year That Time Forgot

Just like that the holidays were over, and we were back at school to start my second grade. The grade two teacher was a big stern looking old lady called Mrs Nhema. She was terrifying to look at. She had an extremely large head and small beady dark eyes hidden behind green glasses with black amorphous spots that reminded me of the markings on some snakes. I couldn't help imagining that she could be the wife of a 'Binya'; legendary giants that roamed the forests capturing naughty small children; and roasting them in a giant wok before devouring them for dinner.

She shared the same surname as the chief of our district; Chief Nhema. Although I had never seen the chief; I had heard that he was a huge dark man with over twenty wives; over fifty children and over a thousand cattle making him the richest African man I had ever heard off. I imagined the Chief sitting on his big throne wearing a traditional African garments and a big lion skin over his shoulders and a crown made of the head of a lion with its mouth wide open; baring sharp massive canines. I was sure he would be a formidable ruler; dispensing justice with a swish of his cane with a handle of a golden baboon. I would have given anything to see him; just once but the chance never came up.

The fear of my grade one teacher was nothing compared to the fear I had for this monstrosity of a human being. My my fear of her was only tampered down by her nephew who had joined us in the second grade. He was at town boy from Salisbury present day Harare; also chubby with a friendly face that looked like he didn't have a care in the world. He was smart; well dressed, his uniform fitted well, was brand new and not a hand me down like the rest of us had. He was full of confidence and he seemed totally happy with himself. Town boys always had this easy-going look and manner about them that I really envied. I wished I could be like that one day; not have a care in the world and just live life and be happy all the time.

His name was was Christopher and we immediately became friends. We had one thing in common which was that we both lived on a farm. Chris as we called him loved to draw. He was very good at it. Every free moment he had; he had a pencil and pad in his hand; drawling something; a car, a man, a house and sometimes whole scenes of things. In no time he had filled out the whole pad with the drawings. Every kid liked to look at his drawings and we all tried to copy his technic. I even got quite good at drawing cars; but I quickly got bored with it; because I didn't see the point of all that drawing.

Chris wasn't just good at drawing; he was also very smart like Piye. He just seemed to know stuff; even stuff not in books like what was going to happen at school long before anyone else. If there was going to be a football match with another school; he would already tell us before it was announced at assembly.

To my utter surprise and delight Mrs Nhema was not the monster that I had imagined her to be. She was the exact opposite. She looked stern; but in fact, was soft and sensitive. Her voice was crystal clear; soft and gentle like a stream of water running over smooth rocks and pebbles. She scanned the classroom; looking at every face as she called out the register. I had the impression she was more like a mother hen; watching over all the chicks round; fierce to intruders; but gentle to her chicks. She had no favourite in the class; not even her nephew Chris.

Much to my disappointment; Precious had not showed up at school. Later; Piye explained that Mr Mbele; her father had been promoted as headteacher at another school and they had to move to that school. For me this was a punch in the stomach and I felt it. She had been someone to look forward to it everyday at school. Although; I had never mastered enough courage to speak to her; now that she was gone all hope was lost. As much as I loved school; the chance to see her beautiful face was a driving force; that made sure I never missed a day of school; if I could help it. Without her; I wasn't quite sure what I was going to do.

I soon forgot about Precious as the second year was all serious learning. Everything was piled in on us. Geography; Maths; telling time; History; English; Shona. For the first time I actually had to use my brain especially when it came to telling time. All sorts of new ways of looking at things opened up. It became clear that there was something bigger than us out there; and we were being prepared for it.

Sure enough my intuition was confirmed when John found a stereoscope with pictures of London. To see the pictures in a stereoscope; you held the stereoscope over your eyes so that the rest of the world was shut out and then you clicked a small lever on the side of the scope. The first time I did, I felt like I had been sucked into another universe. In that world there were pink soldiers wearing red coats; black trousers and big black hats as tall as a woman carrying a bucket of water on her head. There were strange looking red buses and cars going around a big circle with tall pointed pole in the middle. Click. Most amazing of all; were the young women in mini skirts and tight bell bottoms walking in lush green fields; their golden hair sparkling in the sun; they looked just how I imagined angels would look like. When the pictures went all the way round to the same pictures again, I handed the stereoscope back to John. The bright sunlight nearly blinded me; and I was back in our familiar world. But that experience had blown my mind completely.

A few months later as if by some sort of divine destiny during one of the school holidays; Uncle Ben handed me an envelope. In it was a ninth birthday card. It had a picture of that very same world, and I realised that world was real and one day I wanted to see it; and school was the only way to get there.

Sooner or later John got bored with stereoscope and decided to break it apart and find out how it worked. John did this with anything he found. Once he had found an old radio and he had disassembled it into pieces to find out if there were small people inside. For this he had got into trouble; but that did not stop his inquisitive mind. He took the lenses out of the stereoscope and discovered that he could use them as magnifying glasses.

We had so much fun with those magnifying glasses. At some point we decided that we were going to be scientists and were going to do some experiments. Everything went under the magnifying glasses; leaves, drops of water; hands eyes, grains of sand anything and everything.

One day we even decided we wanted to find out what everything was made of. First we decided to take something that we could cut with a knife until the smallest part was left. This we did with a stem of grass. But when it got to the smallest part under the magnifying glass it got clear that the knife was not able to cut the smallest part even though we were quite sure it was possible to cut it with a much smaller and thiner knife.

So, we thought of smashing a grain of sand with a hammer on an anvil. We pounded the grain of sand into a fine powder. Then carefully brushed away all the large pieces until on the evil was only the tiniest spec that could be seen under the magnifying glass. We could not imagine anything being smaller that; because the spec disappeared when we tried to look at it without the aid of the magnifying glass; and reappeared again under it. We decided that was it. Everything was made of the tiniest spec of dust. We were so pleased with our discovery.

John went on to make more discoveries; he found out that if you held the magnifying glass between the sun and your hand the hand got too hot to carry on like that. Soon he had discovered that he could start a fire when he held magnifying glass between the sun and a piece of paper or a tuft of grass.

Starting a fire with nothing, but a piece of glass and the sun. I thought it that was a real big deal; so I thought about it all day. A shepherd has plenty of time on his hands and I had done most of my thinking walking behind those sheep in the bush. By the end of the day, I was sure I had an idea. I had decided that there was already enough fire in the universe and all that was needed was the right tool to tap into it. I had often wondered what was in the space between the earth and the heavens. Yes, I could feel the air between my finger tips; but I was sure there was something else; that we could not see; I had no idea what to call it; but the magnifying glass was enough to convince me I was right.

Once or twice when we were out herding cattle by the big rock, a strange thing had happened to us. It had been a clear day, without a single cloud in the sky. The sun had been particularly hot that day. All of a sudden a dark shadow had passed over us; and out of nowhere for no more than a couple of seconds; a ghostly shape of an impala had pranced across the paddock and disappeared into thin air. The impala had not been real; and yet several of us had seen it.

What could do this to us, on a bright clear day if it wasn't something that came out of the clear blue sky. Some invisible energy that came from somewhere travelling through space and went right through us. I was quite sure that it was the same energy that John had managed to focus to make a fire; not the simple fact that it was the sun's energy focused into a point causing something to heat up.

Grade two finished without a hitch. Mrs Nhema had turned out to the best teacher I had ever had; kind and caring. By the end of the year; I was convinced that she was more like a great Aunt taking care of the lot of us; as if we were her own kids. I had learned that appearances were deceptive and it was not good to judge a person by what they looked like; but by how they treated me. She had been nothing; but kind to me and word had even got as far as home that I was a good clever little boy.

Chapter 9 The Beginning Of The End

The third year of school started like a fiendish explosion. By then I was old enough to know that things sometimes just happened; for no particular reason at all, and sometimes you just got caught up in the storm whether you liked it or not.

It all started in the summer holidays over Christmas when everyone came home from town on holidays. That December had been; unusually hot and wet. The dam had swelled up so high we thought it was going burst. The spillover pool had filled up so high it looked like in small lake. It had filled up with catfish and uncle Ben did not like this one bit. He ordered that the catfish be removed from the spillage pool in case they swum up into the dam and ate all the fish.

A drainage ditch was dug to drain all water out of the spillage pool. From long before sun rise all the men and boys on the farm and converged at the dam carrying picks; hoes and shovels. A long trench was dug from the lower slope of the spill pool and at the very last moment; carefully connected to the spillage pool by knocking out the last bit of earth separating the trench from the pool. A torrent of water gushed down the slope across the road towards the river. When almost all the water had drained out; there was mass writhing dirty muddy catfish left in the middle of the spill pool. They soon churned the little water left into a quagmire of slimy slithering mud. It was as if the mud was alive with a mass of catfish slithering over and under like giant snakes.

Uncle Ben had not expected this many catfish so on seeing this mass; he was stunned and dit not have an idea what do with them. He stood there with one hand on his chin; and another resting on the handle of a pick. For a man who was a teacher in a high school; he liked to get his hands really dirty every once in a while. Always turning up to a job like this; in a fine clean shirt; nice trousers and a pair of gumboots. Of course by the end of the day; his clothes would be filthy; but the next day he would be in fine clean clothes once more.

For religious reasons we did not eat catfish; but it was not in our nature to waste anything; so like a true master he came up with a plan.

"Who's the fastest between you boys?"; he asked looking at John and I.

I knew that he already knew the answer to that question; because of the way he was looking at me. It was always a wonderful honour to be singled out of the group by him. It meant that I was special, had something extra to contribute and made me feel very proud. I put my hand up.

"Run to the Shumba's farm and tell them to come and help themselves to the catfish from the spill pool. Tell them to pass on the message to the Maposa's so they can pass it on to the people from the reserves".

"What are you going to say?"; he asked me to repeat his instructions back to him.

I repeated his instructions back to him; and he said; "Good. Run along!".

I ran as fast I could, it was uphill all the way to the Shumba's; but I didn't even break a sweat. I knew that I could run for miles like this; without needing a rest or a drink. Eager to impress; so they could all be amazed how fast; I was. I raced across fields, grassland taking as straight a route as I could; not even caring if I stepped on a snake or not. The desire to impress made me fearless and in no time at all; I was on the Shumba's farm delivering the message to Mr Shumba himself.

Then I turned round and ran straight back. The run back was easy. Downhill, my every step was twice as long as when I was going up.

Uncle Ben almost didn't believe I had delivered the message so quickly; but before long people started descending on the that dam; some walking and some on bicycles. The whole morning people were arriving, catching the huge catfish with their bare hands; loading their buckets; full to the brim with catfish.

After nearly all morning of watching people come and go; we were bored and hungry and took ourselves back home for breakfast. After breakfast we took the cattle we had forgotten all about all morning.

After letting the cattle out we sat on the big white Rock relaxing for a while. We were exhausted from all the digging and running in the morning. A group of women carrying baskets laden with catfish walked past us in the distance heading north towards the villages. They balanced the baskets perfectly on their heads leaving both hands free to walk normally chatting; laughing and gesticulating wildly with their hands. They walked single file, one behind the other following the twisting and turning of the winding path. We watched the women walk until they were hidden from view by some bushes.

My eyes drifted back to the cattle. They were munching the soft grass on the riverbank; and were in no hurry to go anywhere. They seemed to be making up for lost grazing time. I followed the group of cattle with my eyes, at the back of my head looking for something, looking for Afrikanda. For sometime Afrikanda had begun playing up. He would disappear during the day; no one would know where he was; the next morning he would be back grazing outside the kraal.

He could not be kept in the kraal at night either. He simply smashed a hole in the kraal and by morning he was gone. I soon learned; that the reason for the strange behaviour was that he wanted to go out and mate with the cows from neighbouring farms; especially the Shumba farm, who did not have a bull of their own. He smashed out of our kraal, trudged all the way across the farm and smashed his way into the Shumba's kraal as easily as he had smashed out of his.

The problem was that a couple of weeks earlier,; when he smashed his way into the Shumba's kraal, he had left a big gapping hole in their flimsy kraal; allowing all the cattle to escape and devour their crop. Mr Shumba was not at all happy and came round demanding compensation.

That day the only work that had been done was strengthening the walls of the kraal with bigger thicker poles. When the work was finished the kraal looked like a fortress. Uncle Bill supervised the locking of the kraal gate that evening and boasted that even an elephant or rhino could not smash his way out of that Kraal. No-one disagreed; the kraal had never looked more solid.

Over dinner that night Uncle Bill continued boasting; the way we fixed that kraal; Brother nothing can escape from it.

"Bulls don't fly do they!", he joked.

"Because; that's the only way he would be able to get out; by flying like bird".

The next morning; to our huge surprise and disappointment; Afrikanda had broken out of the kraal and vanished. He had managed to stick a horn in between the thickest set of logs that made up the kraal wall and left them up; making a gap that he simply pushed his way through and and got out.

Uncle Bill was livid. His anger knew no bounds. He paced up and down shouting and cussing.

"That bull is possessed"; he said angrily. "He's completely mad. I will kill him; I promise you".

He complained furiously that he'd had enough of that bull, and he did not know what to do next. The next thing is going to do is attack one of the children he said displaying a rare concern for the cattle boys. I was quite sure the only reason he was angry about was that he had been outsmarted by a bull.

Mr Shumba had been back on our farm; before breakfast; even more angry than the last time. That day, we were told we were to help with the harvest and did not need to look after the cattle.

The next day we were back on normal cattle duty. Afrikanda had disappeared again. We just thought he had gone to the Shumba's again; a couple of days went by but he never returned. It seemed as if he had vanished off the surface of the earth; without a trace never to be seen again.

Several days later uncle Ben went on a trip to Ndanga, and re-appeared back on the farm with small Alsatian puppy and another head of a cow to smash up for dinner.

The small puppy was a feisty little thing; with razor sharp teeth. He liked nothing more than chasing us around the yard and biting our legs and feet whilst we ran for dear life. Even though he was small and young, we were no match for his speed; and by the time we found something to climb to get out of his reach, he had taken a few bites on the legs and drawn blood. For some reason; John decided to call it Sizwe after Uncle Sizwe.

The loss of Afrikanda was a big blow to us all. It left a big empty hole in our lives. We no longer had a bull to be proud of. We just had boring old cattle. It was like a farm without a soul. We consoled ourselves with the knowledge that we still had his two sons. They were still too young but we knew they would grow to be just as big one day.

One of the bullocks was black and almost a carbon copy of Afrikanda. His small horns were already showing signs of the beautiful symmetry and proportion of his father's horns. He promised to be a great looking bull in a few years. The other bullock, almost the same size and age, was cream coloured and a good size for a bullock. His mother was Uganda the cow that had fallen in the dam whilst drinking water and never managed to get up again. She had to be butchered on the spot; rather than leaving her there to drown. Uganda's son, was a fine looking bullock except for the fact that whilst one of his horns was perfect the other pointed straight down the side of his face. This was a big disappointment to us. How would he be able to fight with only one horn when he was a mature bull.

John had named the black bullock; Bullet as the bullock was as perfect as freshly minted bullet. Perfectly proportioned, with a shiny black coat. He was going to be an even bigger and stronger Afrikanda. The cream coloured bull; John had named him Rhino, on account of his single useful horn. With Afrikanda gone; one of these bullocks would have to take his place and become the bull of the farm. To us, it was pretty obvious that Bullet would be the successor.

I thought we did not have to worry about making our choice for a good few years and was shocked when one morning after breakfast soon after Afrikanda's disappearance; uncle Bill gave the order for one of the bulls to be castrated that morning.

I had long arrived at the conclusion that adults were entirely irrational and insane beings. They lived in a parallel universe to us, imposing draconian rules on us without even taking into consideration how we felt about anything. They never talked to us about anything; as if they thought we idiots without any opinion of our own. They just gave orders without regard of what we thought about anything, and every single time, we followed the orders without question. Sometimes we didn't like what we'd been asked to do; but we did it anyway.

We let the cattle out of the kraal and drove them to the rock. We all got ready to catch Rhino and bring him to the rock to be castrated; but much to our shock and surprise, uncle Bill stood high on the old white rock and shouted.

"Catch that black bullock and bring him over here!".

We just stood there looking at him; unable to comprehend what he had just said. I would have sworn he had a big smile on his face; except, with him it was quite hard to tell whether he was unhappy about something or whether he was having the time of his life.

"You boys, didn't you hear what I said. Don't stand there like a bunch of morons. I said go and catch that black bullock and bring him over here; now!"

John glanced at Rhino; then back at Bullet and back again at Rhino and started to say something; but his father cut him off before even one word could come out.

"Go!"; he ordered vehemently.

We ran towards where Bullet was grazing. I could feel my whole world collapsing around me with each and every step. I couldn't believe what was happening; the most beautiful bullock that was going to grow into an amazing bull was now going to be turned into nothing; but an ordinary ox. An ox use to pull a cart; or plough the fields. Not a prized fighter like we had dreamed he would become. I had little respect for uncle Bill; because I thought he was a fool; but from then on I had no respect at all. How could he do this to us. It was easy to see that he had chosen Bullet because of his obvious similarities to Afrikanda; but to leave us with a lame one horned bull was the cruelest of all acts.

We surrounded Bullet so that he could not escape. Steven; put a rope around his horns and we walked him to the rock. Once on the rock, ropes were tied to the front and back legs and he was pulled down. He went crashing down on the rock on one side.

Even for a young animal, he was very strong. Just about every male was present at the rock to help. I looked around for the man from the dip whom I had seen do a castration before; but I did not see him. The last time I had seen him do a castration on a sheep no less, he had with him a big tool that looked like a pincers; that he used to castrate the animal; but he was nowhere to be seen. I thought maybe Uncle Ben had invested in our own pincers from town so we could do the castrations ourselves and I got very excited about this. Maybe one day we could get to try it ourselves.

Instead to my horror Uncle Bill brought out the kitchen knife, that had been wrapped in some dirty old cloth and started sharpening it on a whetstone.

I was horrified, and was asking myself when had the decision changed from castrating to killing the animal; besides we still had plenty of meat from the cow's head brought back a few days earlier so what did he want to kill the animal for?.

There were man holding ropes on both ends, and two straddling his stomach so he could not try to stand up. Jason was holding the sharp hones and commented that the horns were quite sharp.

"We will chop the ends of those as well", Uncle Bill suggested.

"Jabulani, go and borrow a hacksaw from the workshop, run along!".

Jabulani was sent running, to fetch a hacksaw. Jabu and uncle Bill were not the best of friends either; and uncle Bill did everything he could to pick on him and exert his authority. Jabu started running. He was the fastest amongst all of us; but only for short distances; for long distances he would have struggled. Uncle Bill; kew that yet he still chose him. He, continued sharpening the knife and checking its sharpness against his thumb; for a while.

"Right, hold him down and make sure he can't move. Steven, hold his legs down on the ground so he can't kick me"; Uncle Bill ordered.

Then he moved in towards the bull, kneeling behind his stomach near the rear end, and picked up the testicles of the bull with one hand, then he sliced open the scrotum and cut each testicle out, tossing each to the waiting dogs.

The bullock bellowed in agony; bleeding like a slaughtered pig. Uncle tied up the sacks with a string and said, that will do.

He stood up nonchalantly and groaned from the stress of kneeling down for a few minutes. He wiped the blade on the bullocks belly and tossed the knife on the rock.

Presently; Jabu got back with a hacksaw in one hand and handed it over to uncle Bill.

"Right; lets have a look at those horns. Yes they are very sharp. Hold him down boys. One of you here; help hold down its head!"

He hacked about a couple inches off the end of each horn. By now Bullet was forming at the mouth.

"Set him loose boys!"; he ordered.

Bullet lay there for a little while; then struggled to his feet, then made his way off the rock and went off to stand in the shade of an old thorn tree.

The dogs licked the blood of the rock clean. Bullet just stood under the thorn tree; motionless. Watching the bullock in such a terrible state; even John who never shut up was speechless.

Is he going to die I; asked. I had observed; through years of cattle herding and shepherding that when an animal was going to die, or give birth it usually took itself to a quiet hidden spot away from all the other animals. Bullet, appeared to have done the same thing. He appeared to be in bad shape.

"No; he's going to be fine", came the answer from Steven. "Give him a few hours and he'l l be as right as rain"; he added.

Bullet didn't look like he was going to be alright to me. The situation looked hopeless. I loved the farm; but I was traumatised by what I had just seen. I didn't care if I never saw another castration like that in my whole life again.

However; Bullet recovered quickly and by the end of the day he was already grazing and apart from a swarm of flies that followed him around all day he looked pretty much okay. I was stunned to notice that he didn't seem that much bothered about the loss of his testicles. He wasn't try to look for them or acting like he was missing something. I was quite sure if it had been me that been castrated like that; I would have been very upset about it.

But; jokes aside, I could not understand how uncle could make such a poor choice. A bull with one horn was no good to us whatsoever. We had a reputation to keep.

From that day on, things just kept on going from bad to worse. Uncle Ben started talking about building a house on the hill again. For years and years he'd gone about building a mansion on the hill; but nothing had ever been done about it. During dinner one evening, he announced that he wanted to start clearing all the trees on the hill the next day to make way for the construction of his mansion. He explained that he didn't want any trees in front of the house because it was going to be so grand that he wanted it to be seen by everyone for miles around.

The next morning; even before breakfast; several large trees on the hill had been chopped down. There were trees that had been there since the beginning of time as far as I was concerned and they had all been cut down; but nothing in my life hurt me more than seeing our favourite two tsuma trees and our old 'mutohwe' or chewing gum tree chopped down. That morning I felt every blow of the axe that went into that small tsuma tree; as Steven reluctantly cut the tree down. For the first time in our lives we had protested and begged Uncle Ben not to cut the small tsuma tree down. Jabulani and John, who were more confident that I was; begged and cried; uncle Ben just waved them away. Steven hesitated.

"Are you sure, you want this tree to be cut down?"; he had asked almost begging him to change his mind.

"Cut it down; man!". Uncle Ben commanded, impatiently.

Uncle Ben; was a highly energetic man; never resting for a minute; always busy doing one thing or another. Once he got an idea in his head; he was like a run away train; there was no stopping him. Steven chopped the beautiful little old tree down. It was the only one of its kind on the farm; or anywhere else for that matter. It was like seeing an old grandmother murdered right in front of our eyes. An old granny who had looked after us; given us rare treats for years. Now she lay dead on the ground; good only for firewood. Something died in me that day. When word got to Auntie Lizzy and Gogo Madube what uncle Ben had done; they were livid.

"Ben how could you do this. How could you cut down the children's fruit trees. What will they eat now?"; Auntie Lizzy had asked him angrily.

"They have lots of guava trees?"; he had replied.

The tsuma was a sweet juicy fruit whose size ranged from the size of a small marble to the really big marble. The tsuma's ripened in the middle of winter, when guavas were long gone out of season. The tsuma and the chewing gum fruits were a really important supplement to our diet in the cold dry winter months; when food was scarce. There were three types of tsuma trees on the farm, and for each type we had only one fruiting tree of each. The rest of the trees were sterile and never produced any fruits. It was a delicate and fine balance because the loss of any one of those trees would have left us with one less fruit tree; something we could ill afford. We had lost two in one day. The little old tree that produced the sweetest most beautiful of all tsumas; which when ripe was a beautiful yellow perfectly cylindrical fruit about half the length of a grown person's pinkie; or nearly the size and almost the same shape as an olive.

The other tsuma tree that was cut down was our real bread and butter and old favourite; it had grown on a large old ant hill, and produced copious amounts of large super sweet fruits, that were delicious and filling. It was that tree we visited when we were hungry in the winter months. Now it too; lay on the ground dead. Just like that, gone. Something that had stood for years and years; and all of a sudden it was reduced to firewood.

I had loved and worshipped uncle Ben up until that morning; but when he cut that little old tree down, our favourite 'tsuma' tree the rarest tree of them all so that his fancy new house, not even built yet could be seen for miles around; I lost almost all the respect I had for him. The two tsuma trees were pretty special, one had sweet fruits any other used to produce large copious amounts of large almost golf ball size sweet fruits. In the cold winter months and long dry season these trees would flower produce fruits and ripen right when there was little other food like maize, in the field or in the house. For as long as I could remember the trees had been our source of top up meal, when hungry after school John and I headed out first to these trees and gorged ourselves on the delicious fruits. But; now just like that they were gone. I had no idea what we were supposed to eat now that they were gone.

My childhood brain tried to figure out why he would do something so cruel. Did he not realise we needed those fruits, or did he just do it on purpose; besides the trees were nowhere near where the house was going to stand yet they had to go. As a kid I understood there to be two kinds of adults, cruel adults that beat you up for no reason and kind adults that protected you from the beatings. He wasn't much of a beater, but that single act was far more cruel than all the beatings I had ever had; put together.

So it was, that even before breakfast had been served, Uncle had managed to cut down the most important trees to us on the farm. The emptiness that followed that act; was unbearable. It was as if someone had died. John and I looked at each other; we were the real ones affected, because we lived on the farm all year round never going anywhere else except for those rare occasions when were seriously ill or something out of the ordinary had happened. We looked at each other and did not say anything, only the eyes spoke of a deep pain that no words could express. It wasn't about the trees, it was about the act of cruelty and the lack of empathy that hurt the most. How could he not see that what he had done was going to hurt us.

To add insult to injury he had ordered the big 'mutohwe' tree, the chewing gum tree to be chopped down as well, and the cruel axe had come down on it. At that point I knew something was wrong with the man and I lost all sense of respect I had for him. The chewing gum tree produced fruits that when ripe split open like a flower bulb, and each petal was wedge shaped like an orange wedge. Each wedge was dripping with a sugary syrup that oozed out and dripped down the bulb beckoning all creatures, to come and feast. To eat you simply picked the bulb, and broke of each wedge as you do for an orange wedge and chewed the tough wedge squeezing the nectar out of the wedge with a sucking action. The sugar hit the back of your brain and sent you into a world of joy and happiness.

To see that tree lying on the ground, now only good for firewood was like seeing my own mother lying dead on her death bed. God seemed to have deserted us and left us that day.

Why had Uncle done this, if he cared about us why would he do such a thing. It did not make sense. That day I learned one thing, that adults were completely mad and never to be trusted. As children we couldn't say anything even if we didn't agree with what was happening. We had no voice, because saying anything would be considered disrespectful and carried a huge risk of being beaten to a pulp. So we bottled up the injury to carry it along for the rest of our lives.

From that day on, nothing in our lives was ever the same. It was as if the winds of change had finally arrived, and just swept the world we knew away. Things had always been the same, unchanging stable rhythm of life, for as long as I could remember. The sun came up, I went school, I got back home from school, I took the sheep and cattle out, saw a snake or two; nothing had ever changed. That day though; there was something else in the air. I could feel it.

After the 'tsuma' trees and chewing gum tree had been cut, we pretty much avoided the hill until the town people had gone back to town as it was too painful to see; where once the trees had stood there now there was nothing.

Things were changing around us so fast. Afrikanda had disappeared without an explanation, our fruit trees cut down and a flurry of activity on the hill where the new house was going to be built.

Uncle had explained it all, the house was going to be at the top of the hill. It was going to have two sitting rooms, a dining room, kitchen two toilets, and five bedrooms. A toilet in the house had been the strangest thing I had ever heard. Our current toilet was a shack situated about two hundred yards from the kitchen hut, you had to walk miles; about two hundred yards really; to get to it and after dark, nobody used it, they just went to the side of the house and peed against a bush or against the back wall of one of the houses.

Once one of the women had nearly been bitten by a snake whilst walking in the dark with a dim lamp to the toilet. So most people figured, it wasn't worth the risk. This toilet was a deep pit, covered by a concrete floor with a small triangular hole in it at one end. If you looked inside the hole on a good day, you could see millions of maggots writhing about in it. I used to have nightmares about falling in in that pit and I often imagined that was what hell was like if you could get to it, yellow and full of maggots. It smelled like hell too.

Once; a chicken had fallen inside that hole, and all attempts to fish it out had failed, the poor bird had eventually died after a couple of weeks of marching up and down the big pit and dodging poos as they dropped down the hole.

It was fairly disgusting affair. So, to imagine that this stench would be in the new house, was beyond comprehension. Not one, but two stinking toilets in the house. I was sure that was a very bad idea.

Chapter 10 England

For all the surprises that had happened that holiday, nothing had prepared me for what happened next. Even as I could feel the winds of change blowing from the east, nothing had prepared me for what happened next during that crazy summer holiday.

It was probably the last week of the summer holidays and the mood was both sombre and electric at the same time. There was excitement about going back to town, excitement about going back to school, sadness thinking about friends going away and sadness about the loneliness that would follow.

We had just got back home from turning the animals in that evening. All the adults were sat outside in the warm evening twilight; chatting. The fireplace in the middle of the yard, which was used on nice evenings like this was burning steadily with a big three legged pot called a 'bodo' bubbling away.

My nose detected meat, potatoes and my stomach started rumbling. Auntie Ruth was busy doing just about everything at the same time as usual. The woman was a complete machine who worked non stop from the time the sun came up to the moment she lay down to go to sleep. The food smelled wonderful; wafting all the way from the middle of the yard to the edge of the yard a couple of hundred yards out. Whenever there was meat we knew the meal was going to be good.

As soon as the adults saw us, uncle Ben called my name out.

"Nkosi, come here!".

"Sit down there!"; he said pointing at a spot on the ground.

My heart started pounding in my chest. To be singled out usually wasn't a good sign. I thought I was in big trouble until, he called my sister as well.

"Nomalanga, he called , you too, come here, sit down next to your brother!"; he ordered.

I knew something was up; but what?; this had an ominous characteristic, had someone we knew died, were we about to be sent off somewhere. My young brain was working hard to figure something out, had something happened to Gogo. No, she was sitting on a reed mat right there; next to Uncle Ben and all the other adults.

Uncle Ben put me out of my misery and pulled out a neatly folded piece of paper from his shirt pocket and said.

"This is a letter from your father in England. He want's to know how you're both, he said. He wants you to know he is married again. He has found a new mother for you".

'Manje uthate ikhiwa?', "Has he married a european woman?", Gogo asked.

"It says here she is West Indian?".

"Ngum'India. She is Indian?"; Gogo asked again, by now sounding very confused.

"No, mama!"; uncle Ben cried out, now already exasperated with his mother.

"Likiwa elivele eWest India. No, she is a white from West India".

"No, she must be West Indian, white, black, Indian".

By the time, the adults had finished debating I had no clue whether my new mother; was white, black or Indian, European or what!. I didn't even know what an Indian looked like. So, I figured if it's England she must be white. In my head, there was only one black person in the whole of England and that was my father. How would they have got there. I imagined people must have travelled for miles just to see this one black man. It never occurred to me that there could be other black people there as well, where would they have come from, the place was so far away you could only get there by plane.

After what seemed like a long debate, Uncle said, "Congratulations. It looks like you have a new mother!".

Then he added, very casually as if he was describing what was going to be for dinner. Now that you father is settled, he might want you two to come over and live with him in England.

"Go and play!", he said dismissing both of us with a wave of his hand.

These words uttered so casually, picked me up and shook me like a rag doll.

"He might want you to come and live with him in England now that he is married!".

Just a few little words and my whole world had collapsed around me. I had never entertained the thought of ever seeing my father again, let alone live with him in England of all places. The place was so far away, so different from our world, I didn't even dare to think about it. The suggestion that I could one day see him and live with him, and have someone to call 'Baba' was so completely amazing. I played and replayed those words in my head; what Uncle Ben had said; it was like sweet music to my ears; and so terrifyingly unrealistic it sent shivers down my spine.

But these feeling came at a huge price, suddenly the world I had known and loved so much, a place I never even dreamed of leaving, my beautiful farm wasn't enough anymore. There was more, there was England. I had seen England in those pictures on the stereoscope. The red buses, the beautiful buildings and the pretty young women with golden hair in mini skirts. I couldn't imagine a more wonderful place to go and live.

Chapter 11 Mrs Chirashe

I had long observed through many years is a herd boy and a shepherd that nothing made sense. Sometimes things just happened out of the blue for no particular reason at all. You could go for ages without any trouble at all and then for no reason at all; all at once you lost the sheep; you got told off or beaten up for it. If you were really unlucky you stub a toe on a rock or walked straight into a nest of wasps and got stung in the eye. That had happened to me more times that I cared to count.

And as soon as the trouble had started it would disappear once again. Uncle Ben had put the idea in my head that my father might one day want me and my sister to come and live with him in England.

A few days later I walked straight into a branch full of wasps nests and got stung in the eye; I lost the sheep and got told off; but worst of all the nightmares began. I didn't know who I was anymore.

The holidays finished and we went back to Fort Milton school. I was now in grade three and nearly ten years old, one of the oldest boys in my class. It was the year that I was closest to being the happiest a human being could possibly experience and the last. It was a year so perfect and pure that its beauty was etched in a special place in my memory; so that I could go there any time I felt sad and find perfect bliss.

We had a new teacher; for grade three. Her name was Mrs Chirashe. She was young and beautiful with an angelic voice. Her voice was so soft and light; it had the effect of lifting you up like a kite and flying you away to far corners of the world, on soft cushioned wings. She stood in front of the classroom and introduced herself writing her name on the blackboard with a delicate fluid motion. No one made a sound; I guess they were all mesmerised by her beauty as much as I was.

She had a very light brown complexion; and her skin seemed to glow with the radiance of jewel. There was not a single blemish on her skin; her face and her legs as if she had been freshly created; by the gods themselves that very morning and sent to us; as an example of their finest creation.

She wore a crispy clean white blouse and a long navy blue skirt that flowed down past her knees hugging her body very closely. She wore white open high heel shoes so that you could see the painted nails on her feet. On her waist she had a big white belt, with a shiny silver buckle.

She was so beautiful and pretty, she looked as if she had come from a different world. I had never imagined that there was person this perfect and beautiful in the world.

"Good morning class. My name is Mrs Chirashe". She said, with her angelic voice that took my breath away.

"I will be your grade three teacher this year"; she smiled beautifully and swivelled round in those fine shoes and sat down on the chair behind the teachers table.

"Let's take the register"; she said.

"Audrey Shanje!".

"Present!"

She looked up and smiled after calling out each name.

"Zandile Chirashe!".

"Present!".

Everyone looked up at the girl who had answered. This was a new name we were not familiar with.

Mrs Chirashe looked up and smiled; proudly and joyfully at the girl.

The girl; giggled happily.

Zandile Chirashe. It didn't take too much to put two and two together and figure out that the girl and Mrs Chirashe were related. The girl had the same complexion as Mrs Chirashe. She had all the characteristics of a privileged life. Her smile was infectious; when you looked at her smiling happy face; any pain you had inside just melted away. She too was very pretty.

After school that day; all I could think about was Mrs Chirashe. She was so beautiful. My imagination took me many years ahead to a time when I was older and rich and could ask her to marry me. It had not occurred to me that she was already married.

A couple of days went by and each day I could not wait to get to school and see her. One afternoon she set some work for the class. You can leave when you finish; but don't forget to hand in your exercise book.

Before long everyone had finished their work and handed over their exercise books and left for the day. She sat behind her table and carried on working and I sat there and pretended to be still doing the work whilst taking furtive looks at her hoping she might take notice and talk to me.

Whenever she looked up I looked down and pretended to be working. After playing this game for a while I decided it was time to go home and if she didn't want to talk to me it was fine; I stood up and walked to the table and handed in my exercise book.

To my absolute surprise she put her pen down on the table looked up at me and smiled so beautiful and so graciously I felt weak at the knees and nearly melted away into the floor. I stood still not quite sure what to say or do.

"Your name is Nkosi isn't it"; she asked smiling

"Yes it is"; I said; trying not to sound like an idiot.

I was looking at her face; her eyes I was trying to record an image of her face in my memory that I would access when she was not around and enjoy every minute of the day.

"Tell me about yourself"; she said smiling. She had one arm on the table and the other on her chest. I could see her hand move up and down as she breathed. She looked at me and talked to me as if; as if I was someone worth talking to. No adult other than Gogo, my grandmother had ever shown me that kind of interest.

I was amazed; that she knew my name already and that she was interested in anything I do say. I adjusted my weight from one foot to the other trying to find a relaxing position and saying something important.

"Where do you leave she?", she asked after a brief delay.

That was easy for for me to answer.

I explained that I lived on a farm; pointing in the direction of the farm.

"Do you have any brothers or sisters?" she's asked.

"I have a sister at this school"; I explained.

"Just one sister!"; she observed; surprised that we were such a small family.

I already knew what the next question would be and I knew what the answer to give.

Everybody always ask that question; whenever the conversation got to that point and I always answered the same way. What followed was always the same.

"What do you parents do?"; she asked.

I explained that my parents lived in England I didn't bother to explain that only my father lived in England and that my mother had abandoned us remarried and I had no idea where she was.

"Will you be going to stay with them, in England?"; she asked.

It always amazed me when people asked; me that question. Did they not realise that you didn't just pack your bags get on a bus and go to England. Coming to think of it the more I thought about it; I had no idea how anyone got to England. It seemed so far away and such a different world that going there was a one way ticket, never coming back. I really had never allowed myself the luxury of contemplating the possibility of such an event ever occurring.

I didn't answer. My eyes met hers and to my surprise I didn't look away; I just stared straight into those dark brown eyes and I fell into their whirlpool. She was completely unperturbed by my steady gaze. I wanted to absorb the image of her face; eyes, everything about her;

deep into my memory; so that I would never forget what she looked like.

She smiled; a warm and kind smile. My hand moved automatically to my chest; because when she smiled my heart skipped a beat.

"I better not keep you any longer Nkosi". She stood up and put her hand on my shoulder.

"I'll see you tomorrow. Take care of yourself. Everything will be alright", she said.

"Good bye Mrs Chirashe"; I said and left.

The shadows were already getting longer when I left school which meant that it was already getting late. My eyes were full of tears and I hoped that Mrs Chirashe had not seen then welling up when I said goodbye to her. What kind of man would that make me, crying in front of a beautiful woman like that; like an infant. I was infuriated with myself.

I had no idea why I started welling up; but I knew this one thing I was totally in love with Mrs Chirashe. I felt different; I felt like I could walk on water; like I could fly like a bird. I was so energised I didn't feel any fear and when I got home late I didn't even care if I got told off. Nothing could hurt me, because I was in love with the most beautiful woman in the world; Mrs Chirashe.

By the time I got home the sun was already low in the horizon and turning into its familiar orange glow. I didn't bother going home for lunch as dinner would be served within the hour or two at the most. Besides I was neither; thirsty no hungry. I was in the happiest place in the world, all created in my on mind. All the way home I had imagining myself grown up; happily married to Mrs Chirashe with our own kids and a nice yellow Citroen; the one with the big lights that looked a bit like a tortoise; and had a suspension that allowed to go up or down. As I approached the kraal I could hear John driving the cattle and a sheep to the kraal for the night.

"Hey Nkosi!"; John called from behind a thick bush.

"You're late!"; John remarked impatiently.

I ignored his rudeness.

The number of times that I had looked after the animals and turned them in my own whilst he was at school or somewhere else; he had no right to complain; I thought to myself. The cattle were grazing in the clearing between the gum trees and the kraal.

"Where are the sheep?"; I asked when I didn't see them. Over there by the crater; he said. They were grazing in the short grass around the big pit. The lambs were skipping about and jumping in and out of the pit; their perfect white coats glowing in the orange evening sunlight.

"Nkosi"; John called from behind a bush in a terrified voice. I thought he had seen the biggest snake that ever existed.

"Come and see this he screamed!".

I ran around the bush and found him squatting down with a short stick in his hand poking something gross on the ground.

"What is that I asked completely?"; horrified.

On the ground were two balls with thousands of spindly wriggly white worms. They writhed faster and faster every time he poked them with a stick.

"What are they?; where did they come from?"; I asked disgusted by the sight in front of me.

"I did them came; the reply". His face was ashen grey as if all the blood had been sucked out of it. It was the first time that I had ever seen John looking; worried about anything. Normally, he could handle any situation; a promise of a good hiding from his mum or from uncle Bill didn't faze him one bit. I was quite sure that he even relished a little bit of controversy in his life. Living life on the edge gave him a buzz, never really doing what he was told to do and breaking apart every piece of equipment he could lay his hands on; to find out how it worked.

"Do one, he ordered!". I was thinking the same thing myself. So I did one, and found a nice short stick from a bush. I squatted down and poked around to check if there were any worms; but to my relief there were absolutely none.

The sun dropped behind the horizon quickly afterwards, like it normally did whenever it got to this point. It turned into a lovely bright reddish orange giant ball; then the next thing was you could literally see it dropping over the horizon; changing from a ball into half a circle then a small wedge and and finally completely disappearing. Another day was gone and you only had a few minutes to drive the cattle and sheep in the kraal before it got completely dark. You certainly did not want the sheep disappearing at this time because it was impossible to find them in the dark.

Fortunately; at this time the animals tended to keep together and hang around near the kraal all by themselves; as if they knew it was time to bed down for the night. We quickly went into auto. John rounded up the cattle and I took care of the sheep. We were both eager to get home and break the news about what John had found in his stool.

That evening when he broke the news to his mother, Auntie Ruth there was shear panic and pandemonium. No one had ever seen anything like it before. Auntie Ruth could not finish the cooking that night. Auntie Sibo had to do the rest. She was panicking and babbling senseless words. Gogo was much the same. She thought that her grandson was rotting away from the inside out. That very night uncle decided that they would take John to the hospital in Salisbury the very next morning.

John was gone for what felt to me like a life time. Without him; the farm was the loneliest place on earth. I was afraid that he was never going to come back. The longer he stayed away the more I worried that because; he had been away from school for so long he would be unable to beat Elliot in the end of term exams. Elliot and John had an intense rivalry that dated back from the first year at school together.

Their rivalry was known by the whole school. Elliot was the son of the headmaster and was a really clever boy. At the end of each term either John or Elliot took the crown of taking the first position in all the exams combined. Elliot had come first twice in a row and John had not been very happy about it. Somehow he had fought back and taken the crown from Elliot in the last term; only to lose it in the following term. On one occasion the rivalry had even reached fever pitch, and the two of them decided to settle the score in a physical fight by the river near the school. It was quite nice to watch a fight, and not be the one in the thick of it. John had won that one as well. I knew better because I had been in a one or two scuffles with him. He was quick.

His punches were effective and he would; expectedly throw a high kick for a good measure. He was not afraid to get into a fight either. He had one of those remarkable faces that looked battle hardened and fierce all the time. It was a face that greatly belied his great intelligence and sharp perceptive mind. His view of the world was completely different from mine. He was confident; fearless and smart. He bulldozed his way through anything life through at him; without spending a minute worrying about it. I had no idea how he could do that; I felt everything deeply and the pain lasted for an eternity; however; so did the joy whenever it decided to show itself.

Life on the farm was certainly boring without him and when he was away I missed him terribly. We had our occasional differences and I sometimes hated the fact that he got away with not doing his fair share of looking after the animals. In any case I didn't really mind; but I never quite figured out what it is; that he was doing or where he was when he was not with me looking after the animals like he was supposed to be.

Despite the solitude life carried on is usual. Being alone gave me so much time to daydream and make up all sorts of wonderful and weird imaginary situations. I never tired of it. I imagined I was all grown up had a wonderful house; a bit like the Maposa's house, with electric lights and married Mrs Chirashe and we had four or five beautiful children of our own. The whole day would go by, minding the sheep whilst whilst my mind was completely in a world of its own. Then it would be; time to turn the animals in; and it was time to snap back into the real the world.

I enjoyed school so much I could not wait to get there in the morning. I turned up an hour early; ready and eager to learn and to see my beautiful Mrs Chirashe. Classes with her were amazing. She spoke softly and never raised her voice to anyone. She didn't need to because no one misbehaved in her class. Her voice was soft and mesmerising. Most of the time she taught from behind her teachers table; only standing up to write something on the blackboard.

She rewarded my friendship with errands; sending me out to ring the bell or distributing balls and skipping ropes from the PE cupboard. Sometimes she would ask me to clean the blackboard. I relished the responsibility and the attention she was giving me. But best of all were the afternoons when everyone had left and it was just me and her in the classroom. She'd come over to my desk and help me with my maths; fractions and ratios.

For no particular reason, I detested Maths. It bored me to death, it was hard at first; but once I had figured out the method, it became too easy to want to do anything with it. Once, Piye had explained how to calculate the speed a car drove; given the distance and time it took to get from one place to another. Once you could do one distance and time, you could do them all; and that drove me insane. It was like cheating the universe, robbing nature of its hidden mysteries and I didn't like that one bit.

When she had finished coaching she would go and sit at the back at her table and we'd talk like old friends. On a couple of occasions Zandi came back to the classroom to collect the keys for the house from her aunt. They had moved into the old deputy teacher's house. The first time that Zandi, had come back Mrs Chirashe had introduced her to me very graciously.

"Have you met my lovely; niece Nkosi?". I had smiled; trying to look really casual; so that Zandi would not think I was obsessed with her aunt. Zandi, had simply looked me up and down; smiled collected the keys and skipped off slamming the door as she sped off. I had the impression she didn't like me very much, but it didn't bother me much. It wasn't her that I was interested in.

I was the happiest I could be in those few afternoons I spent with the woman I loved so deeply. I was even beginning to think that she felt the same way too. She talked to me as if I was another person, not just a little boy. She was interested in knowing about me as a person. It was the most wonderful experience feeling to have another person be interested in me in that way.

One afternoon after I left Mrs Chirashe class after saying goodbye to her; I made my way across the yard. To my surprise Zandi and Diana who lived next door to each other and inevitably became friends were making their way home together and had just walked past the big Jacaranda tree just past the assembly line. They looked round and saw me behind them and stopped. Zandi whispered something to Diana, and they both giggled. I couldn't believe my eyes I was looking at probably the two most beautiful girls in the school maybe even the world right there in front of me and they were waiting for me. I'd never spoken to Diana before in three years at the school. I wondered what they wanted with me.

I noticed they had exactly the same complexion. They were also exactly the same height; but Zandi was slightly plumper. Diana on the other hand was sleek and slender with the majestic long neck and a face that was both beautiful confident; intelligent; but most of all aloof and clearly beyond the reach of a farm boy like myself. Although, she was extremely beautiful, she was a year older; the daughter of the headmaster; and whilst I always made a point of falling in love with pretty girls I didn't even permit myself to think about her in any way other than how pretty she was; she looked to me beyond the reach of anyone.

I wanted to turn round and go back the other way, as I was quite sure that Zandi was going to tell me off for being in love with her aunt. I braced myself for a verbal thrashing. I knew what she was going to say.

"Nkosi, my aunt doesn't love you. Leave her alone. She's not your type. Go back to your cattle and sheep; you stupid little boy".

Instead she called my name in a rather coy voice and what I thought was a very rich and interesting accent.

"Hey Nkosi"; Zandi said in a coy husky voice.

I looked at her; then at Diana the back at her again. I had never stood face-to-face with her like this and so had never seen Diana's face that close. She was so pretty she was on another level; beyond human scale. Not a blemish on her skin and not a hair out of place. She was smiling. Her teeth were perfect white and straight. How was it possible to be so beautiful, I wondered if it hurt a little bit to be so perfect. She had black eyes that gleamed like pearls.

Her face was soft and gentle; with an inquisitive intelligent look. She didn't say a word; just smiled. I smile back and for a brief moment I thought I had made a connection with probably the most beautiful girl in the whole world. It was quite amazing, I had not even expected her to look at me; let alone smile. I was quite sure no-one could fall in love with such a pretty girl; she was too beautiful too perfect; too good for anyone.

"Where is that handsome brother of yours?", Zandi; asked rather demanded to know. Her voice had suddenly become sharp and authoritative and caught me by surprise.

I was going to say none of your business; one because I'd never thought of John is being handsome and two; because I had always thought of myself as very handsome and to to hear that stupid girl call my cousin handsome instead of me really made me bitter on a scale I didn't think was possible; but I controlled my anger.

I didn't want to offend her; I had too much to lose and besides I was still rather relishing the smile Diana had given me; so I took the bait and gave a more considered; response.

"Well I said, he is in Salisbury".

"Salisbury", she exclaimed. "What is he doing in Salisbury?"; she demanded to know.

I wasn't prepared for that question.

"He is not very well I said; I decided to lie; he broke his arm?". I couldn't exactly tell a girl like that; that worms had come out of his stomach and he was rotting from the inside out.

"Oh, I am so sorry I really like your brother he is so; handsome?".

"When you see him, tell him to hurry up getting better and get back to school".

Both, girls laughed; and turned round and started walking away.

I stood there rooted to the spot for a moment; processing what had just happened. I was consumed by a jealous rage. I was not in love with Zandi nor with Diana so I had no idea why I was so jealous. Practically frozen to the spot with envy.

The girls looked round and saw me still standing on the same spot and giggled once more; bending forwards with laughter.

I never spoke to Zandi again after that day. It was as if she had been wiped out of the existence from my vision and memory. What is worse is when my cousin John came back from Salisbury I never even and remembered to tell him that he had secret admirer and very beautiful one for that matter. So intense was my envy I shut everything out. It didn't make sense to me that she thought John was handsome and she wanted him and not me. I was in her class for goodness sake, so how could she fancy someone from a different class. She had wounded me and I took revenge by shutting her out of my mind.

John had never shown any interest in girls apart from one girl, Bella. She too was in his class and I think he might have fancied her immensely; but he never said it; just an occasional hint here and there; like how she had smiled at him, how she had asked him a question. Diana was also in his class and he had never even mentioned her not even once; even though she was clearly the most beautiful girl in the whole school.

One afternoon quite uncharacteristically, he appeared near the grade three classroom; speaking animatedly to Zandi and a group of other girls; then he casually said goodbye to them all and left with no display of any emotion; as if he might have said goodbye to bunch of his friends. He didn't seem to care for, or worship girls in the same way that most of the boys did. He walked, always with his head held high, with purpose, as if he was marching towards some definite goal. He seemed to be always preoccupied with something, and not a single moment to waste. Whilst I frittered my every waking moment in endless reverie; his mind was busy working away like a machine.

I finally figured it out. My cousin John, had been a mystery even to me; who grew up with him and saw him every day. His secret was that he was cool, and that's why Zandi and Diana were besotted with him and not with me. I could not even understand where my own irrational behaviour had come from, and realised that maybe, I had been jealous of him all my life and never known it until then.

The next morning after witnessing John's triumph with the girls we attended the daily assembly as usual. It was held outside in front of the school bell that hang from a small ancient tree.

We stood in straight lines each class in one row demarcated by a line of bricks. Each class in one row; girls to the left and boys on the right side and starting with the grade ones at the front. I was in grade three and had two rows of kids in front, who might as well never have existed as no-one paid attention to anyone in lower grades than theirs. I din't know the name of a single kid in a lower grade.

The teachers also stood in a single row in front; facing us with the headmaster roughly in the middle; leading the morning ceremony. The ceremony usually included announcements about unpaid fees and kids that would be sent home; kids that had broken some rule or made some infringement and were to be sent to the headmaster's office for punishment.

Mrs Chirashe was in her usual pristine white blouse and blue figure hugging long skirt. She sparkled beautifully in the morning sunlight. She was standing right in front of me only a couple of rows ahead. I was sure she spotted me and smiled a little. She was looking radiant; my heart skipped a beat and I remembered the endless depth of joy I had felt when I looked into her eyes on that first afternoon I had stayed behind. She looked even more beautiful that now I considered her a trusted friend. I now knew that she was married and that Mrs meant that someone was married. Piye had explained it quite simply, if a lady is called Mrs then it means she is married, if she is not married then she is called Madam or Miss. How did he know all this stuff, I wondered.

Her husband was a tall handsome man; also very light in complexion. Apart from Dreyfus I had never seen an African man that light; in complexion. They were a very beautiful couple. The fact that she was married did not alter my feelings for her one bit. I just didn't think about it. That morning I noticed the two of them were not standing side by side as the usually did. Next to her was Mr Hungu, teacher renowned for being a great Maths teacher.

He was a short guy with a head as round and as a big as a full moon, if not bigger. For that reason he had been nicknamed him Mr Big Head; and that's what everyone called him. His enormous head rested on a pair of enormously broad shoulders and virtually no neck. I had never forgiven him for battering Simon all those years back when we went swimming without permission and I hated the very sight of him. I was quite glad he wasn't my teacher and it would be a few years before I was in his class. But; what happened next; if I didn't like him before; I certainly loathed him after it; abhorred him completely.

I had been watching Mrs Chirashe face; as I did as naturally as a bee flies towards a flower, as naturally as a sunflower turns towards the sun, completely unconsciously. Just before the headmaster started going through his list of boring announcements Mr Big Head leaned over towards Mrs Chirashe and whispered something in her ear, she turned her face towards him and giggled quietly. Their eyes met and their faces came so close they were almost touching as they both shared a personal moment. For a few brief seconds; her eyes never left his nor his hers.

I glanced towards Mr Chirashe who had leaned over and was watching the whole thing, his face contorted and twisted in a vicious rage; fists clenched and grimacing like a dog about to bite someone.

Even as a small boy, I knew that, the way his wife and Mr Big Head had looked at each other; meant only one thing. They were in love.

I felt like someone had stuck a spear through my heart and twisted it. I nearly fainted. I felt a cold chill take over my body and the energy I had been riding on for so many months seemed to fizz out of my body like a balloon that had been popped. It left me weak and unable to stand on my on.

Shaba kicked me in leg and nodded as if to say, look your girlfriend is cheating on you. Or, he might have just been saying, look, there is something going on between those two teachers; but that's not how I felt. What could I do, I was a kid. I hated Mr Big Head so much; had I been older I would definitely walked up to that line and knocked him out cold.

The two exchanged a couple more words and laughed quietly between themselves; completely absorbed in each others world; like two young lovers. Over on the other side, Mr Chirashe was fuming like mad bull; there was practically smoke coming out of his ears. He was glaring at them as if he was ready to grab one of them and throttle them right there and then. This pleased me immensely as I hoped it would be Mr Big Head he would throttle.

I have no idea what was said in that assembly as I spent the whole time watching the two young lovers bathing in their loathsome sunshine. It made me feel sick. When the marching drum started I walked back to my classroom like an automaton. I could not feel, see or hear. Time stood still. My love for Mrs Chirashe had made me feel invincible; like a young Zulu warrior. I could do anything; go anywhere I wanted fearlessly; because I was in love. But in one short moment; everything was gone, I was once again an empty shell. A lonely; skinny half starved; poor farm boy without even a pair of shoes. I felt so ugly and horrible; so weak and useless as I watched the woman I loved; lost to me for ever. The happy world I had constructed in my head with Mrs Chirashe had suddenly and without warning been razed to the ground by Mr Big Head's big bulldozer head.

In class Mrs Chirashe was positively animated. She had a twinkle in her eyes. Her voice was like music to my ears and every movement she made was like a dance of the stars. She looked even more beautiful; now that she was completely unavailable to me. Every so often she would glance longingly at the door and I wondered why. I didn't have to wait too long to find out. Soon enough the door; opened slightly and the giant head belonging to Mr Big Head popped through the side. Mrs Chirashe's face lit up like a bright star; immediately instructed us to carry on working quietly and she would be back shortly.

This happened a couple more times during the day and we were pretty much left to our own devices that day. At lunchtime she disappeared altogether; and never came back to the classroom. By then I had recovered my senses a bit more. It wasn't her I was mad with, it was that horrible big headed short man that was the problem. Overcome by curiosity; to find out what was really going on, I convinced a few of my friends to walk with me past her house and try and find out what had happened to her. With everything that I had seen that morning I suspected something had happened to her. She had not been herself the whole morning.

As we approached her house which was next to the headmaster's house we could hear the noise of pots and pans crashing; then the booming voice of a very angry man. He was threatening to kill somebody. There were male voices, more muted voices saying calm down. Sit down. Calm down; man. From the window I could see a man; very light complexion pacing up and down throwing his arms around in the air.

I knew exactly what was happening. Shaba mentioned that he thought that Mr Chirashe was having a fight with his wife. I wanted to saying; keep up; but he was my friend. Whatever was happening; it seemed to be well under control. We tiptoed slowly; past the house down towards the river. As we went past the big trees I spotted; the figure of Mrs Chirashe standing in the middle of the field holding a long forked branch with one end resting on the ground and the other pointing skywards.

She looked so forlorn and seemed very upset. I told the boys we should go and ask if she was okay.

"Are you crazy?", Shaba retorted. If he didn't think I had feelings for her before; he sure did now; I thought to myself; but I didn't care.

"Do you want get your ass whipped by the headmaster tomorrow morning".

As far as I was concerned I didn't care if the headmaster killed me the next morning, I would do anything for Mrs Chirashe. I would die for her.

It broke my heart to see her standing in the middle of that field; under the burning hot sun all alone, looking so distressed. She looked like a bright lone flower out of season; growing in the baking sun; no water; no shade and would die out there; under the hot sun.

"Come on!"; Shaba said; literally trying to drag me along; but I would have non of it and I dragged him instead. As we approached her; she tried to wipe the tears off her face; with the back of her hand and looked away so that we would not see the tears in her eyes.

"Mrs Chirashe, are you okay"; I asked in as concerned voice as I could master.

"I'm okay boys she sobbed, please go home!".

We didn't move.

"Go home!"; she ordered pointing towards the river; her voice sharp and and almost angry.

We started walking reluctantly. I walked in silence. My mind completely absorbed by what had just happened.

I thought about the events of that day all night and for years after. It dawned on me as I lay there before falling asleep; that Mrs Chirashe did not have any feelings for me whatsoever. To her; I was simply a poor little kid whom she felt sorry for and was trying to be nice to. I had misunderstood our whole relationship. For some strange reason I did not feel angry with her; instead I was grateful for the months and months of so much kindness and attention she had shown me. I was grateful for the way I had felt that whole time; because it had felt good and when it was gone; it left a big hole in my heart. That kind of love never really dies, it simply fades into the background; a part of you; as important as an arm or a leg.

That night I had a dream. I had lost the sheep and walked for miles and miles through lion infested jungle; then when I had nearly given up looking for them, I parted some branches and there in front of me was; the greenest smoothest valley I had ever seen. The sheep were in their flock, happily grazing away whilst the lambs scampered about in the warmth of a gentle hazy sunshine. It felt so real and I woke wondering what it all meant. Was there a green field; waiting for me somewhere out there in the distant future?.

Since the fight between Mrs Chirashe and her husband; I never stayed behind to watch her whilst she marked the exercise books; whilst I pretended to be hard at work doing sums or reading all the while waiting for those precious few moments when she would speak to me. In any case since then she had changed. The dark brown eyes that had been so vibrant when I looked into them; all those months ago; seemed somehow sadder. Even, her soft angelic voice seemed quieter and more distant. She laughed less and smiled reluctantly. I felt sorry for her and never forgave Mr Big Head for this betrayal.

The year was drawing towards the end and yet I had hardly noticed any time passing. Mrs Chirashe had completely absorbed my every waking moment and time had passed by quickly. The first end of the term was always very welcome period. As there were no exams at the end of the first term so it was completely stress free. Not that the exams worried me; but it was still nice not to have to do them. The last few days of school not much happened in the classroom. The teachers were out most of the time attending endless meetings. Sometimes the prefects would get us all out to perform school duties like picking up the rubbish or fetching water from the river for the teachers. Sometimes we would even be asked to bring some tools from home to cut the long grass back on the football ground and around the school yard.

School holidays arrived with a bit of mixed emotions; caught between wanting to see my school friends everyday and wanting to see the town people. As it always happened; it didn't matter much; how much you 'will' the day to come or not to come; sooner or later the day arrived. That was the nature of time; it carried on going forever forward; no matter what happened in ones life. Time didn't care if you were happy or not; it didn't care whether you loved or didn't love; whether the sheep got lost or not; it just carried on doing what it wanted to do; relentlessly marching forward.

On the last day; the head master called out assembly as usual, and dismissed us to go off on our holidays.

"Enjoy yourselves and get back to School safe; the next term"; he announced.

Once we left school we didn't think about it at all; until it was time to get back to school again.

Chapter 12 The Descent into the Abyss

The day after the school holidays began; started like any other day; but by the time it finished; my life had been completely turned over and under. I knew neither; whether I was coming or whether I was going.

I felt like a pebble; cast into a whirlpool; spinning down into the abyss. I had lived with the dangers of sudden death from a snake bite; or attack from a wild animal; being swept away or drowning whilst crossing a swollen river. I had actually experienced that very thing; nearly being swept away by a swollen river. A year back towards the end of the year; after a long dry season one day it had started to rain. We were in the classroom but the teachers was out; so as soon as it started raining everybody stood up and started jumping up and down. I happened to bump into this tall boy who immediately and without warning started throwing punches at me.

Unfortunately for him; I had been fighting since day dot; and my reflexes were quick and sharp and I dodged and blocked everyone of his fists. Everyone was already cheering; as I moved backwards blocking everything and trying to plead with the boy to stop. But he called me a small boy and said he was going to teach me a lesson. That really annoyed me so I let him have my signature move and punched him in the mouth; he cut his lip badly and was bleeding profusely. There was nothing like a bit of blood to stop a fight dead.

Whenever it rained like that they always let us off early so that we could cross the river before it go to swollen. I was walking with my friends and my sister was right behind us with her friends. When I crossed the river it was bone dry; but just as we got on the river bank I heard my sister scream and turned round to see her ankle deep in water that was racing down the river at an unbelievable speed.

Wondering where the water had come from all of a sudden I glanced up the river to see a wall of white swirling water with whole trees descending down the river. My sister and her friends just stood there like idiots holding hands; paralysed with fear not realising the wall of water descending towards them. I ran back in the water; screaming to them to get out; grabbed hold of her hand and pulled them out. Just as we climbed over the bank I looked back to see a whole tree pass over the spot they had been standing. I felt sick; I just looked her afterwards and wondered what I would have done if she had been taken away. I was quite sure I would have thrown myself back in the river until I got her out or until we were both taken.

Nothing had prepared me for events that took place that day. One tiny moment changed the course of my life and made me the person I would become.

The town people had arrived late that afternoon. John and I had real trouble trying to decide whether it was late enough in the evening to turn the sheep and cattle in for the night or leave them whilst we ran home to greet the town people. In the end we decided not to and left them alone; dangerously too close to the crop.

Everyone had jumped out of the Peugeot 404 and I found myself surrounded by people smiling and singling me out as; if I had done something special. I enjoyed the attention; but a little voice in my head warned me that something was not quite right.

Where is Nomalanga; Lindiwe; my cousin from town asked; then after she gave my sister a big hug. She broke the news that brought me down to my knees and nearly made my heart explode in my chest.

"You two are going to England"; she said.

"Wait; what!'.

"Yes, that's right. Your father wants you to come and live with him in England"; added Uncle Ben lifting me up from the ground with ease and holding me up high. You are going to fly in an aeroplane; over the seas all the way to Europe.

That night it was all everyone talked about. That my sister and I were going to leave Rhodesia (present day Zimbabwe) and go and live in England. It was quite incredible. Suddenly; because we were going to live in England; we elevated from law ranking nobodies to superstars and all of a sudden everyone was interested in us. Everyone was telling us about the wonderful things that were going to happen and all the wonderful things we were going to have. We were going to live in a nice house; wear nice clothes; fly in an aeroplane fly across the sea. It was all too much.

"You two are so lucky"; they said.

At that point, my mind had completely shutdown from shear emotional overload and all I could think of was that; I hoped there would be no sheep and cattle for me to look after in England. Even as my small mind wondered what they ate in England for food without cattle and sheep, I was quite sure there wouldn't have any; besides I thought; it would definitely be too cold for cattle and sheep. I smiled to myself on the inside, that would be really nice, no cattle; no sheep.

Uncle Ben explained that my father hand written a letter to him asking him to arrange for Nomalanga and I to get passports as soon as possible to be able to get on an aeroplane and fly to England. We could even be gone by end of the year or within a couple of months even.

I should've been happy more excited; but I guess I was in too much of a shock to take it all in. Instead I felt numb; as if all emotion had suddenly been sucked out of my body. Sitting; on the kitchen floor; listening to everyone saying how wonderful and exciting things were going to be for us; completely unaware of the emotional turmoil that had raged in my head for all of my living memory. All my entire existence; the only thing I had really ever wanted, more than anything else was to see my father. I could have given anything for just one minute with him; and to hear that this was going to happen in a few months. That was too much for me to contemplate.

So I just sat there and listened, unable to speak; unable to feel anything. The more I thought about the more unreal it sounded. Still everyone was so excited about it and I went along with it and started believing it really was going to happen.

For the next few weeks they didn't stop talking about how my sister and I would be going to England in a short while. However; it didn't really make much of difference to me; because I still had to work hard on the farm; like everyone else, I still had to go and look after the sheep and cattle. However; I got the impression that uncle Ben was paying me more attention that usual. I guess he wanted to make sure that I would be okay until we were delivered to my father in England; safe and sound.

By the end of the second or third week things started to move very quickly. Uncle Ben took Nomalanga and I along; with aunt Sibongile and uncle Percy to Gwelo (present day Gweru); to have our passport pictures taken. I had to look smart; so I was given a nice clean shirt, tie trousers and some old hand me down shoes that I polished till they were so shiny I could see my face on the leather. Uncle Ben, said I looked like a young English gentleman.

By then I had more time to think about things; and was starting to really believe that this was it. Nomalanga and I were going to join my father and our stepmother in England. I have no idea why; but for some reason I had never given much thought to my own real mother; other than wonder what she looked like. No-one ever spoke of her. It was as if she had never existed at all. Sometimes I felt as if we had just appeared out of thin air; completely motherless. Gogo had mentioned her exactly once to me; explaining how my mother had handed my sister and me over to her with a bag of terry nappies and a big baby towel and said.

"Here are your grand children, Madube. I'm leaving!" and just like that she had left and that was the last time anyone had ever seen or heard from her. I was four or five when she told me that story. Knowledge can be a bad thing sometimes; because up until then I had always thought Auntie Ruth was my mum; so when Gogo had told me that story; I had cried uncontrollably until somehow Nomalanga had managed to calm me down. From that day on; my consciousness had awakened, and every day was a journey with only one goal; to get to see my father. Fortunately; I had been blessed with a memory that recorded every detail; every tree; bug; rock; blade of grass; everyone and everything, so vividly I could access it any time I wanted; and I could not wait to share my experiences with my father in England.

The trip to Gwelo had been amazing; and duly the pictures arrived; then there were forms to fill and a few more weeks of going backwards and forwards. Finally, the passports were ready. I was nine years old and I looked handsome; really handsome kid. I was ready for England.

Enough time had passed and enough had happened for me to feel more confident that this was really going to happen. I was beginning to be very excited about the journey. Even though a small part of me was still doubting. Maybe a part of me felt it was all too good to be true; but with the passport ready I was sure uncle Ben could not have gone to all that trouble for nothing.

At last, I was going to meet my father and I was going to find out for myself what it really was like to have a parent; my own real parent; the excitement was unbelievable; like being taken from the dung heap and sat on Chief Nhema's throne; given a golden cane and told; now you are the Chief of this district. I used to see the other kids; even as big as John, when they were getting, tired or upset or ill; how they would just throw themselves in their mother's arms and whinge and whine, and she would just take them and hold them tight. How I wanted to be held tight like that, I could almost feel it from a distance. No matter how much an uncle or Aunt cared about you, they can never hold you so dearly as a mother holds their own child. It was only a matter of time before I could enjoy that kind of love and warmth myself. I was slowly starting to feel like I was on top of the world.

The passports were great with their brand new shiny green plastic bind. There was a picture of me in it, nine years old with a tie looking so good. It was the only picture that had ever been taken of me. I was excited beyond belief. Happiness was just around the corner. No sheep; no cattle. I had heard so many stories about terrible stepmothers; but I really wasn't afraid; because somehow I was quite sure that my father would never let anything bad happen to us. I didn't worry about white people either except maybe that my English was not very good and I was not going to understand them; but I was sure I would learn it.

Most of the things I had heard about them were good. Uncle Bill used to always go on about how smart they were to build all those amazing things; like cars and aeroplanes and light bulbs; which drove absolutely mad because I was quite sure, between John and I; we too would be able to build planes and cars when were older. After all we built our own toy cars and aeroplanes as kids; so it would be no trouble to do so when we grew up.

"They are going to ask you where you come from"; Mandla said.

"You are going to say".

"I come from Rhodesia".

"How old are you; and you will say I'm nine years old".

"No; ten years old; you'll be ten when you go because you were born in August"; Lindi who had a knack for numbers and knew everyone's birthdays corrected us.

When the passports arrived Uncle Ben told us that, all we were now waiting for were tickets to arrive. Your father will send them from England. Once the tickets arrive, you will be on your way. That night I could not eat or sleep; from shear excitement and disbelief. My whole body was alive; buzzing and tingling with excitement. It was really going to happen; we were really going. I was simply the happiest kid alive on the planet.

Every waking moment of my life from then on was spent thinking about what life would be like in England. How would I cope with having to speak English all the time; would I forget how to speak Shona and Ndebele. Would I survive cold, the incurable Spanish flu, which Auntie Ruth had explained should not be a problem as it only affected European people. I didn't think I'd ever miss the farm, the sheep and the cattle; the back breaking work in the fields; but I was sure that I would miss school yes and the wonderful times during the holidays. The hard work and the hard times on the farm; uncle Bill; I was really looking forward to putting all that behind me.

At the same time while all this stuff about my sister and I going to England; uncle Ben had started building his hilltop mansion. The top of the hill was levelled and long trenches were dug and filled with concrete. This he explained, was going to be the foundation of the house. He explained, that there would be two seating rooms east and west; so we could enjoy sunrise in the morning and sunset in the evenings. There was also a separate dining room; a large kitchen, two toilets and five large bedrooms. We would all live in the same house. The foundations just looked like some sort of giant puzzle to me; nothing very exciting and I certainly didn't see how that would be turned into a house.

Soon the holidays were over and it was time to go back to school. The plane tickets had not arrived and uncle promised us that the tickets would arrive during the term and he would come and collect us to take us to the airport.

Although I was cautious to only tell my closest friends of the possibility of leaving school and going to live in England, it didn't take long for the whole school to find out what was happening to us. The reaction from the other kids that I knew was remarkably gracious. Everyone I knew was happy for us; and thought we were quite lucky to be going somewhere so nice.

At home home; we had been elevated to hero status and could do no wrong. I didn't mind the attention or the respect that came with it. It wasn't fashionable to be mean to the cool kids who were heading out for a great life and a better world overseas. Auntie Ruth was quite sure that the tickets would arrive during the school holidays, and that this would be the last term we would be going to Fort Milton school and we should probably say goodbye to all our friends; so at the end of the term we said goodbye to everyone. Mrs Chirashe shook my hand and held it in both her hands and said she was sad to see me go. She said not to be afraid; because we were going to have a wonderful life in England.

"You are a clever boy Nkosiyetu. You will do well and you will soon forget all about us and make new friends in England".

I smiled broadly and shook my head; to say I was never going to forget her; ever.

The term ended; but the tickets had not arrived. The town people came back to the farm as usual. My heart was in my mouth pounding like a hammer inside my chest. I was praying and begging God to let uncle have brought the plane tickets with him. But; to my big disappointment, there were no tickets. Instead; he said.

"Congratulations. You have a baby brother in England. His name is Sifiso!". Then he went back to talking about his mansion. There was no mention of the tickets. There was no explanation. I thought maybe; he just forgot to mention it and would explain in the morning.

That night, the nightmares started.

The nightmares were graphic and as detailed as a bioscope. It was hard sometimes to distinguish them from reality. In the nightmare the tickets had arrived and it was the morning when we were leaving for the airport. The truck; an old greenish blue jeep similar to those used by the Rhodesian police I had seen in Gwelo when I went there for the passport pictures. The jeep that we were going to travel to the airport in wouldn't start; so I had to get out with the others; to push the jeep to kickstart it. We pushed the truck along and faster and faster it went and it started; but instead of stopping to let me back on the truck; it drove off at speed without me. I ran after it; screaming at the top of my voice for it to stop; but the truck kept driving away kicking up dust that choked my throat and lungs then I woke up dripping in sweat; choking and tears streaming down my face.

That night I had been more terrified than I had ever been in my life, it was ten times worse than the experience with the black mamba or with the hyenas; in fact it was a hundred times maybe even a thousand times worse. It ripped me apart into small pieces and threw those pieces in the garbage pit in a big heap. I tried to tell myself that it was just a dream; but the more I tried to convince myself the more I was frightened by the possibility that the nightmare was a warning of what was really going to happen.

Every night was torture night. It was always the same nightmare; with a slightly different twist sometimes we had hitched a lift to the airport and the car would breakdown just before getting to the airport and we would see the plane fly away without us; whilst the man tried to fit a tyre on his car. Sometimes we would get on the bus; and the bus would take off in the wrong direction and not to the airport where it was supposed to go.

Weeks went by; but the tickets never came and soon the holidays were coming to an end and the town people would be going back to town and to my deepest embarrassment I had to go back to Fort Milton School and face the the kids I had said goodbye to; and tell them we didn't go England. I expected to be made the laughing stock of the entire school for the rest of my life there. I wanted the ground to open up and swallow me; I wanted to disappear into nothingness; anything to stop from going back to school and face becoming a laughing stock; a loser of all losers.

The dreaded day came, and as I arrived in school that day I expected every kid to be pointing their fingers at me and laughing. I prayed for the ground to open up and swallow me whole. I had always been one of the first to get to school because; I loved school so much; but that morning; I couldn't bring myself to get there and took as long as I could. The fear of being taunted and laughed at was too much.

No man can run from his destiny; and eventually I had to get to school. I walked into the classroom. The class was already settled and Mrs Chirashe was taking the register.

She looked up and saw me.

"Oh; Nkosi she exclaimed. I thought you'd be gone to ..."; she said.

Noticing my broken face and the tears streaming down my face; she stopped talking, got up from her sit at table and took me in her arms and hugged me in front of the whole class.

"Welcome back, Nkosi. We would have missed you too much anyway"; she said.

"We'd have missed him too much; wouldn't we boys and girls"; she said turning to the class. Her; own voice faltering as she turned to sit down and gesturing me to take my sit.

The whole class responded; "Yesi; Missi", "Yes Miss".

I had never known a love like that!.

To my utter surprise; not one of those kids said one thing about what had happened to us. Not one of them laughed or joked about it. It was as if nothing had happened. All my fears had been completely wrong. I could not believe the generosity and kindness of my friends and the other kids in just leaving that subject alone. I was sure they had left that subject alone; because they knew that it would be too painful for us to even talk about. I was grateful to those kids for not mocking me; more than they could ever imagine.

Even though we had been promised we would go to England and I wanted so much for it to happen; somehow deep down I had always known that it wasn't ever going to happen. To everybody else it just looked like my father didn't really want us with him England. I dared not think about him in this way; but from that day on I decided not to spend another second of my time and energy thinking about him. My heart had been burned and turned to stone; a black rock. I was going to grow up and live my own life on my own. I was done with the lies.

I had lived my whole life on the farm; all nine or ten years of it; survived drowning in the dam at the age of four or five, numerous encounters with deadly snakes; a hyena attack; survived almost being swept away by a swollen river. It hadn't all been bad; I had also had wonderful times, but I had done it all because I had dreamed that one day I would see my father; that had given me the courage and strength I needed to survive. But a new chapter in my life; had now begun; one without his shining beacon.

The mind is a monster that lives in our heads. No-one can shut it down by will; shear conviction or whatever. It will do what it likes; no matter how hard I tried to stop thinking about what happened; I would find myself thinking about it and remind myself to stop. I didn't want these thoughts in my head; but still they came into it; I figured by a process of introspection, my father had lost interest in us; that's why he had not sent the tickets. His new wife had given birth to a son; my brother; Sifiso. All of a sudden everything made sense, fitted together like a jigsaw puzzle; the long delays the false promises when it came down to it he had a new family now and he didn't want us in that picture.

The realisation of this was like a dagger through my stomach. I wondered why if there really was a God. Why would he'd do this to us. Some children lose a father or a mother; but to lose both, that was phenomenal, a real curse from the devil himself, and the proof was right there in those recent ugly events.

I wondered why God had saved me from the mamba and so many other snake encounters, why he had let me save my sister from being washed away by a wall of water in a flush flood only to punish us like this. All sorts of weird theories would spin around in my head for hours on end; whilst following those damned sheep every afternoon after school. I had now got to the point where I hated every minute of it. To have come so close from escaping the mindless waste of time and energy following sheep around; and then thrown right back into it was a punch in the belly that I felt at a deep physiological level that I developed an ulcer from it.

Whilst the kids at school had been kind and so generous the story was completely different at home. We dropped from being super heroes back to much worse than where we'd been before all this palaver started. We became the laughing stock of the entire family.

Someone started peddling a lie that I had said that Rhodesia had become really boring and couldn't wait to get to England. Uncle Bill mocked me with this every chance he could get. I wonder if he had invented the whole story as a way to push me down back into the gutter where I belonged. That man hated me so deeply sometimes; I imagined he could quite easily take me into the forest and strangle me and leave my body there to be devoured by hyenas and jackals. However; the hatred was mutual; I didn't like him much either. I had so little respect for such cowardly behaviour. For a big old man to target a small child and abuse him in any way shape or form was despicable, I thought. I was sure the only reason he didn't do something really bad to me was because; he was afraid of uncle Ben or aunt Lizzy. So he did, the next best thing; mock me at his leisure.

As the months went by, everyone forgot about our little demise and gradually stopped talking about it and making fun of us. But; for me the battle carried on inside; like a shell shocked warrior, it went on and on; whirling around in my head for years, eating at my heart until all that was left; was a cold black heart of stone.

Chapter 13 Bed Bugs

When the town people had gone back to town the farm was almost empty. Whilst most of the time we slept on the floor; during the term with everyone gone back to town; there were enough beds to sleep on. One night I couldn't go to sleep; because every time I turned and tried to settle something was pricking my body. When I got up in the morning my whole body was covered tiny red spots that were itchy as hell. I didn't realise I had been bitten by bed bugs. I went to school as normal; but when I got back in the afternoon I decided to find out what been biting me all night and put an end to it.

I look recruited my little cousins to help find out. Unbeknown to me they had been bitten as well, and turned out this had been going on for a while. Their bellies were covered with the same bite marks. I was mortified; how could anyone allow this to happen? There had to be hundreds of them to cause so many bites. I told my little cousins to hunt for the culprits and together we went hunting for them and discovered them hiding in the small nooks and cracks of the plaster on the walls of our bedrooms. Some holes were covered in a fine cob web behind which were hundreds of eggs. We got small sticks and used them to squish every last bed bug and their eggs we could find in the cracks of the wall.

Some of the bugs were so engorged with blood, they popped like berries as we squished them and blood splashed across the walls. It was quite satisfying to see. However; for some reason I was not happy because I could not figure out how the bed bugs could climb all the way from the wall; walk all the way across the floor; climb onto the bed and bite us and suck our blood all night and then; before we got up in the morning they had managed to climb all the way back down the bed and walked all the way across the floor and climbed all the way up the wall finding and climbing into cracks in the wall to hide. There had to be more bugs on the bed itself.

We checked the blankets, mattress and there was nothing. It was quite a mystery. I thought they were playing hide and seek with us so I went under the bed to look. To my horror of horrors; the whole underside of the bed; all along the bed frame was teaming with thousands of bed bugs crawling around. It was disgusting. I told my cousin, Violet to look under the bed. She was so disgusted she jumped up from underneath the bed knocking her head on the bed frame really hard; making the little ones collapse on the floor with laughter. I told Vio we had to carry the bed outside and squish the bugs there. I didn't want to squish them whilst lying on my back whilst they mild around above my head.

We lifted the mattress off the bed and rested it against the wall. We carried the metal frame bed outside into the sun and laid it upside down. We started squishing the bed bugs and they popped splashing the blood they had taken from us the previous night everywhere. Every bug underneath the bed was fat as ripe red berry. It was disgusting; but there were just too many bugs to squish by hand. So I decided we should burn them. We collected some straw and laid it along the bed frame. When everything was covered; I took match and set fire to each corner of the bed.The flames took hold quickly and travelled along the bed frame in very little time. As the fire burned we could hear the creepy crawlies sizzling and popping from the heat of the flames. In a couple of minutes all the straw had completely burned out and reduced to ashes. I took a straw sweeper swept the ashes off the frame. The metal had been singed and blackened but to my absolute delight there was not a single bug or egg left in sight. I was overjoyed with my solution; it was simple but effective.

When the metal frame had cooled down we carried the bed back inside; put the mattress back on. We were never troubled by bed bugs ever again.

Chapter 14 The Big Crunch

Life doesn't stop because you've failed or lost something or someone you love. The sun still comes up at the beginning of the day; spends the whole day torturing you; turns orange and goes back down at the end of the day as it has always done since the beginning of time. My pain; in my failure to go and live in England; even though I felt it everyday and it never really went away; the experience had made a man out of me. It was as if I had been forged in the fires of hell; and come out new; hard; bitter and uncompromising. Overnight I had fallen from being uncle Ben's number one boy to being Mr Rude; Mr Naughty; Mr doesn't listen. It was back to the early days when I'd been scapegoat for everything. Apart from Gogo; there was no one else on my side; but I didn't care; I just did what needed to be done to survive until I was old enough to leave and do my own thing. But; no-one had ever told me that childhood would last an eternity. It went on forever and I hated every minute of it.

After the fall from grace life on the farm was a lot harder for me. Physically I was there mentally; I was nowhere. Auntie Ruth, tormented me with renewed vigour and somewhat more confidence. Hers was a subtle kind of mental attrition; making up stories that did not exist and watch me suffer for it. She was an expert in the art of subterfuge could change from downright angelic, to cruel lies at the drop of a hat.

I used to have nightmares about her refusing to take me to the hospital after I had been bitten by a snake. Of course these were just nightmares; because if there was one thing she was good at it was making sure all the children; myself included were well fed; healthy and all the wonderful things a mother does for her children. However; when it came to making sure we were happy; that was not one of her strongest points. She never laid a hand on me personally except the one time when I thoroughly deserved it; when I had pretended to have seen a lion and screamed so hard she came running all the way to the paddock; to see what I was hollering about. She really did care.

My feelings about here were very strange. There were moments; when I just wanted to wrap my arms around her like John and my little cousins did; but I didn't. I suspected she wanted to keep me at a distance; to stop me from getting too close; in case her on kids got confused. The kindness and empathy that she showed me when I was ill was unbelievable; she would have gone to the moon and back just to make sure I got everything I needed to get better.

Uncle Ben was too busy building his mansion on the hill to care about minor things like our feelings. He never explained to me why the tickets never came. He spent all summer directing the building and piece-meal destruction of more fruit trees around the mansion. Not only had he cut down fruit trees; but he also cut down wonderful timeless old musasa trees on the on the hill. To us these were sacred old trees that had been there since the beginning of time and I was sure that the spirits of our ancestors came out at night and danced around those trees and protected us from evil. I imagined; once before the whites had driven all the dangerous animals like rhinos and lions into game reserves behind electric barbed wire fences great lions had rested in the cool shade of those trees. To see them cut down and gone made me so sad. The hill was now scarred bare patch of shrubs and vines that covered the hillside; and an ugly sprawling building site.

The house was already beginning to take shape. Uncle insisted on taking any visitor who turned up on the farm to the building site to show them everything; describing each feature in great detail. What amazed me most; were the two small toilet rooms in the house. There was no hole in the ground and the floor was already concreted over. Try as much as he could to explain to everyone most of us could not understand how it was possible to have a toilet without a hole in the ground. Where would the poo go.

John had lived in town when he was ill and understand the whole thing and finally explained it to me in a way that I could understand. We had actually gone into the house and he had literally shown me how it would work, step by step. When he was done, I realised; it was fairly simple; but very clever. Get water to wash everything away. Quite ingenious.

Since his illness John had become quite distant. I just never saw much of him anymore except when he occasionally popped out to play. He spent most of his time studying. Whilst I spent all my free time looking after cattle and sheep. I didn't bother complaining about this; but I never stopped thinking about what wicked stroke of fate had put me in that position. It was as if I was living in a nightmare and one day I would wake up and everything would be okay; I would be living with my mother and father and sister. Except; it wasn't a nightmare; it was a real as reality could get. So I just got on with it.

The farm was changing, John was changing and I too was changing.

The town people came home, Christmas came then Christmas went and it was the beginning finally of another year.

15 The House on the Hill

Within a few months of the new year; all the sides of the house had been completed and and windows fitted. The house stood atop the hill like giant ancient ruin. I the evenings the sun set right behind the house on the hill, that Auntie Ruth called the Little Hill. We could see the silhouette of the house with orange light bursting out through the windows of the roofless building like some primitive site inhabited by ghosts. It was quite surreal.

It was almost the end of the term; when one day after school a big lory arrived loaded with triangular shaped timber frames.

We abandoned the sheep where they were grazing and ran up to the top of the hill following the truck to see what was being delivered. The timber frames were unloaded and placed on the ground next to the house. Soon after the unloading was done the lorry driver waved us good bye; got back in his lorry and then drove off without spending another minute on the farm. It was the strangest behaviour I had ever seen. Normally; when someone had travelled such a long way they would stay overnight; eat something; get some rest and then go back the next day.

John who again; somehow knew what had been delivered explained that the wooden frames for the roof. I had no idea where he got that idea from; but I feared that he was right. Over the next week the timber frames went up on the wall and finally the mansion with its timber frame roof started looking more like a proper house. Even just with the wooden frames it looked majestic; sat there on top of the hill.

One day we came back from school and the entire roof was on the house. A greyish white asbestos roof that gleamed in the hot sun. The house was magnificent. I had never seen a house so imposing; so completely and unbelievably divine in its appearance; on top of the hill commanding the whole countryside like some old master. All of a sudden; just like that; we had the most beautiful house that I have ever seen, and it wasn't even finished yet. How much more amazing was it going to be when it was finished. It already made the Maposa's house look pretty ordinary and they had a really fine house. We were all excited about it; immensely proud of it and couldn't wait to move in.

The building site had become our playground for many months and every day either on my own or with John tried to get all the sheep nearby and play around on the site. Once one evening we found the petrol concrete mixture and decided to play in it; turning it on and tumbling ourselves until we were totally covered in dust. It was very stupid; because after a while we couldn't breathe because of the cement dust. That game didn't last very long.

Other times we played in the empty rooms or just climbed the walls and surveyed the horizon that we could see around for miles. We could see the school from the top of the hill. From the farm house the long massive buildings of the school transformed into the size of a matchbox. It was very strange how distance; made something so large look much smaller than it really was. There was no way all those school kids could fit into a matchbox; and yet from where we were standing, that's exactly what they were doing every day.

Our favourite game though was the tractor tyre downhill roll. We had found a big old tractor tyre discarded near the new house and we'd push that up to the top of the hill right next the new house. One of us would climb into the base of the tyre whilst the other supported the tyre upright; then held onto the sides of the tyre real tight. When ready, the person supporting the tyre would give it a gentle push and let go and the tyre rolled down the gentle slope gathering speed and if you were lucky the tyre would go roll down the one or two hundred yards down the hill along the clear track, all the way to a field towards the Shumba's farm. John; being always the crazy remarkable guy; could steer that tyre whilst being spun round like a top and manage to guide it down the track where he wanted it to go.

I; on the other hand, had no idea how to steer the tyre; being able; only to hold on tight for dear life whilst the tyre went where the tyre wanted to go. The only problem was that just off the track to the right of the path was about an acre of land, clear flat Savannah with elephant grass as tall as a man, and dotted every few feet in the whole acre were six foot deep holes about the three foot wide and four or five feet long. Cows were not allowed anywhere there and they seemed to know not to venture near there themselves. Uncle had explained that the pits were there to plant orchard trees. I had no idea what an orchard was; but I could remember that the pits had been there for ever and were lethal; if you accidentally fell in one of them. One had been used to bury one of our dogs when it had gone bad and was brutally put down. It was a real bad thing that they did to that dog.

Many years back when I was five or six; one of our dogs called Rexy had gone bad and was stealing chicks and eggs. It had all come to a head when Rexy and another one of our dogs called Jinja were suspected of stealing a lamb and devouring it. The grown ups were not really sure which dog had done it. One morning; Uncle Ben devised a plan to catch the criminal. They got the two dogs out in the yard and offered them an egg with a tiny bit chopped off the top of it to make more enticing. Everyone gathered around to see what the palaver was about.

At that point; the workshop man tried to diffuse the situation by offering an explanation for the disappearing chickens.

"Gara membwe inodla, huku? - by the way do impalas eat chicken?"; he asked earnestly.

We laughed till our sides hurt; but that didn't help the two dogs one bit.

Uncle Ben; put the egg on the sand in the yard and ordered the two dogs to eat it. The dogs were very hesitant; so uncle brought out the whip and whipped them hard.

"Eat!"; he ordered.

"Eat that damn egg; damn dogs!".

Jinja; who was quite a smart Labrador mongrel refused to eat. You could see his little brain ticking over and saying, No! No!, "I don't like the look of this!; I don't like the look of this at all!".

Rexy, the medium size black mongrel on the other hand; could not resist the egg; and devoured it; thus exposing himself as the chicken and lamb thief. Unbeknown to us; he had just sentenced himself to death. After that show; we headed to the field near the orchard pits and there; whilst everyone worked harvesting 'nyimo' Jugo beans, and the dogs lay in the cool shade of the big old fig tree. Rexy was fast asleep; presumably chasing lambs in his dreams. All of a sudden the men started removing the hoes from their handles and chucking them on the ground and pretended to be digging whilst slowly moving towards the sleeping dogs. At first I was wondering what they were doing; but when they reached the dogs they started pounding Rexy with the thick wooden handles of the hoes.

That dog howled, and yelped and growled and grimaced and whined in agony. He tried to get up; but a hoe handle as think as a baseball bat landed in the middle of his back; bones crunched as his back broke and he crumbled back to the ground. They kept pounding that dog whilst he yelped helplessly in agony until; finally there was only the sound of the hoe sticks going thud; thud on the pulverised flesh of that damned dog. He was gone. Silence. Silence; like I had never heard before fell on that field that morning.

The women and little children were so upset and so traumatised that they decided to leave that field and go back home. Rexy's body was summarily tossed into one of those pits and covered with a bit of earth and that was that. We left to take the cattle and sheep out for the day. For some reason that field was never planted again. Although; it was a sunny cloudless day with blue skies; a darkness seamed to hang over the whole farm; that day.

To top it all up; only a couple of weeks after that dreadful event with Rexy; Jinja and was caught red handed; attacking a lamb and injuring it so bad there was no choice; but to let them devour it. Animals like humans can be quite cruel too; he made short work of that lamb as if he was a wild animal. When we broke the news to the adults; uncle Ben took him away and left him the 'Boterequa' mountains. He said that Jinja was later found by a nice white farmer who took him in and looked after him. Years later when I actually saw the Boterequa mountains; I was quite sure the jury was still out on that one.

The fig tree was one of my favourite trees. It produced clusters of super sweet small figs that when ripe turned a bright purple or red colour. It was an old tree with a tree trunk the width of a small African hut. The only problem with it; was that its branches were covered in a flaky white skin, that made it as smooth as glass and deadly slippery. This was a good and a bad thing. It was good because it meant snakes could not climb the tree so it was safe for us; bad, because one slip and it was a long way down to the ground. However; this didn't deter us when the figs were in season. We scaled the tree; skilfully holding to the thin; but strong branches; getting to the delicious figs and gorging ourselves on them.

Anyway; back to the tyre; rolling the tyre down the hill was by far the most favourite game we played around the building site. With all the comings and goings of trucks bringing materials to the site, the track had been pulverised into a nice dusty clear road perfect for rolling the big old tractor tyre. We didn't mind being completely covered in dust; we'd go to bed completely covered in dust; but like magic in the morning we'd be clean again. I had no idea where all that dust had gone during the night. This was so common; that one of the Shumba boys had told me that if you woke up with your feet and legs covered in dust; it meant that; a witch had bewitched you in the night; got you up and rode you like donkey to perform which craft in the next village. Of course I didn't believe in that rubbish; but it did take me a day or two to figure out why it was that we went to bed filthy and woke up squeaky clean.

One evening we had been rolling down the hill for a long while. Even I was getting quite good at keeping the tyre in the right direction; leaning this way and that way at the right time and the tyre went where I wanted it to go. Of course it was hard to keep the dust out of our eyes and mouths; but the thrill of going down hill inside a tyre would not deter us.

When it was John's turn to roll down; he got in settled and shouted for me to give the tyre a little push. The tyre rolled downhill, steadily gathering speed. John was in perfect control; but all of a sudden he must have lost his concentration or something; the tyre hit a small bump jumped up in the air and headed straight for one of the pits. I was screaming John, do something you are going to fall in the pit. The tyre gathered speed. I thought John was going to die right there in front of me. Then, boing, the tyre went straight over the first pit; boing; straight over the second then plonk, it rolled straight in the middle of the third pit.

I ran as fast as my legs could carry me; covering 200 yards in a few seconds. I expected to find limbs scattered everywhere from one pit to the next. Instead as I got to him; John was crawling out of the pit; laughing and screaming with delight.

"Did you see that?"; he had his arms up dancing and laughing wildly. He put is arms on my shoulders and I joined in his victory celebration. He had cheated death itself. The big old tractor tyre had wedged itself in the ends of the pit with the bottom of the tyre barely touching the ground. It was a miracle that the pit was just the right size for this to happen. John had simply stepped out of the tyre as you would do from a car or bicycle. At the bottom of the pit was a small mound of earth covered with short grass. It was Rexy's grave.

I wondered why uncle Ben needed such big holes for his orchard. Once; when showing a prospector who was prospecting for water for a new well for the big house, with his forked stick uncle Ben proudly announced that there was going to be a great big orchard there. There were going to be orange trees; mango trees; lemon trees and all sorts. Even as he explained I wondered; but why such deep holes in the ground. In my years and years as shepherd and cattle herder I had noticed that in the wild; most of the time the seeds did not need to buried under ground; they just grew from where they had dropped on the ground; all they needed was a bit of water a few leaves and straw over them; the rest they took care of it themselves growing into trees all by themselves. I wondered if it was something special about oranges they needed six foot deep holes; where a man or cow could accidentally fall in and break its neck.

A few months later; the house was by all accounts complete. The inside of the house had been plastered and was as smooth as glass. One of the sitting rooms had a green cement floor whilst the other sitting room, which was adjacent to the kitchen had a glossy yellow floor. All the construction work had finished, and there were no longer any men busy around the building site. All that was missing was the paint work and the flushing toilets that John had described to me.

Chapter 16 The War

I started grade four, my fourth year in primary school in total fear and trepidation; because the grade four teacher, was the renowned decrepit old man called Mr Shamurefu. His reputation for beating and punishing school kids was legendary. He was known as the butcher of Fort Milton school on account of his cruelty. He had been a teacher for more than 30 years at the same school. Auntie Thembi used to say that my father and her and everybody else in the Fort Milton area had been taught by that man. All of them had at one point or another been canned to a pulp by him. Everyone was terrified of him. He was known to keep whips and canes of all sizes and description in the cardboard; both in the classroom and back in his school house that he used for caning the school kids.

I had long wished the day would never come when this horrible man would be my teacher; but that dreaded day had arrived.

Time is cruel and unforgiving master. Forever; relentlessly marching forward; whether it leads you to pain and disaster, it doesn't care. It takes you there, drops you there and leaves you to deal with it. You either come out on top; or sink never to be heard from again.

My experience with the teachers had not been too terrible. Apart from my first grade teacher; whom I think we just got off on the wrong foot; I had pretty much liked and got on well with all my teachers. So; when the day finally came; I was pretty much resigned to my fate and had decided; he would have no reason to beat me; if I didn't do anything wrong. That's how I had survived most of the time; it didn't work all the time; but it worked most of the time.

It is true that every dark cloud has a silver lining. That silver lining came from good old Piye. By then someone had nicknamed him King Piye, on account of has long rain at the top of the class. During the previous year; one day he had been asked to go to another class and explain a difficult Maths problem. It just so happened that this class was Mr Shamurefu's class. Piye had gone there, solved the problem and got back a hero.

He wasn't a single bit scared of Mr Shamurefu. The boy commanded the most respect from everyone who came across him. He was not only clever; he seemed to know everything, even things that were quite general like the headmaster going to say at assembly that day. It was a mystery where he got his information from.

His stories about life in Salisbury were fascinating. He never seemed to stop talking about Salisbury and had such a wealth of information about everything. I could not figure out how anyone could keep so much knowledge in their heads. He surprised me; because he was completely without any fear and concern about Mr Shamurefu. I explained to him all the things I had heard about him and his reply was.

"He's okay; he taught my cousins last year and none of them got beaten". "Besides"; he added.

"He's only going to beat you if you do something wrong".

It was nice to hear someone else's point of view; but I knew perfectly well; you didn't need to do anything wrong for people to pick on you. But his attitude impressed me; and I felt a lot better about meeting Mr Shamurefu.

The first day of school started with assembly as usual. The headmaster made his announcements and threats to expel any kids who didn't pay their school fees by the end of the week. Being excluded from school for not paying fees was one of the most degrading and the demoralising experiences. We had been sent home once, and had been marched right back with the money for the fees the same morning. The shock had been bad for us and for the adults as well; because the fees were never paid late again.

I searched for Mrs Chirashe; but was shocked and disappointed to notice that she was not in the row of teachers in front. I had instinctively searched for her; hoping to bathe in the delightful radiance of her beautiful eyes and incredibly beautiful looks; but she was not there. I looked for her husband in the line of teachers stood in front of us; but he was not there either. I swallowed a lump in my throat as panic began to set in. I looked down the direction of her house in case they were late and were walking down; but there was truly no sign of them. My heart was racing, my head was spinning. I could not believe this was happening. Mrs Chirashe was gone.

Mr Big Head was still there. I didn't care about him, and at least I didn't have to worry about him for another two years as he was the grade six teacher.

I didn't hear anything the headmaster announced afterwards; because I was so upset that Mrs Chirashe was gone. Now she was gone; I didn't have anything to look forward to going to school anymore. The marching drum started beating; and I marched back to the classroom like a machine; my eyes filled with tears. The grade four classroom was right next to the assembly area so it was a really short march back to the classroom. The grade four classroom was at the end of the long block and was much bigger than the first three classrooms. It had a row of four large windows on the eastern side; which on crispy bright mornings; let in bright warm sunlight into the room.

The teachers table was in the same place as all the other classrooms; on the right corner of the classroom as you walked into the classroom. Nestled, right in the corner was the classroom cupboard. I wondered whether it was full of canes instead of PE equipment.

On the teacher's table rested the period bell; the bell that rang between all the different lessons. It was a large bell made from a golden coloured metal with a brown wooden handle. We were all excited about it. Maybe one day; we would get a chance to ring it and I guessed good behaviour was the price we had to pay to be able to ring that bell. If that was the only price; I had no problem with that.

This class was also different from the other classes. There were no benches and tables. Each pupil had their own little weird desk that you could open up and put things inside. Each of us had their own chair. I had the sense that we were now grown ups. Not little children anymore. Own desk and own chair. That was pretty awesome.

Mr Shamurefu walked into the classroom and immediately the class, stood up and fell completely silent. It was so quiet you could hear a little mouse scurrying along the concrete floor; if of course one did appear at that very moment.

It was a true tribute to his reputation; and he did not have two tell anyone to be quiet. Pupils just behaved around him without him having to say anything to them. He glanced in the direction of the class and carried on walking towards his table without uttering a word.

I noticed that he was quite an old man with a complexion that we called medium; not dark and not particularly light. His face was not as I expected; fierce and vicious; but to me looked old and wise; like the picture of my grand father, I thought, who had died decades before I was born and whose picture hung on the wall in uncle Ben's dinning room.

Mr Shamurefu stood behind his table and looked at us. "Good morning class"; he said.

"Good morning sir"; we replied.

"You may sit down"; he said softly.

He was a fairly tall; lanky man with a very slight wobbly gait when he walked. His brow was heavily wrinkled; but behind it all, I could see that he must have been a good looking man when he was young. He's crisply ironed checkered shirt hung loosely over his thin torso and was tucked inside his brown trousers. He looked smart and quite cool. I had the impression I liked him instantly and saw no reason at all to be afraid of him. I always judged people by how they looked and had figured out many years back, that most of the time you could correctly; tell the persons character just by looking at their face. If the heart was rotten so was the face. Uncle Bill was a great example; his face was fixed in a permanent snarl; that was there even when he laughed at his own silly jokes.

It was amazing how quickly I settled down to the job of learning. Grade four was quite a big jump from grade three. The Maths was harder and there was more of it; triangles, Pythagorus, ratios; percentages and all that rubbish. I understood it quickly; but saw no use for it at all. If I could count the number of sheep and cows we had on the farm; that was enough for me. On the other hand I enjoyed English and history so much. The grade four English and History books were packed full of interesting stories that took me to places where I could just forget that I even existed. I loved the story of the boy Blue who; not much older than I was; built a space rocket. Unfortunately for him it had exploded and covered him with a blue ink. The ink would not wash off; so for a whole term, his face was blue. His friends had nick named him Blue. I had laughed until my stomach hurt, when I read that story.

Every subject was tougher and more challenging; but it was more fun at the same time. As the weeks went by it was quite clear to me that Mr Shamurefu was not the monster that he had been made out to be. In fact he turned out to be the exact opposite. He had a kind of gentleness and calmness about him that commanded attention and respect. He gave me the impression that you wouldn't want to do anything he might consider wrong; for fear of discrediting yourself by embarrassing yourself in front of him rather than the fear of getting caned.

It seemed to me that he would give everyone the benefit of the doubt. To me it was quite obvious that he was a man that demanded reason and understanding than respect through fear. I thought he almost had special connection with his pupils. He never once had to shout at the whole class to be quiet.

This was not the man that had been described to me. Was it possible that he had changed that much over the years. I didn't much care; but, I was glad that he was my teacher. And it didn't take too long for me to gain his favour. The usual trick worked. It was always to work hard; get good grades and behave impeccably at all times. I was older, more experienced and somehow knew how to survive. The school was my domain of expertise; it was the place where I thrived.

As with all other classes Mr Shamurefu taught all the subjects , expounding his vast knowledge slowly and deliberately. When he explained something; it was like he was addressing you personally as individual; holding your interest every step of the way. At the end of the term the first term, the immutable King Piye once again took the first position with relative ease. Chris who had joined us from Salisbury in grade two fought him hard, coming a close second. By then; I had accepted that I would be relegated to a distant third. Piye was a serious guy but; Chris; on the under hand was a fun loving guy who enjoyed drawing above everything else and he was very good at it. Everyone gathered around his desk when he was drawing something particularly amazing. We all tried to emulate his technique; but only Chris could draw like Chris.

Mr Shamurefu always addressed us as if we were adults and not little children. He gave us instructions without threatening us with punishment if we failed to do what he asked. In return; I think he expected us to behave in a responsible way.

One day Mr Shamurefu called me aside and explained that he had taught my father once and he had heard what had happened to us the previous year. He said that he felt very sorry for us. But whatever happened didn't matter. I was a clever boy and not to worry about it; everything was going to be okay in the end.

He also added: "I can see you're struggling with your craft work. Don't worry about it; your brain is more academic and that's what you should concentrate on. But; some of these boys", he added; "Will never be able to amount to anything; so they have to concentrate on the craft work; so that they're able to make things with their hands, and sell them at the market. You on the other hand will go to college; maybe even university and study to be a teacher or even a doctor!".

I was so proud that he thought so highly of me; but was totally surprised that someone so far removed from my life even knew of my personal circumstances. Mr Shamurefu was talking to me as if, I was someone worth talking to, not some good for nothing child. Here was a man whose reputation preceded him; for all the wrong reasons. Instead of being the monster I had heard of so many times; he was the kindest and wisest of men. I felt so good despite everything that had happened; and hearing this from him, I felt that if I could only just keep pushing forward things might just work out, in the end like he said.

The second term had just begun when Shaba claimed he had seen a crocodile at the dam on Mapfumo farm. He claimed that it was huge, about the length of the classroom. No-one believed him; but the curiosity got the better of us. For me it didn't matter much as the Mapfumo farm was pretty much on the way home; except for a little bit of a diversion south west instead of directly west. I was also very curious to see what another dam ,other than the one on our farm would look like. I had always thought we had the only dam in the area; but finding out that there was another one somewhere else, my curiosity got the better of me despite the memory of the beatings for one such infraction all those years ago. So; completely putting aside our experience of the crocodile; in the first grade, a group of us joined the boys from the reserves and walked the two or three miles to the dam; all the while discussing the many ways to run for it; should the crocodile try to attack us.

We had no knowledge of crocodiles whatsoever; apart from the many stories we had heard about them; and a chance to see one for ourselves was irresistible. We crossed the river and followed a narrow winding path snaking its way through the thick trees and small bushes; so we walked in a single file. I had never been to that part of the thick forest that covered the whole area around the river before. The scenery was both exciting and frightening at the same time.

To my left the land started to rise gently higher and higher and was thickly forested with young trees; most of them with trunks no wider than a man's legs. It was a pleasant hot day; the constant shade of the overhanging trees turned it into a pleasant stroll; our minds completely absorbed in the task at hand. We let our six sense takeover the job of looking out for immediate danger like stepping on a snake. This was all territory of the famous Tariro river lion that was known to take the odd drunk now and again. No-one; I knew had ever seen it; but it was always at the back of our minds. I often wondered what I would do if I ever came face-to-face with the terrifying beast; but my brain would not allow me to think past that unimaginable point.

Soon the path made a sharp bend to the right started sloping down towards a dark ravine. It was an eerily quiet and quite frightening place. Everyone stopped talking at this point as if expecting some wild creature to jump out and attack. Quite, suddenly as if a massive giant curtain had been opened, the path cleared and in front of us was the dam. It stretched for nearly half a mile west. In the distance its water was shimmering under the bright hot sun like a lake of liquid silver. Close by the water looked dark and deep with gentle waves rolling across it endlessly is if it was alive.

Phil; who was in front put a finger on his lips and we tiptoed forward. You don't want it to hear us coming otherwise it will disappear under the water; Phil whispered.

As we came round the side of the dam wall; there was a loud splash and a plume of water rose from the dam.

Did you see that did you see that; Shaba screamed excitedly. Ripples spread out from the spot where the crocodile had dived into the water. There; in the middle of the dam was a trail of ripples where the crocodile was swimming towards the other end of the dam. Apart from the shape of a log and the ripples trail I really did not see anything mildly exciting or dangerous. I had come to see big gnarly teeth, and vicious evil yellow eyes but all I saw was a log and ripples of water. This crocodile; was proving to be a very disappointing mystery.

A flock of wild ducks; alarmed by our approach lifted off from the water; the spray from the wings dropping down and glistening like pressures jewels creating a transient rainbow in the shimmering sun.

I was a bright clear day, with not a single cloud in the sky. All around us apart from the ducks everything was quiet and still. As we walked I noticed from a different angle and much closer to the water in the dam looked crystal clear; clean and good enough to drink. Apart from a cup of tea and corn bread in the morning, not a single morsel or drop of water had passed between my lips. Seeing that water; looking so cool and fresh made me feel thirsty. However; no matter what, there was no way I could drink any water other than from the well at home or the water dug out from the dry river bed. Sometimes when heading home after school after a whole day without a drink we'd be so thirsty; that when crossing the dry river we'd use sticks to dig the sand on the riverbed until we reached the water table about a foot down. After a few minutes the hole would feel up with nice clean water; which we'd scoop into our mouths and quenched the thirst. Unfortunately; on one or two occasions; I found out that my hole was right next to a cow pad and in fact consumed water that had sipped through it. It never did us any harm though.

Our search for the crocodile finished; we decided to go and look for wild fruits of the famous chewing gum tree. The boys from the reserves were quite familiar with area and knew where all the good fruit trees were. They led us up the hillside where there were all kinds of fruit trees. There were 'matamba' monkey orange trees, with their perfectly round green fruits just; which when ripe turned yellow so that it looked like someone had deliberately hung loads of tennis balls in the trees. The shells of the fruits were as hard as rocks. You needed a rock to smash one to get to the delicious gooey sweet fruit inside. There were the blood red 'nhunguru' governor's plums with purple berries the size of golf balls and the famous 'tsubvu' tree with its black olive like weird but tasty fruits. Shaba casually pointed out that was the tree where that boy; had bean bitten by a black mamba and died.

I had never stopped thinking about what happened to that boy. So hungry; he had taken himself away from the group and decided to go and find some fruit by himself.

He had climbed that tree and disturbed a mamba that had probably been hunting for small birds that feasted on the 'tsubvu' fruit. He had seen the snake; but too late. It had bitten him and it had taken only the time to climb down the tree; walk and crawl a few yards before he was overcome by the venom and died. We were in grade two when that happened. One morning the headmaster had announced that Tahaka Mukonoweshuro had been bitten by a mamba and died. As a result the headmaster had sent everyone home that day.

Tahaka's death had made me realise how lucky I had been to have survived so many snake encounters and it was always a complete wonder why I hadn't been bitten. Once just like Tahaka; I had decided to top myself up with the odd rare winter guava. I had learned that in winter long after the guavas were out of season, there was always one or two guavas left; growing slowly to ripen over winter and those guavas were the sweetest of them all. In my haste I had got up that tree without the usual precautions of scanning the tree for dangerous snakes.

The guava tree was evergreen; it's foliage as thick in winter as it was in summer. I had scanned the tree for the tell tell yellow spec of a ripened guava and spotted it; then without taking my eye of it climbed up to claim the prize. It was large yellow and I could already taste it in my mouth, its delicious reddish pink flesh and small seeds. I picked the guava only to find that the birds had made a small hole on one sided and completely devoured the inside. As I turned to look for another I found my face centimetres from a small green mamba. It was in the familiar now familiar squashed 'S' shape which I thought it coiled into that shape to get away from me as far as it could without actually moving away. I had simply ducked hard and leapt straight down to the ground the couple of meters from the short guava tree.

Another time; it had been whilst with a whole bunch of my cousins just enjoying a good old climb, when suddenly I reached for a branch and right there; no more than a few centimetres from my face I saw the little green and black snake called a Boomslang; compacted into a tight S shape. Although I was quite high up the tree; I preferred to fall to death than die from a snake bite; so I had just let go and just dropped down like a stone. As I fell I had looked up to see the snake strike the spot where my head had been half a second before. But as luck had it; I had hit every branch going down and landed softly on the ground; with only a few minor scratches.

It was with these thoughts that I stared at that tsubvu tree and carried on walking up the hillside deeper into the forest. The hillside was bonanza of different fruits; but we were focused on one fruit, the 'mutohwe' chewing gum tree .

The hillside was somewhere where hardly anyone ever dared to climb; because it was also mamba territory and the fruits were abundant. I had never seen anything like it. Finally halfway up the hill we got to the chewing gum trees. There was a whole cluster of them; not old and tall like the one uncle Ben had cut down; but small and bushy with thin spindly branches that looked like they could barely support the weight of a small boy. The trees were packed with big, fruits dark as honey combs; bursting with the thick sugary molasses that infused the perfectly symmetrical triangular wedges of the fruits. They looked so delicious I could practically taste the juices from the ground before I even touched one.

Being one of the skinniest boys in the group and quite sure also the best tree climber of the lot; having practically lived up trees on the farm I was up one mutohwe tree as fast as a bushbaby. Once up there; I found getting to the fruits on those thin spindly branches; hard work. I picked some fruits and threw them down to eager hands on the ground.

"Me, me"; each one shouted excitedly.

"There; there"; shouted Piye; pointing at branch with the biggest juiciest fruits clustered on branches no thicker than a man's thumb. I edged forwarding, balancing precariously on the spindly branches to reach the best fruits. The best fruits; I stuffed in my pockets and the rest I threw down to waiting hands on the ground.

Some of the fruits were dripping with sugary trickle like honey. The sticky trickle coated my fingers making it even harder to hang on to the thin branches that could barely support my weight. The I saw them; right at the end of a thin branch, the biggest juiciest of them all; some had opened up like petals of a flower, oozing golden brown trickle that looked just like honey. I carefully edged my way towards them; testing the branch with my feet and when I was sure it could not take any more of my weight I stretched out my arm to grab the tiniest of the branches with the fruit so I could pull it towards me and pick each fruit off and stuff it my pockets.

The was a loud crack and with not even a second to react, I was flying through the air. The next second I could taste the soil mixed with blood in my mouth. It was salty. The wind had been knocked out of my chest and the lights went out. It was a warm and dark place and I was flying out in space amongst the stars. The sky was carpeted with stars and I was reaching out to catch one with my hand. I bumped into some knocking them out of the way as I flew higher and higher.

Then I felt cold hands on my face. I could hear all sorts of noises as if I was back in a buzzy classroom.

"Is he dead?"

"Nkosiyetu!". Finally I heard, Piye's voice shout.

"Are you ok?"

My left wrist was in excruciating pain; I sat up; spat the blood and soil out of my mouth. Run my tongue along my teeth to see if I had broken any. The were all there and there were none loose. Faces were gathered around, at first looking concerned, then smiling. Phil described the fall in detail.

"You dived for the fruit, got them and then came down like a stone hitting that branch and that branch and that bush on the way down!".

My friends couldn't help chuckling a bit.

"You are very lucky"; Shaba said; once one of the boys from my village fell from a tree and landed on his legs. His legs were pushed right into his stomach and he was never able to walk again.

Piye explained that; when you fall over; as soon as touch the ground you should roll over. I didn't say anything. I was in too much pain and just wanted to get home and lay down; my whole body was aching; but my wrist was in excruciating pain. I was sure I had cracked or broken a bone in the wrist.

"Here", Phil said, pushing a few more fruits into my already bulging pockets; you actually managed to grab these before you fell.

We made our way down the hill. Everyone except me was cheerful; gorging themselves on the sweet nectar of the chewing gum fruits. I had completely lost my appetite and my pockets felt heavy and sticky from all those fruits. The stalks of some the the fruits had found their way through the holes in my pockets and were scratching my legs irritating me immensely. But such was the delightful quality of the fruits I dared not throw them away; because I knew that John and the kids at home were going to really appreciate them.

We followed the path that wound along the whole length of the dam and then veered left towards the villages. Solomon from the Shumba farm and I were heading right to join the road home. We followed another winding dusty track that took us back to the main road and were on our way home.

The sun was already low by the time I got back to my farm and the cattle and the sheep were already being headed to the kraal for the night. I was in too much pain to even bother helping with locking the animals in for the night. I walked into the kitchen and emptied my pockets on the old kitchen stove. My wrist and hand now swollen to about double its normal width and the pain was unbearable. Auntie Ruth was crouched over the fireplace in the middle of the kitchen blowing on the fire to get it going.

One glance through a cloud of grey smoke; is all she had needed to tell that something was wrong.

Without saying a word, by now tears running down my cheeks because of the pain, I took myself to my previously bug infested bed; but now completely bug free thanks to my ingenuity. I threw myself on the bed in one of the rooms in uncle Bill and auntie Ruth's house and pulled my feet to my chest and tried to fight the pain.

It was at times like these that I really missed having parents. One of the main problems of not having parents was that communication with adults at home had to be subtle. I had to convey what I wanted to say, not with words; but with gestures; changes in mood and sometimes completely irrational behaviour and left it to the adults to interpret what it is; that I wanted to say.

It was also because adults were a completely different species to us children. They lived in their own cosy little world; where they spoke to us; but we as kids were not allowed to speak to them unless spoken to. We had no rights and no opinion about anything. Regardless; in any case; I couldn't have confessed that I had gone off the track to collect some fruits and fallen out of a tree and nearly broken my arm. She would probably have broken the other wrist as punishment.

As I lay there in agony the thought that kept racing around in my head was my old recurring dream with Auntie Ruth where I was bitten by a little green snake and she refused to take to the hospital; saying; we just don't have any money. I knew I had done my part, communicated that there was a problem; and it was all up to her to figure it out and fix it. Even though I knew that Auntie Ruth was an amazing woman capable of the most wonderful kindness, I couldn't help thinking like that.

Once when I was ill, I suspect from malaria or something like that. She and Steven carried me several miles to the school hospital and back. I was no more than four of five years old at the time and they had done this journey at least two or three times. The last time Steven had the wonderful idea to put a blanket in one of the two wheel burrows on the farm; and pushed it all the way to the hospital and back with me in it. Even as I was ill it had been enormous fun sitting in the wheelbarrow all that distance and back. I got better and Aunt Ruth had selected a big fat chicken from the brood; slaughtered it and cooked a delicious meal; served with her speciality; brown rice cooked in peanut butter. That meal was so wonderful and the way she talked to me; so kindly I wanted to just put my arms round her and tell I loved her and really preferred her when she was nice and kind; but for some reason I didn't. The day after I was well enough to go back to the sheep; and she was immediately back to being completely indifferent.

At other times however; she turned, now she spread most malicious rumours about me about being rude. Once she had said I had sworn at her and called her 'Ruthless'. Even though I did not know any swear words; let alone say them in front of her. Between her and uncle Bill, when they were on the war path and I stood in the way, I paid the full price. Some years back when I was eight or nine something had really come to a head.

One day uncle Ben had come home from town, on his own and stayed the night. I had slept on his floor to keep him company and explained all the goings-on on the farm when the town people were not there. I had explained how I looked after the sheep and cattle everyday tirelessly never complaining and yet; the thanks I got for it was endless accusations of being rude and naughty and disobedient. To my horror of horrors uncle Ben had repeated everything I had said to Auntie Ruth and uncle Bill the next day. I had assumed that I was telling him everything in confidence; but I had been wrong.

When he left to go back to town the next day uncle Bill and Aunty Ruth were not happy with the little brat. They said that I had made them look bad. My innocent conversation with uncle Ben had backfired in the most unexpected way. It had not been my intention to discredit them at all; I had simply been expressing the truth as I saw it. I brushed it aside; because I had long made a theory; that you could not keep trouble away for any amount of time. Sooner or later whether you prayed everyday or sinned, it didn't matter; trouble would still come for you.

Unfortunately for me; I had not prepared myself for what happened next. The next morning; unbeknown to me uncle Bill had hashed a plan to meet out the best punishment he could imagine. In the middle of the night; maybe three or four o'clock in the morning; long before even the most eager of all cockerels crowed; I was suddenly woken up by him and told get up and go and wait outside. Reluctantly I had unwrapped myself out of my old blanket and left it in a pile one the reed mat.

Where are we going; I had asked unable to fully wake up.

"Shut up and get ready"; uncle Ben ordered; "or I will pummel you good".

Outside it was peach black, nothing moved and it was eerily quiet; apart from the odd lightning and distant rumble of thunder.

I thought this was it; this was the night when uncle Bill was going to take me into the forest; hit me over the head with a hammer or strangle me and leave me there to die and be devoured by hyenas. There were three or four places he could do it; and I thought to myself; if we headed in the direction of any of those places I would run for it. I had no idea where I would go; maybe I would run away and work in the mines in Wenela eGoli, in South Africa, I thought to myself. I knew I could outrun anyone; even the devil himself so that's what I was going to do.

I waited outside in the yard whilst he got ready. He was wearing his blue overalls and gumboots; whilst I was wearing my old pair of shorts and an old shirt that had long lost whatever colour it might have had once. Neither of them had ever been washed from the time they had been handed down to me by one of my cousins; not that I had any idea they ever needed to be washed.

He ordered me to follow him and headed out towards the kraal. So, he wasn't going to kill me after all. Out at the edge of the yard, Steven and Jason were waiting for us. We walked in the dark to the kraal. It was a particularly dark night; but just as well I knew the path to the kraal so well I could have easily got there by myself blindfolded. Then uncle Bill ordered me to help harness the oxen and go and plough the fields near the hill a couple of miles from the kraal. I thought he had lost his mind completely. First of all, we had a tractor for this type of work, what was he doing getting me up to do this kind of work in the middle of the night. The penny still had not dropped that this was some kind of punishment.

I got in the kraal and expertly drove four oxen out of the kraal; stepping on wet cow pads that squelched between the toes of my feet and felt quite horrible; but I was used to this by now. I now knew even the most horrible filthy cow dung mixed with urine; all gory fluids from cows and rain to form a horrible muddy bog could do no harm to my feet. I could just wash the cow dung off my feet when we crossed the river on the way to the hilltop fields. I helped attach the oxen to their harnesses whilst he held up the old oil lamp from the kitchen; cussing and spitting hot ambers the whole time.

The oxen ready; he ordered me to lead the oxen to the hilltop fields. The oxen were harnessed together in two rows and I had to walk in front of them whilst holding a leash attached to the middle of the yoke.

"Move", he ordered and whipped the cattle hard. It was a particularly dark moonless night, and even the stars were hidden from view by dark clouds. I could barely see what I was stepping on. From the word go I was stepping on sharp stones and sticks unable to see what lay on the ground. I wondered how long it would be before I stepped on a snake and was bitten and dead within a few hours. So; this is how he was going to do it; make it look like an accident; I thought to myself. No-one would ever know. I was starting to get worried; what was on this man's mind?

By the time we got to the hill top my feet had been lacerated by sharp stones, sticks and I had even stepped on the sharp thorns of one of the nastiest plants of all on the farm. This was a plant we called the 'devils teeth'. It was an innocent looking creeper that spread itself over a wide area on the ground, sending long arms in all directions like a giant octopus. Its seeds lay flat on the ground with two, three or four sometimes even five thorns about half an inch long sticking out of the top of each seed.

Each seed was about the size of a medium size dung beetle, about the size of a grown man's top half of the thumb. Each thorn was irregular in shape, some were shaped like a blade, others like a nail and yet others like a pyramid spike; but all of them were as sharp as needles. Even in the day time when you lost concentration and suddenly realised you were about to step on one; and quickly tried to avoid doing so, only putting a tiny bit of weight as you stepped on one; the pain was still unbearable.

The worst part was putting full weight on the hill part of the foot over one of those seeds. Those three of four thorns drove into the base of the foot like a nail through a sponge. God, the pain was unbelievable; it felt like the whole body had been smashed by a massive boulder; leaving just the head poking out.

If you've ever unwittingly; stood barefoot on a red hot amber under the heel of your foot and felt a slight discomfort; which grew into quite a bit of pain. By the time you realised you were standing on a red hot amber; the damage was done and the pain that followed was excruciating; lasting almost a minute or two. Well; the pain from stepping on a devils teeth thorn seed was about a hundred times worse than that.

"Walk straight; walk straight; you stupid boy!"; uncle Bill shouted as I nearly lost my balance pulling one of those the seeds out of my burning right heel. The pain had knocked the wind out of my chest and I had started weeping; quietly. I could hear him huffing and puffing behind.

I could hear him saying; under his breath; "I'm gonna make him suffer; you'll see; I'm gonna make this boy suffer!".

He was already working himself up into a frenzy. I was wondering what I had done wrong to deserve this.

"I said walk straight, you dog of a child ('imbwa ye mwana')"; he screamed. We had reached the rocky hill top fields and I had just stumbled on a rock sticking out of the ground and lost a wedge of skin of the front of my right toe; and I knew it was bleeding profusely even though I couldn't see it in the dark.

I burst out crying loudly.

"Shut up, or I will beat you to a pulp!"; he ordered; irritated with my crying.

I did as he said, sniffling like a sick baby, tears streaming down my face and bogeys dripping uncontrollably from my nose. I stopped by the plough that had been left in the middle of the field, while Jason and Steven attached it to the yoke. Steven carried the lamp, Jason guided the plough whilst uncle Bill carried the whip to whip the oxen. My job was to guide the oxen up and down the four hundred yard long field, in the dark without a light, barefoot. I knew these fields well, and I hated them. There were the same fields four or five of them where one of my town cousins; Joseph had claimed to have been bitten by a snake; because he was too lazy to work. It had turned out to be nothing; but I still hated those fields and tried to avoid them as much as I could.

Once the plough was attached to the harness uncle Bill ordered me to start leading the oxen forward taking a line along the middle of the field. Things didn't get any better for my battered feet; when I started leading the oxen down the middle of the field all the way to the end and back up again and again. My feet we getting stabbed and cut by old corn stocks cut from the previous harvest but still sticking out fo the ground like, short stakes on war camp. I cried openly now, not caring any more about his threats. The pain was too much and I had no idea how much more of the cuts and lacerations my feet could take. I could just imagine the entire skin coming off so I would end up a completely immobile cripple, never able to walk or play football again.

"Shut up, stop your crying!"; uncle Bill shouted from the back.

A peace of mud went flying past my head and bits of mud rained on my big afro hair. I tried to be quiet; but I couldn't. My crying was comforting, I was talking to the wind, telling it to "Please go and let my father know that I will die today; come and save me".

All of a sudden in the darkness I made out the shape of the skeleton of snake, it's white bones perfectly discernible even in the dark. I saw it too late, my right foot stepped right on top of those bones, the entire length of my foot was on those snake bones. I erupted, screaming; not just because of the pain; because I believed this was the end for me. I was terrified I was going to die. We had always believed that the bones of a snake were just as poisonous as the snake bite itself. So we never touched, or even went anywhere near them, and now I had stepped on one and a couple of the bones had penetrated deep into my feet.

"Uncle Bill was livid, stop the crying; right now. You filthy mangy dog. I'll give you something to cry about!".

He brought the whip down my back. It stung like the devil.

"I said shut up", smack; down the whip came down, "I said shut up", down it came again; again and again until, I was out of breath and stood there unable to make another sound. The oxen, just stood there and watched the whole thing, didn't even make one attempt to move.

"Now lead these cattle again; quietly, or I will kill you, I promise!"; uncle Bill ordered.

I carried on, my senses were now crystal clear, I could see better in the dark, the silhouettes of trees in the distance, which normally would have frightened me now looked the most beautiful of all old friends, I could hear each ox breathing heavily, I could hear; the plough wearing away at the ground like a gently melody, I could hear uncle huffing and puffing behind me. I could tell he wasn't finished with me yet. I wondered if the poison from the bones was beginning to work now. They had always said you see your whole life flush by clearly like film before you die. Was this what was happening to me?

I guess, I was just out of luck that morning. At the end of that very row where I had stepped on the snake bones; I walked straight into a small thorn bush just slightly taller than my hip; but packed full of the most healthy looking thick needle sharp elephant thorns as tough as nails. It was at the end of the row where you turn to start another row and the momentum of the turning with oxen breathing heavily behind me; I walked into it at some speed. It's impossible to describe the pain of hundreds of thorns driving into my feet, legs; hands and belly all at the same time.

This time I didn't scream because I was afraid of dying; I screamed because of the shock of the pain. Imagine fifty people standing over you and sticking a needle each where ever the liked on the lower front half of your body hands and arms at the same time. I instinctively sat down and tried to pull branches of thorns out of my feet. Uncle wasn't having none of it. He came running from behind the oxen.

"Get up, stop crying!". He yanked me up. Probably the first time he had ever physically touched me.

The whip came down again. I screamed louder.

The whip came down harder. I screamed even harder.

Again and again the whip came down.

He was now in a complete uncontrollable frenzy, but so was I. I was now completely resigned to my fate and he was going to have to kill me to shut me up.

He threw the whip on the ground and slapped me hard.

He kicked me in the groin and slapped in the face and my screams became epic. I was quite sure even my dead Aunt buried half a mile from there would be able to hear me; if not I was ready to die and be buried right next to her.

"Stop; stop; please stop; Uncle Bill!"; Steven and Jason finally begged him.

He was not quite finished with me.

He punched me in the stomach.

I was now doubled over; in dire agony. I tried to scream; but no sound came out.

I was down on my knees; puking like sick puppy. Nothing came out except bogeys and spit.

Now Steven and Jason were wrestling with him. "Stop, he's suffered enough!".

"No"; he shouted.

"If he has suffered enough; then he has not suffered at all. Let him suffer some more. I will kill this boy today!"

He was out of breath. His frenzy now fully unleashed.

"I will kill this dog of a child!".

"Stop, Baba vaJohn; Stop John's dad!"; they begged.

"I will kill this, boy!"; he hissed.

I was now on my haunches. My hands clutching my stomach; try to suck in a breadth of air. The air was humid and warm. The ground; damp and cool. I could see my dead ancestors hands stretched out; reaching out to me. They looked peaceful. They were calling me to them; they were saying; "Come home; we're ready for you"

I waited for the final blow. The one that would finish me like good old Rexy.

"Go on. Do it. My father will hear about this!"; I said to myself.

"Go on get out of here!"; Uncle Bill; shouted throwing a piece of freshly ploughed mud at me; "Get out of here!. Satani!"

I hobbled back home in the dark, and rolled myself in my old blanket. For the first time in my life, I wished I was dead. I had been a fighter up until then; but uncle Bill had beaten the will out of me, he had won. I thought that if I died at least my father would come back from England to bury my body, I thought. He would cry for me, and I would finally find peace. It never occurred to me that it was my own father's brother meeting out this cruelty on me, I knew he was; but I never somehow thought of him that way. I just saw him for what he was, a coward and a monster; picking on a child no bigger than a tooth pick, and I hated him with every last inch of my tiny little body.

Something strange had happened to me after that horrible night. I completely lost all memory of everything that happened the days and months following that horrible event; right from the very morning. It was as if someone had taken a cleaver; and chopped off a whole chunk of my life away; but unfortunately the event was recorded in my memory like strip of film to be relieved again and again ad infinitum.

The thought of that horrible night had provided some distraction from the pain; but I had snapped out of as quickly as I had gone into it. My wrist was throbbing hard and I pulled my arm up close to my chest. That relieved a little bit of the pain. The door cricked open. Most of the green paint on the wooden door had long flaked off, leaving a patchwork of flaky green and grey wood work. The bottom of the the door was jagged where termites had chewed off the wood. It left a gap where a determined small snake could easily push through and find its way into a comfortable warm bed. It was a real wonder no snake had ever entered that house; seeing there were always snake trails in the yard where a snake had dragged its body across the sandy dusty yard whilst we slumbered in the middle of the night.

Auntie Ruth came into the room, holding a dish of hot water and a small dish cloth. I snapped out of my time warp; quite pleased to see her.

Come on "Bhudi" Nkosi; let me have a look at that arm. She said softly turning on the charm and speaking in the most gentle voice you could imagine. She placed the dish on the floor and kneeled beside the bed. She took my hand gently and pulled it slightly towards her.

"Let's have a look now". I grimaced in pain. "Oh dear, or dear, what happened?"; she asked.

I didn't really know what to tell her, and I was quite sure she already knew the answer. The room was already getting dark with the last of the daylight fading away and I pretended I had not heard the familiar cattle calls and whistling as the cattle were driven to the kraal; to avoid answering the question.

"Who is going to get the cattle in!"; I sobbed.

"Don't worry about that"; she said; the boys will bring the cattle in; you just worry about your hand.

"Oh that looks pretty bad, let's hope you haven't broken a bone!". She folded the dish cloth into a thick rectangle and dipped it in the hot water and squeezed out all the hot water to make a hot compress. Then she pressed it firmly against my throbbing wrist until the heat had gone from the compress. She repeated the process until the heat was gone from the water. The gentle heat soaked into my throbbing wrist dissipating some of the pain. She stood up and said.

"There, that should do it. Let's see what it's like in the morning".

She lit the small oil lamp on the long darkly stained side board with fancy china and crystal glasses and silver wear. She walked to the door, held it open and looked at me and said.

"I'll send your sister with your dinner, you can use a spoon to eat with the other hand". Then she gently closed the door and left. Poor woman; no-one should be forced to look after another woman's child in the way that Auntie Ruth was forced to look after my sister and I. Simply not fair.

The next morning, my whole left arm was twice the size of the right arm and hurt like mad. Auntie Ruth decided that it must be fractured and the only way to find out for sure; was to have an X ray done in Selukwe. After a brief discussion with uncle Bill; they had decided that none other than uncle Bill would take me to the hospital in Selukwe. Of all people in the world; he was the last person I wanted to spend the whole day with; but I was in so much pain I had no choice; but to say nothing. Steven had to start the old tractor and drive us the four or five miles to the bus station; all the way north across half our farm and the Samukange farm. Auntie Ruth went into her bedroom and brought out a red headscarf which she expertly tied around my neck and made a sling and placed my left arm so it rested in the sling across my chest. My arm immediately felt a lot better.

Steven took the better part of too long trying to start the tractor. That tractor was a nightmare to start in the morning. The easiest way to start it was to have two or three people push it downhill and kick start it. But, every now and again they had to use a crank shaft to start it. The crank shaft end was pushed and locked into a position on the engine drive shaft. Then turned as hard and fast as possible until the engine burst into life. As soon as the engine started the crankshaft had to be removed otherwise it would be totally impossible to remove it whilst the engine was running. It was all about timing and if you missed the timing by a second the engine could easily rip your arm off. Finally, I heard the tractor start; Steven let the engine run for a bit before letting uncle Bill know he was ready to go.

The day after that I was back at school with a sling from the hospital; expertly tied around my neck supporting my arm that was bandaged firmly with a crispy clean white bandage. I was an instant hero, amongst my friends.

I recounted the story of the long narrow bridge that the bus had to cross on the journey to Selukwe. The narrow bridge had no sides except for short vertical blocks that looked like bricks painted a brilliant white. As the bus approached it, the bridge had appeared narrower than the bus. Everyone was wondering how that huge bus was going to get across. I recounted; how the driver drove faster and faster as we approached and descended towards the bridge. The suspense on the bus as we got nearer and nearer bridge was unbelievable. Not a single voice spoke, just the sound of the bus engine as it revved up and sped towards the bridge could be heard.

The driver who obviously had done it many times before was revelling in the fear of the passengers. He kept glancing back and laughing as the bus gathered speed downhill towards the bridge. My heart was in my mouth; as the bus went over the smooth concrete floor of the bridge. It wasn't until later that I thought about it that I was quite sure that the bus had to speed up on the way down towards the bridge in order to get enough momentum to climb back up the valley that rose steeply up from the bridge.

My friends listened eagerly as I explained the dangerous mountain crossing called Boterequa on the Selukwe mountains; how when I looked outside the window of the bus I could see nothing; but a shear drop into deep gorges below; rusty old wrecks off buses and cars; carcasses of mangled rusted lorries and trucks that had dropped off the edge of the narrow tight mountain pass. The look on the passenger's faces had been that of shear terror as the bus crocked and spluttered as it struggled to climb up that mountain pass. Round and round the winding road the bus went meandering up the steep slope. I had wondered; where was it was so important to go; to risk one's life like that. I wondered; if the bus went over the side; they would even be able to recover the bodies. There was no chance; so more than likely they just left the bodies there to be devoured by hyenas.

At one time the bus driver had joked that everyone should get off and push the bus; because it would not manage to get to the top with all those people. Finally; when the bus got to the top of the mountain and it started to descend; it started rolling down the hill like a rollercoaster. As I looked down out of the window of the bus, there was nothing on the side of the road other than a shear drop to the bottom of the gorge. If one of the wheels of the bus had gone a foot towards the edge, the bus would have tumbled down the mountain, and it would have been the end for us. The bus driver was a young man, about the same age as Steven and seemed to be in total control of the big giant wheel and every couple of seconds he was pushing and pulling on the bus gears. How he knew which of the two gears levers to change without looking was a mystery to me.

Then lastly; I recounted the story of the total stranger who had felt sorry for me on the bus and offered me some money. I was quite sure the man was trying to make me feel better and as the bus finally reached level ground in the mountain pass and people heaved a sigh of relieve; the man asked me what grade I was and when I told him grade four he had pulled out his wallet, a small red pouch with a draw string and pulled out from it a coin called a "tikki" worth five cents, a shilling worth ten cents, a twenty cent piece called two "Bobo"; a twenty five cent piece called a two and half "Bobo" and a dollar bill also called a ten "Bobo". He held them out in his hands. He had explained the value of each coin and dollar bill to me and to test me had asked me to repeat the names and value of each coin and dollar bill clasped tightly in his right hand; afterwards. Even though I had never seen so much money in my life, I had remembered them all and got the answer right. Clever boy; the man had said.

Then the man done the expected.

"You can chose anyone one of these coins or dollar bill"; the man had said.

I had instinctively looked at uncle Bill, for approval and he had nodded his head. It was the first and only positive interaction I had ever made with him. By now a whole group of people were watching the goings on with great interest. Some had even stood up from their sits to get a better look. I looked at the money and then I glanced at the man's face. In his eyes I could see the conflict raging in his head. On one hand he wanted to offer me some money, on the other hand he did not want me to take the dollar as it was too much money to him to lose. So I had chosen the twenty five cents instead.

Clever boy, clever boy, the man said as he handed me the coin and hurriedly put the rest of his money back in the pouch.

Later on the way back home; Uncle Bill had asked me why I didn't take the dollar.

I had told him I wanted the big shiny silver coin. The truth was that; when I looked at the man's eyes; I could tell he was begging me not to choose the dollar; because he needed that money to feed his family and so I had chosen the smaller amount.

Phil said he would have definitely taken the dollar bill.

My arm was was not broken, it had just been a nasty sprain. That nasty sprain had led to a chain of events that remained seared in my memory for ever. A bad event leading to good things, a silver lining; I never tired of wondering why things happened at all, and what would happen next. Why did extraordinary things keep, happening to me. What did it all mean, I wondered.

The first term of grade four had flown by so quickly and as far as problems were concerned it had gone without a hitch. Of course, what I considered problems were things like falling out with another kid in the class, being sent to the headmaster's office; basically anything that disturbed the regular rhythm of order at school; my escape route to salvation; everything else, was just life as usual.

The term ended and the long holidays began. No longer did I find the holidays exciting anymore. The town people reminded me of a broken promise. The adults set around the fire hashing out the same old stories they had told so many times before; embellishing them a little; but they were the same stories no less.

I didn't even find uncle Percy's stories of the "maJohny"; white Rhodesian policemen who used to turn up in remote villages on motorbikes to inspect the natives to make sure they were nice clean. They carried sjamboks and if they found anyone dirty; they would whip the living daylights out of them. The natives had learned that when they heard the sound of a motor bike approach; they should run into the bush; hide and watch the Johny make a fool of himself playing with mongrels in the yard. After a while the Johny would give up waiting and then leave a bar of soap for the whole village to use; ready for the next inspection.

The story seemed so far fetched; so far in the past it made us laugh. The thought of a big old Johny playing with dogs whilst all the villagers watched surreptitiously from the bushes; was very funny. In the past I had tried to imagine what Jinja or Pinta; our two dogs would think if they ever saw a white man. Would they run like we had done the first time we had seen white men.

Instead; now I listened out for the bits I didn't want to hear, our story of major disappointment; the lies about what we'd said. I was unhappy when they talked about it and I was not happy when they didn't mention anything in sympathy about it at all.

Fortunately; with the house so close to completion, everyone's interest was more on the house and how long it would be before we could move up there. I wondered what would happen to the old houses when we moved to the big house.

"We should move now!", insisted Uncle Bill; but Uncle Ben would have none of it.

"The electric wiring still needs to done, then the ceilings and there are no toilets yet. There's still too much work to be done before we can move in; Brother"; uncle Ben assured him firmly.

"If we don't move in; thieves might break in and steal, things from the house. They could strip the house of its doors and windows in the middle of the night and we'd never know"; uncle Bill tried to push his point.

I had to say I agreed with him on this point. I couldn't put it past people doing strange things like that. Once; we had found our fattest; plumpest lamb gone one morning. Beside the kraal, we found the contents of its belly and blood socked grass where someone had slaughtered it in the middle of the night. The effrontery of the crime was beyond belief. That someone could have the nerve to disrespect us like that; come onto our farm in the middle of the night and steal my sheep; slaughter it and carry it into the dark night was beyond belief. To my surprise nothing had been done to try and find the culprit. I guessed that the loss of one sheep out of forty odd wasn't worth the trouble; but I always wondered if that brazen low life of a human being would ever return to steal another one of my sheep.

This time when the town people had come home; a sheep had been sacrificed and the meat from it had fed everyone for weeks. It was a nice change from the head of a cow. Long strips of some of the mutton had been cut and then hung to smoke and dry over the open fireplace. In time the strips of meat dried like a strips of leather in the acrid smoke turning them stringy and as black as soot. For some strange reason, the flies that carpeted the walls of the kitchen and buzzed about irritatingly all day and all night long over our dinner plates didn't even bother with the bounty of dried meat hanging over the fireplace. That had really amazed me; why leave all that meat up there and come and buzz over my dinner.

The flies were everywhere in that kitchen and there was no way of escaping them. All you could do was swish them away with one hand, where upon they flew into the air and immediately landed straight back on the plate. Then you had to repeat this over and over again all the way through your dinner. I hated those pesky little things with a vengeance; because I knew they carried germs.

I had thought long and hard about how to get rid of them, even considering burning them. I had imagined gathering a bunch of straw tying it together; attaching a long pole to it then setting it on fire in the kitchen with all the doors closed and then waving the burning torch about burning the wings of the flies as they tried to get out of the way. The flies would not be able to out fly a flame; so I was quite sure that would have worked. But; I didn't go through with that idea; because I could remember once;

when I was maybe four or five when the thatched kitchen roof had caught fire and burned down.

The whole thing had happened so quickly. One morning, Auntie Ruth wanted to start the fire in the kitchen; but she could not find the matches or the matches had run out. So she had asked one of the working girls; Betty to see if there were any cinders left on the fireplace outside from the previous night. Sure enough; there was a cinder left and Betty, being a very resourceful girl; decided to create a small flame with some straw outside and carry the burning torch into the kitchen to light up the fireplace in the kitchen. I tiny piece of burning straw had broken off the tuft of straw Betty was carrying into the kitchen and floated upwards straight onto the edge of the bare thatch. There was the tiniest of breezes that was impossible to feel; but was enough to fan that small flame so that the thatch immediately caught fire.

John and I were still outside playing and saw the whole thing unfold. At first it was just a bit of smoke; so we must have thought it was just the small piece of straw flaming out; but as soon as we saw a small flame start; we began screaming fire; uncontrollably. Everyone ran outside that kitchen, then someone ran back in again to fetch the bucket of water that always stood on the black stove in the kitchen and throw the water on the fire.

By the time they had got the bucket of water the flame was already as tall as small child and as red and angry as a mad bull. The bucket, did nothing to stop the fire. There was panic and pandemonium amongst the adults. Some ran in to start getting furniture out of the kitchen and others ran to the edge of the bush to break branches off trees to beat the flames down with.

Within a few minutes the fire had run up all the way to the top of the kitchen thatch like a possessed demon and began to spread quickly engulfing the whole kitchen roof whilst the man tried to beat the flames down with branches. It was a hopeless situation; in the end all everyone could do was just stand there and watch. Gogo sat on her haunches and wailed, auntie Ruth wept bitterly. When the fire was done; the small yellow radio had been singed; on one side; but remarkably it still worked. Occasionally; we could catch the end of the news and hear about George Shaya of Dynamos scoring yet another goal. The top of the brown cupboard had been turned as black as charcoal.

Soon after that the two beautiful young maids; Betty and Joy had vanished from our lives.

Those flies hatched in all sorts of places around the farm; in the kraal; in that toilet pit, in animal droppings and they all seemed to somehow find their way to that kitchen. Dinner time drove them into a feeding frenzy and they in turn drove me crazy.

Above the fireplace the meat was preserved for a long time. When soaked in water for a couple hours and cooked it was divinely delicious. Auntie cooked the most delicious dried meat in peanut butter source fried with onions and tomatoes and served with sadza. It was a veritable feast, fit enough for the gods.

Sometimes we had dinner sitting around the fire under the stars outside listening to endless stories being recounted.

That night though was special, everyone's favourite food was cooked. From the freshly butchered sheep, tripe, folded into two or three layers around which was tightly wound the freshly cleaned entrails from the sheep's intestines so that the pieces of tripe looked like ribbed sausages. The pieces of tripe done in this way were so beautifully crafted you could not see the ends of the entrails. Served hot straight from the fire, there were so delicious you could feel God's presence; because he was right there with us, cheering us own to enjoy life to the full. This was the meal that we ate more meat in one sitting than any other occasion; because all the insides of the sheep had to be cooked and consumed all at once as they wouldn't keep for more than a day, kidneys, the liver, entrails lungs that were light and airy and felt like rubber all had to be eaten at once in one sitting.

As if we had not eaten enough when dinner was finished, a great big wok was placed on the fire and filled with ground nuts. Auntie roasted them slowly and once they were ready she mixed some salt and fresh water in a cup and poured it over the groundnuts in the wok. She mixed them gently until all the water evaporated coating the nuts with a layer of salt. When done she transferred them to a big basket shaped like bowl which she sent round the fire place with everyone dipping in, grabbing a handful of the nuts and tossing them into their mouths. This was the perfect accompaniment to the meal and washed down with that tepid warm water that stood in a big bucket on the old black wood stove; our bellies were so full they hurt a little bit.

Uncle Sizwe and Uncle Percy who were Big Mama's brothers had also come home that holiday. The two told endless stories and jokes all evening. Everyone loved those two brothers and were always so happy whenever they were home. Even uncle Bill loved them and would listen to their stories intently. He laughed out the loudest throwing his feet up in the air as he laughed with shear unfettered joy. Some of their stories were so funny we laughed until our sides hurt; but some were positively terrifying. Like the story of the man who had survived a crocodile attack; but because the crocodile had tasted his blood, it had tracked him all the way to his hut in the middle of the night, found him and devoured him. The crocodile didn't care about anyone else in the village, it only cared just for that one man who's blood it had tasted. This story was enough to make me want to avoid any and all rivers in case such bad luck ever befell me.

Up above; the sky, was completely carpeted by gazillions of stars. There were stars upon stars; stars behind other stars, bright stars , dim stars; red stars; blue stars lots of orange stars, dark clouds, light clouds; a lot of clouds. There were so many stars and they looked so close it felt like you could simply stretch out your hand real high and collect a bunch of stars in your hands and put them in your pocket.

Somewhere beyond all that I thought; as I looked up; was heaven where God lived with his angels. Life was so wonderful and beautiful at the very moment. I watched as one of those stars suddenly fell down; it's light streaking across the paddock. The next day we had been amazed to find a stream of black rocks strewn in a straight line across the paddock along the path the Shumbas used as a short cut home across our farm. We wondered if a drunk had somehow carried charcoal and tossed it along the path as he walked home in the night. Who would do such a thing, it was a real mystery to us but we quickly forgot about it.

The fire glowed red in the surrounding darkness. Small flames dancing this way and that way; creating colourful ghostly shapes. When the fire was really, hot the flames never seemed to actually touch the wood, the flames seemed to just float above the wood; yet slowly and surely devouring the wood, turning it black then red hot.

Every so often, someone would rearrange the logs in the fire, pushing them closer together building up the flames to create more light, sparks would fly up violently and flames build up for a short period.

It was fascinating to watch huge logs simply burn and disappear. I wondered what it would take to get the logs back from the ashes. I was sure that you could get the ashes back mix them up with a bit of water; but what to do with light and the heat, there I realised it would take a million years to come back with an answer.

For a long time especially in the long winter months. I wondered what heat was, why it was that it disappeared so quickly; the moment the sun went behind the clouds. I had wondered the same about the light. What if I could capture the heat or the light in a box; would I be able to release it later when I needed it, when I was feeling cold in the middle of the night. The more I thought about heat the more I was confused, what was it really I wandered; in the end I decided it was a subject to tackle when I was older.

Light on the other hand, I quickly decided I understood well. I had wondered sometimes whenever I had seen something amazing, whether it would be possible to see it again years later. I knew that some of the light entered my eyes and presumably was absorbed by my brain, but what about the rest of the light which didn't enter my eyes, where did it go. I wondered if I could years later got to the place I had seen something, then fly out really fast; catch up with the light that had left the thing I had seen before and then just wait for the light to enter my eyes again. I was sure that I could, and I was determined to try it when I was older. I knew light was really fast because the room went instantly dark as soon as the light was put out; but I didn't realise just how fast it was.

The harvest had been good that summer we had spent the day cutting the corn and standing the stocks in wigwam shaped corn stacks. This was only the start; the following three or four weeks would see us harvest all the fields on the farm. This was backbreaking work that went on six days out of seven; from first light till the evening. On Saturdays; we stopped working and went to church instead. For us boys, though the work never stopped; after church it was back out on the farm with the cattle and sheep.

Once the maize had been cut the next job was to remove the cob; from the stocks and pile it up on the ground. The next job after that was to drive round on the tractor towing a trailer loading up all the corn to bring it to the great big cement floor, near the workshop where it would be left to dry.

The evening had been long; the fire began to die down and the conversations grew quieter and softer. One person started yawning, then it was another and soon we were all doing it. Auntie Ruth asked John to fetch the paraffin lamp from the bedroom. He disappeared into uncle Bill's house and came back with the old oil lamp.

She lit the old paraffin lamp with a flaming stick from the fire, all the kids stood up to head to the bedrooms, and prepare to go to bed for the night; when suddenly there was an almighty thunder; followed by yet more thunderous bangs. This was strange as it was a clear and crisp night without a single cloud in the sky.

We wondered what was making thunder on such a night. We stood outside rooted to the spot, listening in stunned silence as the night became alive with thunderous after thunderous bangs. Far away in the hills of Shamba, the night sky was lighting up like the distant flash of lightening every time there was a loud bang. No-one had any idea what those bangs were and eventually Auntie Ruth ordered everyone to go to bed. It was like sleeping with the worst thunderstorm you could imagine.

In the morning all the palaver of the previous night was gone. It was as if nothing had happened at all.

Chapter 17 The End Of The Beginning

The school holidays soon came to an end. There was no repeat of the late night stories, no was there a repeat of the cloudless thunderstorm that had passed a couple of nights back. It had been one of the strangest school holidays I had ever had, it was a great relief to get back to school. The work on the farm had been backbreaking that summer and I was truly worn out physically.

All the old friends were still there, Piye who always travelled to Salisbury on holidays and loved to regale his exploits in the big city had the strangest of tales to tell us, the day we got back to school. Usually on the first day back at school; the teachers would stay back in meetings after assembly, leaving us free for an hour or two.

Piye recounted how; when travelling to Salisbury by bus they had been stopped by a roadblock.

"What's a roadblock?"; Shaba asked.

Piye expertly explained.

"The police put a barrier across the road; a long black and white pole across the road so that the bus has to stop. The policemen with guns had then told everyone to get off the bus and stand in a single line with their arms held up in the air".

He put up his arms in the sign of a man surrendering.

"When everyone was off the bus two policeman climbed on the bus to search for weapons. Outside, solders searched everyone. They asked some of the men if they were carrying any weapons and if they didn't answer the were hit in the stomach with the butt of a gun.

One guy was carrying a knife, he dropped it on the ground and the policeman said; what are you doing with that.

The man didn't answer he got butted in the stomach and punched and was carried into a police jeep kicking and screaming".

"What did the guns look like Piye?", even Christopher, who was a seasoned town boy was as curious as us homeboys, were.

"There were two types of policemen"; Piye explained.

"The ones in blue uniform carried rifles with bayonets attached at the end. They did all the searching".

"The other wore police khakis and didn't carry any guns.

I also saw a machine gun, on the ground with a belt full of bullets.It's barrel was resting on a three legs and it was camouflaged"; he went on.

"Kama what?"; I asked.

"That means it belonged to soldiers", explained Christopher who; like Piye; seemed to know things he had no right to know.

"Then what happened"; asked Phil.

"They let us go", replied Piye.

"We got back on the bus and carried on to town. My father said they were looking for "Gandangas"; terrorists".

"What's a terrorist?". We asked.

He raised his shoulders and shook his head. "I don't know".

The door opened and Mr Shamurefu walked in; later than usual with a concerned look on his face.

Not much learning or teaching happened that day.

The whole morning Christopher was drawing the guns that Piye had described and checking with Piye if the representation was correct. Piye explained the changes to make and by lunch time Christopher had drawn the most amazing gun I had ever seen. I had seen a pellet gun once, but Christopher had drawn a rifle with a long barrel, long banana shaped magazine full , pistol grip, and a wooden butt. He had coloured it in just as Piye had described. Finally, he was done.The gun filled the whole page of Christopher's sketch book. It was hard to believe that something that looked so innocent, almost like a child's toy could be a deadly weapon; so powerful it could kill a kudu from hundreds of yards away. It wasn't like a spear; with it's sharp and long blade, which just by its very appearance spelt death.

We finished school early that day roundabout mid day. I could tell because the sun was directly above our heads. As I walked home my mind kept going over the story Piye had told us. The men with the guns; the roadblock and the beatings. I had never imagined another grown up beating another grown up; as a grown up would beat a child. I wondered why the man being beaten did not fight back. Whenever I had a big problem to figure out; I had long found out that walking helped; just walking from school; or just walking behind the sheep my mind worked disappearing into its own little world and somehow; the solution just presented itself out of the blue. It was the same on that day as well; because; as I walked home my mind suddenly found itself many years back; before when one late afternoon we had been playing football on the dusty road between our farm and the Sogwala farm to the south of our farm; when out of nowhere a truck full of soldiers had appeared. The truck looked like a monstrous machine with hundreds of shiny metal spikes sticking out of it in every direction.

We had abruptly stopped playing and drew together to the middle of the dusty road and watched as the truck slowly approached, squinting hard to try and make out what it was. Then as it got within a few hundred yards Mandla had screamed.

"Soldiers; run for your life!"

We had scattered in all directions. Within a few seconds; I had found myself crouched in gully with John and two of the Shumba boys; a short distance behind the barbed wire fence of our farm. I had no idea; how I had got across the barbed wire fence and ended up in that gully. My heart was in my mouth, thumping so hard I thought it was going to explode through my chest; gripped by paralysing fear.

We hid in the gully; expecting at any moment, a soldier to come by and shoot us or chop us up with a bayonet. I must have been about five or six and I was sure we were going to die that day. I was waiting for the moment the bullet would strike, would I feel any pain or would it be instant death. We were huddled together, arms over each other's shoulders; waiting. When after what seemed like a lifetime, we could hear Koko; shouting.

"It's okay come out. They have sweets!".

"Guys, it's ok. Come out!".

Everyone; slowly, emerged from all sorts of hiding places and cautiously approached the truck. The truck was full of men whose faces I could only describe as red and quite scary. Some of them had fiery and red hair and red beard; some had yellow hair that gleamed and sparkled in the sun. But; it was their deep piercing blue eyes that I had found terrifying. The truck was full of them; all smiling; holding our favourite Pascal sweets and beckoning us to come onto the truck; but we were still too terrified to get too close.

Mandla, told us not to take the sweets as they might be poisoned. Although; he had told us in Shona he had used the English word 'poison' and the soldiers had understood our fear at once. A few of them jumped out of the truck.

"They are not poisoned!", see one of them said as he took a sweet out of its wrapper and threw it in his mouth and ground it with his teeth; smiling and making faces. He handed one to Koko who took it; smiling wildly ground it with his own teeth making even funnier faces. Koko was one of the Shumba boys; older than all of us. He had a cleft lip which made him speak really funny; everything he said sounded funny; so we all liked him very much; uncle Percy had nicknamed him Koko Kola; which he didn't mind at all.

Soon, nearly the whole truck full of soldiers was jumping out handing sweets to every kid. Every one loved those Pascal sweets. They were as hard as pebbles; endlessly delicious; lasting so long that in the end you simply had to crush the sweet with your teeth if you wanted to move on to the next one before nightfall.

At night when we had recounted the story to the adults we had been severely reprimanded for taking the sweets.

What if this sweets had been poisoned they had said; again and again.

The big question had remained with me for a long time; until I had completely forgotten about it. "What were the soldiers doing in Fort Milton?".

Years and years had gone by and we had never seen another truck of soldiers again.

As I walked home on my own thinking; I wondered if; the soldiers all those years back; the explosions we had heard few weeks back during the holidays; and the stories of men with guns were somehow; all related. For as long as I could remember; I had always known that war would come to us one day; but I had always imagined it would be a tribal war party; raiding us with spears, arrows and bows, and we would be able to hear and see them coming; giving us time to grab an axe; a spade and a pitch fork to fight and defend ourselves. Guns and trucks of soldiers; that was something else.

As soon as I got home it was back to business and I forgot all about Piye's story.

I quickly changed out of my school uniform; found my catapult where I had left it. It was a new catapult that Jabulani had left for me. He was no longer going to Fort Milton School and had gone back to town with the town people. Jabulani was my cousin and uncle Ben's second son. He was a completely amazing guy; good at everything he did. We called him the man with the Midas touch. He was the best football player at school; the fastest sprinter in the hundred metres race. He was not that tall; but he was big and strong; as solid as a black rhino with an equal temper to match. When he was going to Fort Milton school it was a huge benefit to us; because he completely shielded us from bullies. Everyone knew that if they touched us or laid a finger on us; they would have to answer to Jabulani; no-one dared cross that line.

It didn't matter what he turned his attention to; whether it was making wire toy cars; or catapults; his were the best looking cars or most powerful catapults. It was my rare bit of luck that he had left me his fine catapult; as well as his toy wire jaguar with old shoe polish cans for wheels. The shoe polish cans allowed the car to drive effortless over rough terrain as well as on the sand in the yard. The car was a masterpiece with built in suspension allowing for amazing; cornering and steadiness when driven at speed over rough terrain. Its driving wheel was mounted on a long extendable pole, that could be adjusted to suit the hight of the driver. He had wrapped red masking tape around the wire wheel so it was soft and easy to hold.

The catapult had a stone holder made of soft leather making it quiet, fast and accurate. In the holidays he had managed to down two or three pigeons one taken out in full flight. In all the years only he had managed to pull off such an amazing fit. The pigeons on the farm were permanently on edge. They had learned to be afraid of us; because we hunted them relentlessly. Taking down a pigeon with catapult was practically impossible; but when it happened it was one of the most exciting things to experience. It was a big enough bird and two or three of these made a perfect meal for the whole family. Plucked, gutted and hung over the fireplace until it dried; to be consumed later in the long cold winter months when meat was completely scarce.

I took out the catapult and spent the rest of the afternoon stalking and trying to shoot down birds. I was so close so many times; but as usual I never got to strike one.

That night as we prepared for bed the thunderous explosions we heard a few weeks earlier returned. This time they were louder and more violent.

"They are bombing the mountains again", uncle Bill said in a contemplative tone.

Explosion after explosion came, followed by what I could only describe as a large group of woodpeckers hammering madly away at dry wood in the middle of the night.

"Those are machine guns"; he's said.

"The war has come"; announced uncle Bill in a sad and fearful voice.

Uncle Bill ordered everyone to get inside and go to bed.

The explosions were coming from the Shamba mountains. The Shamba were several miles distant from our farm. On a clear day; from the dirt road between the kitchen and the cottage we could see the dark blue shape of the mountains rise and touch the sky all along a stretch of the horizon. For many years I'd thought that the mountains marked the edge of the world beyond which if you went; there would be nothing and if you carried on walking past them, you would simply drop off into darkness. But; after my first trip to Gwelo I had realised that the world stretched a lot further than I had first imagined when I was much smaller.

The Shamba mountains were also famous for legendary extremely tall ghostly like creatures called 'Dzangaradzim'; that lived up on those mountains and lured travellers to their deaths; by bewitching them with strange lights that went on and off, on and off until a traveller could not help but follow the lights and vanished; never to be seen again.

For a little while longer we stood in the middle of the yard watching the explosions lighting up the sky and listening to the chatter of machine guns firing rapidly.

For a couple of seconds I watched the shape and unsteady flight of the 'dawha' or 'Stupid' bird zoom above the three tall trees at the edge of the yard then completely mis-judge its trajectory and crash land somewhere in the field. This was a night bird; whose name was synonymous with stupid. The bird lived on the ground most of the time. It even made a nest on the ground by clearing a small patch of ground and laying an egg on the bare earth. It barely made an attempt to fly away or defend itself when someone approached it, preferring to close its eyes and pretend to be sleeping. It was a clumsy flier. For it; everything seemed to be a real effort.

Once; we had found one in the evening as we were preparing to lock in the animals for the night. The 'Stupid' bird had been disturbed by the cattle and sheep walking past. It just lay on the ground without moving. John poked it with a stick and it hissed at him opening its mouth wide. Its mouth was deep red lined with a yellow line that went round the inside of both beaks. I noticed that the edge of each wings had claws on it as if they had been feet before.

I felt sorry for the bird because I knew that it wasn't its fault that it was so stupid. I could tell that; somewhere along the line when all the other birds had learned how to fly properly; this type of bird had been left stuck in some kind of developmental limbo; caught between a ground animal and a bird.

Joseph another of my town boy cousins; had thrown a rock at it missed wildly. Mandla had shouted at Joseph for trying to kill the bird; because it was considered bad luck to kill the 'Stupid' bird. All its bad luck and stupidity would be bestowed on the person that killed it. We didn't want any such bad luck on our hands. But what had amazed me was; in the dim light of the evening the rock had hit another rock and caused a spark.

Such magic did not go unnoticed and soon we were all smashing rocks into rocks and creating showers of sparks. We had so much fun doing it. When we were done playing it was already dark. I collected two of the rocks; because John had found out that even; just by rubbing two rocks together you could spot flashes of light. It was fascinating.

I had always thought there was something odd about rocks. I was already sure that the there was some sort of energy trapped inside rocks and now when seeing light flushing as I rubbed the rocks together, I was sure that was releasing some of the energy. It reminded me along time back when we had ventured out to look after the cattle for the very first time; right after I had helped rescue John from drowning in the dam. Let me tell you about that first; because it is my very first memory and the moment that I became a conscious human being; unaware that this was the beginning of something that would last a whole life time.

That day John and I had been squabbling over something all morning and had managed to really annoy Aunt Lizzy; who was busy with the rest of the women around the outside fireplace preparing breakfast. She had said.

"Aren't you boys old enough to go and look after the sheep; instead of playing around here making a nuisance of yourselves?".

To which all the other women agreed vehemently.

Aunt Ruth had promptly ordered the two of us to go and find the man working at the dam and tell them that breakfast was ready. John and I had walked the mile or so down to the dam and found the men digging a trench from the dam to create an irrigation system. Instead of delivering the message we had been sent with John was distracted by the giant expanse of water in the dam and decided he want to explore a little bit.

Slowly we started wading in; I could tell right from the outset something was wrong; the ground was muddy and slippy and we weren't wading in; we were being dragged in. John was no more than a couple of meters ahead and already to his waste when I chickened out and decided to wade back fighting against the slippery mud and gentle tug of a gentle current. By the time I got out and looked back John was I already up to his chest and trying to turn back; but unable to.

He had such a look of horror on his face; I ran towards the men screaming and pointing at John in the water. The men ran so fast in the gumboots; skipping into the water and splashing it everywhere. They got to John just as his head was bobbing in and out of the water like a fishing cork; and pulled him out. He was completely soaked; like a wet chicken after the rains.

Uncle Bill instead of hugging the boy and celebrating he had been saved; was angry; busy trying to find a small enough stick from a branch to use as a whip. He was shouting.

"What are you boys doing here?"

He found one and began to whip his son.

Up until then I had never been whipped as far as I could remember; but seeing what was happening to John and predicting correctly that I would be next; I already started walking away from the scene. When uncle was finished with his son and looked up to find me; there was enough distance between us for him to give up the idea of whipping me because he was never going to be able to catch me.

"Now you boys; go and look after the sheep!"; he had ordered.

Just like that; we had both instantly earned the most amazing job on the farm and we headed out to the kraal to find the sheep.

In order to make a cutting instrument we had to find two rocks, not just any old rock, two really hard type of rock and then smash one rock into another in a very specific way. When done right the rock would split into multiple shards and some of the shards were razor-sharp and perfect for cutting anything that we wanted to cut. However; on one such occasion I had smashed one of those really hard rocks into another; but instead of shattering into many pieces one of the rocks had just simply split in half. I had picked up the two halves and taken a good look at them and to my utter amazement; where the two bits of rocks had split in half were smoking and were sparkly clean as if they had just been freshly created. I wondered how it could be possible that this rock had been lying there since even before my grandfather was born and yet, beyond the rusty red exterior of the rocks, inside they were still as new and fresh as the day they were created.

I held the two halves close to my nose and breathed in. The rocks smelled like fire; but it wasn't this smell that amazed me; but the image that had appeared in my head as I held those two peaces of rock close to my nostrils. In the briefest of moments I saw all around me a sea of black and orange molten rock stretching stretching as far as the eye could see. Then I felt the ground shake with the thunderous steps of giant animals walking, their calls filling the sky like the noise of a whirlwind. I quickly threw the stones on the ground; and asked John if he had heard anything.

"Get inside all of you, I said!"; uncle Bill ordered.

This time we heeded his advice and went inside. We prepared our beds, reed mats on the floor, an old pillow and an old blanket and tried to go to sleep. The guns and explosions carried on in the distance. I do not know at what point they stopped; because I fell asleep with them still going on; but by the time morning came; they were gone.

The morning was quiet and peaceful; as if nothing had happened the previous night. We were just as hungry for breakfast as usual. By the time we were up and ready for breakfast on school days, auntie Ruth had already lit the fire, boiled the water in a kettle to make some tea, and placed the special round cast iron pot over the fire with a tiny bit of water in it. Then she added some mealie meal with a bit of flour; sugar and a teaspoon of salt and a bit of water in a separate bowl and mixed it into a thick moist dough.

When the water in the black cast iron pot started boiling; she took a fistful of the dough and moulded it between both hands; held together as if in prayer so that the dough took on the shape of the hands, complete with finger imprints; then she placed the dough in the pot sticking it firmly to the bottom and to the hot sides of the cast iron pot. When she had gone round the entire pot, she placed the heavy lid back on the pot, adjusted the fire so that the temperature was just right and in a matter of minutes the cornbread was ready and we dived in; devouring it in seconds and washed it down with a cup of super sweet red bush tea.

Nothing could come close to filling up our stomachs as that cornbread on school mornings. Most of the time, this one meal kept us going all day long; until the next meal after school or in the evening.

I never quite understood auntie Ruth; but regardless she was an amazing woman; light in complexion and intelligent looking. Her face was timeless; neither old nor young. She had a mild and gentle personality and never raised her voice to me once. She was capable of the most extraordinary kindness one minute and devastating deceit the next. Regardless of her personality one thing was always true about her.

She always worked so hard to take care of everyone. Tirelessly cooking washing school uniforms; collecting firewood; carrying water from the well in a huge bucket on her head for three miles. I never heard her complain about the back breaking work not even once. During the school term she was the centre of our universe; that kept the farm and the family going during those harsh times.

More than any other time though; it was whenever we were ill; that she shined like a star. Taking great care of us; doing everything in her power to make us feel better. At the end of each illness; when she somehow knew we were on the mend; she always selected one of the best chickens from the brood on the farm; cooked a feast for us; served it with the delicious brown rice cooked in peanut butter; as if to welcome us back from the grips of a horrible illness.

However; as soon as that was over and done with; it was back to normal. And she would go back to her wily ways and a certain kind of ambivalence; as if all that kindness she had shown only the day before; meant absolutely nothing.

That morning auntie Ruth had prepared some African beans for us as well; a mixture of boiled beans; corn; ground nuts and 'nyimo' jugo-beans. She had placed generous amounts in old sugar plastic bags for us to take to school for our lunch. This was a day we would definitely not go hungry.

We left for school. As we descended into the valley between the two Chipembere farms we spotted the Shumba boys ahead of us. They stopped when they saw us.

"Did you hear the guns asked?"; John excitedly.

"Yes, those were bazookas!"; replied Patrick who was one of the most talkative boys I had ever known.

He did not need to explain what a bazooka was; because just the name alone; bazooka; conjured up an image of a very large and loud gun.

I didn't much like Patrick. He was one of those mummy's boys with almost everything going for him. Light in complexion; good looks; clever; so many friends; big family; a father and six mothers. He was very eloquent and able to hold attention of everyone; even though most of the time I thought he was talking rubbish; most of the kids enjoyed his company and what he said. Wherever he went; he had a group of friends around him. He had something to say about everyone and everything; but never came top of his class or anywhere near the top in the end of term tests.

"Those guns that sounded like woodpeckers; are called sub machine guns"; he explained.

I already new what a machine gun looked like, because Christopher had drawn one spewing bullets out of its long muzzle.

"But; who is fighting; who?"; John asked earnestly. It was perhaps the first time I had ever seen John without a ready made answer to any question.

"Terrorists and soldiers I think. That's what my father said". Patrick, responded; shrugging his soldiers.

"What are terrorists?"; John asked again.

Patrick shook his head and shrugged his shoulders again. "I don't know".

We walked past the valley; the road was rose gently towards the school, before descending again towards the river. The road split the Chipembere farm in two, a northern one and a southern farm.

"Look, look shouted!", Solomon pointing towards the barbed wire fence of the northern farm land. There; hanging in neat rows were dozens and dozens of bats; hanging upside down from the barbed wire fence. Their wings folded over their little bodies and heads like some kind of alien creatures. I had never seen a roosting bat; nor had I ever seen one so close; so when everyone started running towards the fence to take a closer look, I ran too. The bat's just hung there; not doing much; except for twitching every so often.

Solomon, poked one with a stick; it poked its head out and snarled; then went back to sleep behind its curtain of wings.

Patrick tried to grab one; but the moment he touched it, it sank its sharp fangs into his finger so deep the finger immediately started dripping with blood. He screamed in agony, withdrawing his hand as fast as he could; but way too late. The bat had already bitten him and hidden its head behind its curtain of wings and gone straight back to sleep.

We quickly decided to leave the bats alone, and continued to school without further delay. Patrick's face had turned ashen grey with the shock and pain from the bite. For once in his life, he had nothing to say. He stemmed the blood by pinching the bite with the thumb and finger of his left hand. Something about those bats had really disturbed me. I had noticed big fat ticks on the wings of some of the bats. It was disgusting, I hated ticks more than any other bugs. I could understand mosquitoes, tsetse flies, bed bugs that bit you, took some blood off you then flew off or crawled off; but the tick was the nastiest of all bugs; it attached itself to a host, be it a man, sheep or cow and stayed there, making itself quite at home whilst feeding on your blood. How could a tick get onto a bat; flying about in the sky at night? That really puzzled me.

As we got close to the river, I spotted a nice thick conspicuous bush; and decided to hide my bag of African beans in it as we always did every once in a while. The idea was simple; taking the bag to school always meant having to share it with with ten other hungry mouths; but if we hid them in a bush and retrieved them on the way home, the most we would have to share with would be a few friends on our way back home; sometimes with with a bit of luck I didn't have to share my bag of African beans with anyone at all; and ate the whole lot myself walking the four or five miles back home.

At school, everyone was talking about the guns and explosions the previous night. Even kids as far as the reserves in the south had heard the guns and explosions all night.

The war it seemed; had started. However; life at school didn't change; much following the guns and explosions of that night. Christopher; our class artist brought the war to life for us with his constant drawings. He drew battle scenes of soldiers with guns firing and bullets flying through the air. He drew soldiers on the battle; lying dead on the ground with tongues hanging out of their mouths and red gunshot wounds on their chests where they had been shot. He draw guns with bayonets; guns without bayonets, he draw small guns and big guns. Someone had even found a drawing of a bazooka on an empty chewing gum wrapper and given it to Christopher; who added this to his next collection of drawings. The bazooka was the strangest of all the guns. It was just a big fat pipe with a lip round one end; a small handle and a trigger. That was it. It was very unimpressive looking; yet it made a lot of noise.

By the time the school day was over I was positively famished. The thought of getting to the bush and retrieving my bag of African beans and nuts got my mouth salivating and my stomach rumbled in anticipation of the delicious lightly salted nuts. Something else also happened to those beans when they had been left under a cool bush all day. They seemed to ferment slightly; softening and acquiring a slightly punchy aroma and flavour. To say they were delicious would not be doing them any justice. They were a divine feast fit for the gods and I was looking forward to tucking in. By the time I got to the bush I was drooling, already tasting the beans in my mouth; I reached under the bush where I had placed the bag and fumbled around for it; not even caring if there might be a snake; but the bag was not there. There was no snake either. I lifted the branches, and looked under, no bag.

Panic set in, I looked around was it the right bush, yes it was, was it the right spot, positive. What in God's name had happened to my beans. A voice inside me was screaming blue murder; if anyone had stolen them I would positively kill them. I looked around on the ground, and I could see lots of hoof marks. Then, it hit me, it was a dip day and lots of cattle had passed this way to and from the dip. Somehow, a cow possibly even Manzuma had sniffed out my meal and stolen it. I had never quite realised how far school was from home until I had to march the whole distance on a starving empty stomach; all the while cussing the damned cow that had stolen my meal.

Every night we were treated to the same fireworks; huge rumble of explosions and rattling of sub machine guns in the distant Shamba hills. After a while we got used to it and it didn't bother us one bit.

The house on the hill top was pretty much completed; but we were still not allowed to move in. Almost every evening after school; John and I played in and around the new house enjoying the echoes from the big empty bed rooms or sliding on the cool smooth yellow and green floors of the two sitting rooms. It was so nice and cool and clean in that new house, we could not wait to move up there and leave our old fly and mouse infested old homestead. We also found the old cement bags made from brown khaki paper layered to create a bag strong enough to carry ten kilograms of cement. The inner layers of paper were clean, smooth and perfect for making exercise book covers. Soon I had every single one of my exercise books neatly covered with a clean brand new brown cover; which Mr Shamurefu was very impressed with.

Even as the explosions and rattle of guns every night didn't change our lives much; we could feel that the wind of change was in the air. Things were happening all around us. Every so often there was a helicopter punching through the air somewhere in the distance. Of course; we ran outside every time we heard one close by, to see what it looked like. Sometimes fast air force jets screamed past in the distance; the sonic boom exploding as it went by; as if the deep blue sky had been cracked open by the giant hand of God.

Soon the sounds of the war machine were all around us; day and night. There was always something happening somewhere far away in the distance; but never directly to us on the farm. An explosion here; guns rattling in the distance; bellowing black smoke rising from some remote village. But; it was at night that most of the action happened; the terrifying dean of hyenas laughing, jackals howling and all sorts of wild animals shrieking all night was replaced with the steady chorus of rattling sub machine guns and rumble of bazooka shells exploding in the mountains.

I knew that the war was coming for us; because at night when we gathered to eat around the fire all sorts of stories were told. Stories of death and terrible suffering. Uncle Bill said that some of the guns were so powerful that even a brick wall could not stop the bullets.

"For a house like this"; he said; describing the kitchen; "a bullet from those guns could easily go right through that wall and out that wall".

It was unimaginable. I wondered what kind of murderous weapon could shoot through walls. You could be killed by a bullet; sitting inside your house; with all doors and windows closed whilst eating sadza or (chibagwe) maize without a care in the world.

Then he went on to describe mines.

"Mines are the worst; mhani!", he said.

"They are killing people; so many people".

The name for the mines; (chimbambaira) in Shona; meant a small sweet potato. The mine he explained, the small sweet potato as I thought he was describing; was set by digging a small hole in the road; then placing it in the hole and covering it up so that when in time when; a car or truck went over the mine; it exploded and killed everyone in the truck, bus or car. I was very excited when I had him describe this. Here was something solid we could really try and we too could be part of the war.

It just saw happened that; the field by the new house had also been Gogo's sweet potato field and that time of the year; the sweet potatoes would be the perfect size that uncle Bill was describing, small and sweet. So the next day after school John and I headed straight for the sweet potato field with a hoe. We dug up a small pile of sweet potatoes; then made a small hole in the ground and buried one. The we jumped really hard over the covered sweet potato expecting to see a massive explosion; but much to our disappointment; there was nothing. The sweet potato had not exploded. We thought maybe we had dug the hole to deep and tried a shallower hole; but still there was no explosion.

"Maybe, it only explodes if it's a tyre of a car or lorry that goes over it"; John suggested.

So; next we tried rolling the old tractor wheel over the small sweet potatoes to simulate a car tier rolling over the mine buried in the soil; but once again; there was no explosion to be had.

We tried everything that we could think of; but the small sweet potatoes did not explode; so in the end we figured out that there was no such thing as a mine and I had no fear at all about walking on the roads in case I stepped on a mine and was killed. We decided those people who got killed were probably killed by something else, may be a bomb or something like that. No sweet potato could kill a man.

Still not satisfied with our findings and conclusion; we decided the next day on the way to school we would meet up with the Shumba boys and ask Patrick what he made of this sweet potato being able to blow up trucks. We had tested it and it had failed. The next morning we caught up with the Shumba boys eager to ask Patrick about the sweet potato mines; but Patrick was not there.

"Where is Patrick?"; John asked.

"Patrick is sick"; Solomon replied.

"Akarohwa nezwishiri - He was struck down by the little birds a couple of nights ago. His mouth went to one side and he can't talk, walk or move!"; Solomon explained.

This was one of the strangest weirdest thing that people from Fort Milton believed in. They believed that a witch could send a flock of little birds to strike an illness into an intended victim; and that person would become ill and die unless some sort of antidote prescribed by a witch doctor was given to him. We were all terrified of such a thing happening to us. I had even seen the little birds once as a small kid; too small to even look after the sheep.

Auntie Ruth had been cleaning some pots and pans outside in the yard late one evening; scrubbing them with a mixture of ash and sand until they were shiny and sparkling new; when out of nowhere hundreds of little birds had appeared flying slowly across the field. They flew erratically; a short distance; of about fifty yards, then landed on a tree or on the ground. They hopped along like this; for a while their wings glowing orange like fire in the setting evening sun. I was watching them and wondering why they were such lousy fliers. Were they young birds or were they just stupid.

When Auntie looked up and saw them; she was panic stricken and had called all the kids to get in the house and closed the door and window shut. We had remained shut in the kitchen until the 'little birds' had gone and it was safe to go outside. I had never seen them again; but every so often the adults would talk about some hapless person in a remote village somewhere being struck by these little birds, contracting an illness and dying within a short period.

That evening after school John and I went to see Patrick at the homestead of the Shumba's. Solomon took us to one of the many huts on the farm and pointed at a small light skinned boy laying half dead on a rickety old bed. The window of hut had a grill with a fine wire mesh net and was open and letting in a very nice cool breeze that evening. Patrick lay there as Solomon had described; curled up like a millipede and his mouth completely displaced to the side of his cheek. The last time we had seen him was when we were laughing at him after he had been bitten by a tick infested bat. I regretted laughing at him then.

"Patrick; how are you feeling?"; John asked.

"Patrick groaned and trying to say something".

John put his hand on his friend and classmate's arm and said; "Don't worry, you are going to be ok, I will see you at school soon".

I was in too much shock to speak. I wondered what could do such a thing. It obviously wasn't the birds because there was a grill on the window; so how would hundreds of birds have got in; beaten him with their wings and got out without anyone noticing. It had to be something else. But what?

Patrick never made it back to Fort Milton; he was taken to a famous hospital in Salisbury; but no-one ever mentioned what happened to him next.

By the time the second term came to an end the Rhodesian government had introduced a curfew in Fort Milton. Uncle Bill explained that the rules of the curfew were; no-one was allowed to walk around outside after dark. This meant that we had to bring the cattle and sheep in and lock them up for the night, much earlier than normal. This; we didn't mind at all. The less time spent following them around the better as far as I was concerned.

Chapter 18 The Helicopter

That summer holiday the town people did not come home. Uncle Ben had decided it was too dangerous to travel in case of road blocks and mines.

The harvest was done entirely by the workers and harvest parties who came in for the day and were done in three or four days. The harvest party was a whole bunch of people; forty maybe fifty people gathered from the villages and came to help harvest in exchange for a full meal and a drink. In three or four days the gang did the work that ordinarily would have taken us the whole of the summer school holidays. I wondered why uncle Bill had never thought of inviting the villagers like this before. It was weird at first seeing all these strangers on the farm, but when they cleared a field of maize before breakfast; it was quite obvious to me this was the best way to get the work done.

Even though that summer holiday was lacking in people; it was filled with all kinds of things. There was no time to be bored and play was no longer the only thing on our minds. The war was making us leave our childhood behind as the world around us changed. The skies were filled with helicopters thundering across the sky in all directions. The day was filled with the sound of trucks and jeeps travelling up and down the roads all day long.

Whilst the days were filled with the noise from trucks; planes and helicopters; the nights belonged to the guns. The rapid chatter of the submachine guns and the massive explosions of bazookas. The explosions were no longer limited to the Shamba hills; sometimes in the middle of the night; they felt so close that if you ran outside in the direction of the shooting for ten minutes you would easily reach the battle ground.

One morning during breakfast we had the most thunderous noise outside. The whole kitchen was shaking; the ground itself felt like it was shaking and the sky sounded like it had come alive. We ran outside to see what was happening. Low above the new house was a great big army helicopter; flying so low its landing skids were almost touching the roof of the house on the hill.

The helicopter flew over the new house; heading straight for our kitchen as we stood outside. It kicked up dust over the fields; made the guava trees shake violently. I held my breath and prepared to die. Seconds later it flew over us, thundering so loudly for a brief moment I lost all sense of being. I was just part of the noise and dust, a small insignificant spec of dust flying round and round. As it went past we could see the red-faced soldiers chatting and laughing happily inside. Its giant blade swishing round nearly blew away the kitchen roof as it went past. I had never noticed that it had another small blade on its tail. I thought the helicopter looked just like a scorpion and wondered what that little blade on the side of the tail was for.

As we stood there watching the helicopter fly towards the school; thankful to be still alive; we heard the thunderous drone of an aeroplane engine. The plane appeared from nowhere above the new house following the path taken by the helicopter. It was flying so low we could easily make out its green camouflage and the two pilots wearing helmets and dark sunglasses. We already knew a lot about this type of plane and just the shear sight of it struck terror in the hearts of everyone. We called it the 'Ray', because its tail was rectangular in shape; like the banned farm instrument we used for loading heavy loads and then dragging them along the ground.

The 'Ray' farm tool was banned because it made deep farrows in the ground; so that when the rains came; the farrows were then dug into deep gullies by the fierce rain water rushing down towards the river after every storm. As the plane thundered past I could feel my whole body vibrate and shake like a reed in water. The noise from the engines was deafening. The back of the plane looked like the plane had been chopped in half and was wide open so you could see all the red faced soldiers sitting down with belts over the shoulders and chests. Two or three more helicopters thundered past, in the same direction following the same exact flight path. By then I was enjoying the greatest show I had ever seen; quite sure by now that they didn't intend on dropping bombs on our house. Those soldiers on the plane had looked so relaxed it looked to me like there were travelling to a specific destination.

Uncle Bill observed that; wherever they were heading; there was going to be plenty of trouble. The aircraft flew east; towards the school and disappeared over the horizon; behind the rising sun.

The day to day rhythm on the farm had remained pretty much unchanged since the war had started; but every night the adults brought stories some distant village being burnt to the ground, of death; whole families lined up and shot by soldiers for not telling them where terrorists were hiding; stories of even schools bombed and burned to the ground. I still didn't know what a terrorist was; but for some reason I always knew that we were not on the side of the soldiers either. Especially if they were shooting families and bombing schools. I thought we were quite lucky; by shear accident of nature; our farm was in the middle; surrounded by other farms and a long way away from the nearest villages. Regardless; with all those helicopters and planes flying around, I was sure that it was only a matter of time before the war came to our farm. Nobody knew what we would do if that happened; no-one had even ever talked about it.

The summer holidays were nearly over and we were gathering the last of the harvest and loading it on the trailer one haystack at a time; when the tractor seized and died. Normally; between uncle Bill and the workmen Jason and Steven; they could fix any problem with the tractor; but they had no idea how to fix that problem. So they sent word to a mechanic in one of the remote villagers to come and help. The man worked on the tractor all day and was covered in oil by the time he got the tractor going again. It was already late and because of the curfew he had to stay overnight.

That night; auntie Ruth cooked one of her finest feasts of chicken and brown rice in peanut butter; followed by roasted salted groundnuts. Whilst we ate; the mechanic; an old man with a thick white moustache called Mr Mangwende; was regaling stories of the war.

He explained, how two trucks full of white soldiers had arrived at his village. It was the first time I had ever heard of the red faced soldiers referred to as white soldiers. I was sure he had got it wrong.

Then he said; "The white soldiers rounded everyone in the village up and made us sit down on the floor".

They asked us, 'Hupi Lo Gandangas?' meaning, where are the terrorists.

When no-one answered; the stood the man up in a line and asked again. "Where are the terrorists?".

"Of course, we could not tell them where the boys had gone. They beat the men up with butts of their guns; but no-one said a word".

"Ian Smith's soldiers are cruel, mhani!" Uncle Bill egged him to continue.

By then I had surmised that the boys were the terrorists; but why was Mr Mangwende calling them the 'Boys'.

"No-one told them where the Boys had gone; no-one; not even a word. You want to know why Bhebhe?", he asked.

"Because; if they had said anything; the Boys would have come back and cut their tongues out!".

"In the end; the soldiers took out their anger on the houses; set them all on fire"; got back on their trucks and left.

"Oh, my God, oh my God; Mai babo!"; uttered uncle Bill.

"And, I'm telling you Bhebhe, we were so lucky. In some villages when people have refused to talk they have shot all the men of fighting age. Twa! Twa! Like that"; he continued demonstrating with his fingers; the shooting action and sound.

By the time the evening was done and it was time for bed; all my questions about who was fighting who had been answered. I even knew which side we stood.

I now knew that the soldiers; with their guns; their helicopters and their aeroplanes were the bad guys. The boys whom the soldiers called terrorists were nothing other than young African men who were fighting on our side. He explained how; once when a village was being bombed, the Boys had appeared from nowhere, caught all the bombs before they hit the ground, and placed them gently down to stop them from exploding. I was so proud to hear about the boys; I wanted to be like them; saving the villagers from the horrible red faced; soldiers. Why did he call them 'ma-soldier machena' meaning white soldiers; they were definitely not white to me; they were a kind of reddish colour as far as I was concerned; but definitely not white. It really annoyed me that the adults decided to ignore what something looked like and decide to call it something completely different to what it really looked like. I knew that if you stood one of those soldiers next to a white car; the car would look white, and the soldier would not look white.

As the guns blazed through the night; I had a better perspective of what was really going on. I could imagine the battlefield in a much clearer way; the terrorists weren't just some sort of fuzzy mystical idea that the soldiers were fighting; they were real young African men. Uncle had mentioned that one of the older Shumba boys had run off with Boys to join the fighting; so that gave me a real concrete picture; of them running through bushes in middle of the night; jumping over dried up river beds; attacking the red soldiers before disappearing again back into the darkness of the night to hide in caves and thick forests during the day.

The fighting went on all night; but as daybreak appeared the guns fell silent and by morning it was as if there was no war going on.

Then night before we returned back to school; just as we had settled to go to sleep; in the spaces between the rattle of the sub machine guns and explosions; we heard singing. The singing went on all night. It was coming from the villages in the south east; miles and miles away from the farm. It was impossible to make out the words; but the tunes were beautiful and evocative and we knew;

that the boys must have been celebrating something special that night; for before that we had never seen or heard them; only the chatter of the submachine guns and bazookas had told us of their presence; here there and every where; but totally unseen.

Chapter 19 The Last Term

I had not noticed how quickly the previous holidays had gone. Apart from looking after the animals we had barely done any physical work at all. That was at least one good thing that the war had brought. We were now back at school in the final term of grade four with Mr Shamurefu

When we were back at school I quickly found out that everyone else had experienced the war in totally different ways. Everyone had a different story to tell.

The boys from from the reserves in the south-east where there had been so much gunfire and singing had changed and were completely different people. They seemed to have grown-up overnight. Piye explained how they had all gone to what was called 'pungwes'; and stayed up all night singing guerrilla war songs. They had all been recruited by the 'Boys' as lookouts called Mujibhas. They had started calling each other comrade so and so. Each had a different code name; given to them by the Boys. Piye was Comrade 'Wise Owl', Shaba was Comrade 'Lightning Jackal' and Phil was Comrade 'Night Hawk' because he had become the best look out of all the young boys.

I sensed an immense sense of pride in those boys. I was intensely jealous; these guys were already taking part in the war and were part of something big. An amazing change that had taken over the whole of Fort Milton; and just because they happened to live in the crowded villages they had been chosen to become look outs for the Boys. Once again; I could not believe that fortune had decided not to favour me with even something as simple as this. I was quite sure I would have made a great fearless look out.

Piye explained that they were not just look-outs for soldiers; they were also responsible watching out for sell-outs and reporting them to the Boys.

"What is a sell-out?; I asked.

Phil jumped in and explained loudly and firmly; so the whole class could hear.

"A sell-out is a dog of an African person who collaborates with the white minority regime!".

There was stunned silence; the whole class just stared blankly at Phil, as if to say, what are you talking about?

Piye jumped in and explained in a language that we could all understand.

"The white minority regime is led by Ian Smith who came from Britain and stole our land. A sell-out is any African person who collaborates with the whites!".

Phew, I was very relieved; I was quite sure I had never collaborated with any white person except that one time many years back when I had accepted a sweet from a red faced soldier and I was sure no-one else knew about it; and I wasn't about to admit it either.

At last; I understood why were were fighting. We were fighting because we didn't like the whites and we didn't like the blacks who liked the whites. It made perfect sense. But; I was now confused about something Piye had said. He had said the whites had stolen our land. We had a farm, and no white person had tried to steal it from us so; I was just a bit confused about that.

This was no time for slow coaches; whilst I was doing battle with my thoughts; Piye had already moved on to something else. All throughout the holidays the young boys had been indoctrinated by the Boys with songs; and speeches from the Boys.

Piye explained how each speech went.

"Forward with Zanu. Abacha Smith and his gang of thieves. Abacha means down. Abacha imperialist capitalist dogs. Down with soldiers. Down with sell-outs. Down with black-whites. Black-whites are black people who think they are white"; Piye explained. "Forward with the people. Alluta Continua!".

Piye explained that whites had come from England and stolen our land. For a second; I almost raised my hand to say I didn't agree with him since I lived on a farm and we had plenty of land; but from the determined look on his face I felt that he knew what he was talking about decided not to say anything.

Only when I was walking home and my brain did what it did best; solve riddles did I suddenly realise that even though we had farm and I was surrounded by farm land all around; the guys who lived in the reserves in tiny huts so close together they looked like bees in a hive didn't have much land. I had no idea where they grew their maize; because the one time I had been to one of those villages I had not seen a single field; only lots and lots of little huts stretching as far as the eye could see. I remembered that when I nearly broken my hand driven through many such villages where for miles around; the grass had been grazed to the ground; every tree had been chopped down and for miles as far as the eye could see; the land was a barren wasteland, dotted only with patches of hut settlements with a few trees near the huts; for shade or maybe to remind themselves what a tree looked like.

But still; what did this have to do with Whites stealing the land; what land had been stolen.

As I walked I noticed that the road had been freshly; 'graded' and were in good condition; presumably to allow the soldier trucks easier access. I was in deep thought when I looked up and so a jet flying almost silently high above in the deep blue sky. This wasn't a war plane. Then it hit me. Mr Smith; the farmer whose aeroplane had served us as a clock to us for so many years had a farm that was said to be the size of a small country; and over a hundred thousand cattle. He needed a motorbike or horse to go around patrolling the animals. That was what Piye meant about whites stealing our land. How was it; that one man had a hundred thousand cattle and so much land when so many lived in reserves with nothing but a little mud hut. I was so glad that I had not embarrassed myself; by arguing with Piye about the land issue.

By the time the boys had finished talking about their experience over the holidays; I wanted so badly to be a freedom fighter and run off with the Boys to join the fighting.

You're too young one of them said; you have to be much bigger to carry a gun. They are really heavy. I didn't argue with him; but I was quite sure; at 10 years old I could have easily carried a gun; I regularly carried far bigger and heavier things on the farm than guns.

The next morning, a camouflaged jeep driven by a lone soldier raced through the school yard which also served as a road heading towards the school hospital next to the school shop.

Even with the war raging on around us every night; school went on every day almost undisturbed; except that the teachers spent most of the time in endless discussions and did very little actual teaching. We spent all our time talking about the war; endlessly drawing pictures of soldiers fighting against the Boys; guns; explosions; bodies everywhere. Everything we had seen and heard about and our own imagination went into those drawings. I loved drawing aeroplanes and helicopters. Ray planes dropping bombs; whilst the Boys below tried to catch them, occasionally missing one creating a huge explosion. Jets racing across the sky at supersonic speed; it was a bit of a stretch I really could see myself flying one of those jets.

Every day the boys from the reserves had a different story to tell about their nightly meetings with the Boys. Things were changing fast; the stories were getting more and more immediate. Uncle Bill recounted a story he had picked up that day; he told how in a village not far from our farm a hut just like ours had been blown to bits by a shell. The shell had gone right through the wall of the kitchen and explored killing everyone inside.

Even as he was telling this story; we were sitting in out own kitchen roasting maize on the fire. I couldn't actually believe that a bullet could go through the wall; even one from a bazooka. I looked at the walls of our kitchen. Sticks covered on both sides with a thick layer of mud. How could a bullet or anything go through that.

Roasting maize was a fine art. I placed my maize perfect distance from the fire where the maize would slowly roast and cook deep inside. Any closer and the top layer of the maize would quickly burn turning black before the inside was even warm. You also had to select a position on the fire with lots of glowing red ambers, a flame was no good. There was nothing in the world tastier than a freshly properly roasted maize cob. In the flickering light of the kitchen fire; gentle smoke rising from the fire we listened to the stories about the war raging all around us and everywhere else in the country.

Some of the stories were ugly and sinister; quite chilling like one about a woman on the bus. This woman was going to visit her family in Salisbury when the bus was stopped at a roadblock. The soldiers told everyone to get off the bus so they could search the bus for hidden weapons and terrorists. When they got to that woman they searched her bag and found a live chameleon wrapped in one of the nappies. The chameleon is a terrifying lizard that looks like an alien from another world. When angry it hisses viciously changing colour making scary patterns; the more angry it gets the more terrifying the patterns; so you just have to live it well alone.

The soldiers had asked the woman what she was doing with the chameleon. They had accused her of being a terrorist and forced her to eat the chameleon alive. The woman had been so traumatised by the ordeal that she had collapsed and died on the spot.

The worst stories were about the punishment metered out to sellouts. Sellouts were hated with such unfettered hateful vengeance; they were made to really suffer all the way to their end. They were killed in the most vicious manner imaginable. The stories of sellouts frightened me; because it sounded to me like our own side were killing their own people. All it took; it seemed to me was an accusation from someone; a neighbour that didn't like the other person that they had talked to the white soldiers. This would be followed by the most brutal beatings and finally execution.

Stories abounded of neighbours turning against neighbours and even family members against family members and I wondered if such a misfortune could befall us. With a beautiful house on the hill; a nice big farm; all it would take was one jealous mind twisting words and making a false accusation. I didn't mind being shot or bombed by a white soldier; but murdered by my own people due to a misunderstanding; I thought would have been the worst misfortune of all and the very thought sent shivers down my spine. I prayed that the war would last long enough for me to grow up and run off and join the Boys and prove that I was on the side of the Boys no matter what.

Every day helicopters and trucks roared in the distance ferrying soldiers back and forwards and every night the sub machine guns sang through the night; supported by the booming bazookas. They were now a nice back drop for getting to sleep. We now knew the sub machine guns by other names; AK-47 or Kalashnikovs or just 'Saboo'.

The headmaster had announced that we should be very careful when walking on the road, if we saw a small freshly dugout patch of ground on the road we should avoid stepping on it; because there could be a mine buried there. I was quite sure if I saw any such patch of ground my immediate reaction would be to dig it up to see what this mine really looked like; then immediately try to get it to blow up. The desire to see an explosion really close; was just so unbelievably strong in all the boys; it was great fortune that we never actually came across a mine.

Weeks went by in the third and final term of grade four. The rains came and quenched the ground of its thirst; filling all the rivers get and refreshing the forests and bushes in the countryside. I knew this was a good thing because all those green bushes provided more cover for the Boys. It also shielded the noise from the trucks; maybe a tiny bit. I still had never seen the Boys; but I knew it was just a matter of time; they would soon come.

We were now so immersed in the war; that every night I dreamt about battles. I was a big boy, deep in a forest with a bunch of my friends; crouched around an AK-47 firing rapidly at soldiers; I was hit in the eye and woke up screaming I don't wanna die. The farm was under attack from hundreds of little helicopters no bigger than a dragon fly; John and I had guns and were shooting them down and they were dropping out of the skying burning up and thick black smoke bellowing out of them. Some dreams recurred many times; like the one where I got shot; in the eye, in leg; in the stomach, or on my butt. I hated that dream; I wanted a dream where I ran gallantly towards the soldiers; shot them and took; their truck and drove it around like mad; but that never happened.

We knew things were getting serious when; one afternoon a teacher came into the class telling Mr Shamurefu to come outside. The teacher told Mr Shamurefu a jeep driven by a white soldier with the two coffins had been gone past heading towards the school hospital. Luckily for us the lunch bell rang. We wanted to find out more about the bodies so we headed towards the hospital; which was on the other side of the girls netball court and football ground.

We stopped at the girls netball court and pretended to be playing whilst what we were really doing was spying on the truck. Two red-faced white soldiers unloaded the coffins; long boxes about the height of a man; and took them into the hospital. A few minutes later they appeared with one coffin which they helped each other load back onto the truck. They went back in and brought back the other coffin and loaded it on the truck. They both got back on the truck and drove across the football ground towards us. The jeep sped past us leaving a plume of dust. I didn't look at it as it went past in case the soldiers noticed that we were spying on them and decided to shoot us.

"I think that's from the fighting last night"; said Piye once the jeep had disappeared.

I could only imagine what this meant.

I didn't see much of John during school time; but that day he joined me at the old 'mupfurwa' tree. I had just finished trying to tell him what we had seen at school; but he said he already knew. When all of a sudden from nowhere; the Maposa cattle appeared in our paddock near the 'mupfurwa' tree. This was one of my favourite wild fruit trees. It's fruits were the size of a golf ball, with a large hard round kernel with three dots on it. Its flesh was green and had the consistency of green bogeys when fully ripe; wet and slimy. You could only eat a few of the bitter sweet fruits; anymore and you would start sneezing endlessly as if you had caught a cold. It was the place we we had seen two mambas fighting; pushing each other until they sensed our presence and disappeared in the undergrowth. John had suggested we should try and follow one; so we could see what root it dug up to try and cure itself of the bite from the other snake.

He said that someone had told him that snakes do that to cure themselves after a fight with another snake; so if you figured out what the snake used to treat itself; then you could use the same root and become a great medicine man. Of course I didn't believe that; but I did wonder if a snake bit itself; by mistake as I had bitten my tongue so many times; would it die. But besides; I was more interested in collecting the fruits quickly; and getting out of there and enjoying how those fruits made us sneeze and speak with an accent like Koko which we found really funny.

The Maposa's had new bull in their herd; Ngorima's son who was the spitting image of his father. We also had a new bull; Afrikanda's one horned son. In size the two young bulls were equally matched. Ngorima's son had lost an eye whilst breaking through a barbed wire fence and the Maposa boys had named him One-eye.

So; One-eye and our single horned bull John had name Rhino squared up to fight. It was the strangest of sights; I wanted to say to them; I knew both your fathers; they were good fighters; today it is your turn; make them proud. But somehow; a bull fight was the last thing on my mind; to see these two young bulls square up somehow did not fill me with any excitement or the pleasure it once did only a year or so before that.

I was still deciding whether to chase them apart; when the young balls locked horns. They pushed and shoved each other. One-eye had his fathers perfectly symmetrical horns; needle sharp. He gored and poked Rhino in the face and at one time managed to insert one of his horns between Rhino face and his downward facing horn causing him such pain and discomfort that he bellowed in agony. It looked like Rhino's downward facing horn was going to snap right off.

One-eye made the mistake of thinking that he had already won when Rhino bellowed in pain and took his eye off the ball for a second. Rhino saw his chance; jerked his head forward and buried his single horn into One-eye's shoulder. The Maposa bull turned tail and ran for it. Rhino gave him a little token chase and stopped and returned to his cows; victorious. That really cheered me up. We didn't think much of Rhino and yet to our surprise he had had proved us wrong.

By now we had got used to the curfew and the nightly fighting. It really seemed like the war might carry on like this forever without ever touching us. No soldier had ever set foot on our farm, and sadly the Boys had also not come. I longed so desperately to see them; even just once. The school day had been cut by two hours to allow us to finish early and get home, well before the curfew.

One afternoon after school we decided to go to the snake hills to find some wild fruits; but as we approached the hills we suddenly caught sight of a group of soldiers resting in the shade of acacia trees. They had stripes of black paint across their faces and apart from the eyes glinting in the darkness of the shade we would not have been able to see them in their camouflage. Piye told us to carry on walking and pretend we had not seen them.

"Walk past them pretend to check a few trees then turn around and head back towards the school"; he instructed. We followed his lead.

That night the fighting had been particularly intense and so close we expected our house to be hit by bullets any minute. However; come morning, when the guns had fallen silent; not a single bullet had touched any of the buildings on the farm.

For weeks the school area had been becoming busier and busier with trucks and jeeps driving past and through through the school. Then one morning after a hurried school assembly; it looked like the whole of Ian Smith's army had descended upon Fort Milton School area. Convoy after convoy of trucks and jeeps drove past the school. We stood by the windows of the grade four classroom and watched them all; mesmerised; and wondering if the world was going to end that day. It was quite clear that something big was going to happen that day.

Mr Shamurefu kept coming into the classroom, fumbling with some papers and going out again and again. Not a single lesson was taught that morning. Then finally; he came in and slumped on the chair behind his table. He tried to say something; but choked up, and no words came out of his mouth.

He cleared his throat and tried again.

"Children; he said softly; gather all your belongings from your desks, everything you own and go to the assembly point; at once".

His voice was shaky; he sounded like he was almost in tears. His face was ashen grey; I thought he looked frightened.

Nobody moved or said anything.

"Children! I said, gather your things and go to the assembly point outside now!".

I packed all my exercise books and a wooden pencil case into an old yellow Bata plastic bag. I left the textbooks because they belonged to the school. We marched out in an orderly line and went to the assembly point. Outside the other children were already standing in line or walking towards the assembly point.

I looked around the school yard and the whole school was crawling with soldiers. We had seen the convoys from the classroom; but we had not seen a single soldier arrive at the school. But somehow; everywhere we looked there were soldiers. To my surprise most of the soldiers were African. They were all tall and handsome looking; in their fine camouflaged uniforms and green berets; shiny almost ankle high boots. They stood in small groups in and around the perimeter of the school; chatting and watching us as we marched in single files towards the assembly point. A small group was sat on the wall around the old bell tree; holding their guns pointing sky high or facing the ground. They were smoking and chatting to each other cheerfully occasionally casting an eye on the procession of kids marching to the assembly point. One of them; a tall young African man whose complexion was as dark as charcoal; but with good features and wearing shiny stainless steal sunglasses pointed at the assembly point with his smoking cigarette; said something and they all laughed.

It wasn't until the line made a left turn; that under the tall jacaranda tree between the classrooms I saw the red faced white soldiers. They were all sat in the cool shade under the tree. Their red and yellow hair looked wild; sticking out in all directions. Some of them had drawn black stripes all over their faces like the ones we had seen the previous day and some had covered their faces completely with black shoe polish. Most of them had thick red or yellow beards.

As we marched past them they just glared at us with their deep blue eyes. It was like walking past a pack of hungry creatures from another world. They looked very serious. I didn't think that even lions or hyenas could be that terrifying. One of them looked straight into my eyes with those deep blue piercing eyes and I felt my heart stop dead. I wondered if this was the end for us; they were going to line us up and kill us all right there and then. Our parents would have to come later to collect our bodies and take them home to bury us.

My mind flashed back to the day so many years back when; we had seen a similar group of red faced white soldiers in a truck. That day they had given us sweets; now they were going to kill us. I thought maybe that soldier with the piercing blue eyes might have recognised me and maybe they would not kill us after all. It was a long shot.

Finally after a few minutes when the whole school was assembled in neat straight lines and all the teachers lined up in front of us looking more distraught and terrified than even the kids were; one of the white soldiers stood up and walked over to the front of the line and stood in the middle where the headmaster normally stood. He was tall; with thick yellow hair that gleamed in the mid-morning sunshine; like fine strands of golden wire. It was as long and straight as the bushy end of the tail of a bull. He was not covered in black paint like the others; and his face was cleanly shaven.

He turned round and looked at the African soldiers standing around the bell tree. He pointed at one of the soldiers and and beckoned him over with his finger; wiggling it fast to tell him to move quickly. The African soldier ran towards him; it was the tall dark handsome one I had seen earlier.

The African soldier saluted the white soldier and leaned his head towards him. The white solder explained something to him; occasionally pointing at us, the teachers and at the snake hills. The African soldier was listening carefully and nodding his head all the time; and saying, "Yes Captain, Yes Captain, Yes, Yes". The white soldier was speaking so fast I could not make out a word he was saying; it just sounded like he was saying tweet, tweet, tweet. At one point his big fat finger seemed to be pointing straight at me. He moved his hand up and down with the finger point straight at me as if to say; him right there is the one. I felt a lump in my throat. I was literally shaking with pure unbridled fear. I was quite sure that he was saying; that boy saw us yesterday in the snake hills; and went and told the terrorists where we were and the terrorists came and attacked us last night. I want you to take that boy and his friends and shoot them.

Even as I trembled like a frozen chicken, from the corner of my eye I noticed Mr Big Head walking past the bell towards the assembly line with his hands in his pockets.

The soldiers sitting and standing round the bell tree all turned to look at him. One of the African soldiers sitting on the bell tree wall stood up and called Mr Big Head over. He pointed jabbed him in the chest a few times; saying something to him that I couldn't hear. I think he was saying "Who do you think you are walking around here; with your hands in your pockets?".

Mr Big Head must have said something back; that really provoked the African soldier; because the soldier slapped him really hard. Another soldier lifter his gun and hit him hard in the stomach with the butt of his gun. Mr Big Head keeled over and the first soldier kicked him hard and shouted loudly.

"Go and stand over there; bloody dog!".

I was delighted. There is nothing in the world sweeter than revenge. Mr Big Head ran like a small child told off by its parents and joined the line of teachers. Humiliated and in pain. If only Mrs Chirashe could see him now; standing there like a mangy dog; no way would she want him now. My fear of impending death had vanished. I couldn't laugh out loud; but I was laughing on the inside. I hated that man with a vengeance; and it had come in the most unexpected way.

The African soldier who had been talking to the white soldier stood up straight and saluted the white soldier again. Four more soldiers approached and stood behind the two in front.

The tall African soldier looked resplendent in his fine, new clean camouflage and black boots strapped half way to the knee. He had removed his sunglasses and I could see he was a very handsome young man. It hadn't occurred to me at that point that he was fighting for the wrong side and I wondered if his parents were really proud of him looking so tall and handsome and able to understand English so well.

Then he started speaking. His voice was loud; clear and confident. He spoke in clear; beautiful eloquent Shona.

"As of now; starting immediately; the school will be closed and will remain closed until further notice. You are all to walk straight to your homes. You must not stop to go anywhere else. You must not run, and if you're asked to stop by a soldier you must do so without fail; and raise your arms like this!"; he said lifting his arms in the surrender sign.

"Some of you think that you are smart enough to help terrorists. Let me warn you; anyone who is found helping terrorists will be shot. Any one caught running will be shot. Anyone caught walking after dark will be shot!".

"That is all; you may go home now!".

The headmaster stepped forward to say something; but the African soldier lifted his hand up with an open palm; the headmaster stepped back in line.

And just like that; the School was closed and we were dismissed and sent home.

I decided to walk home with the farm boys from the northern farms on the main road where all the convoys had been going all morning so we could take a closer look at the trucks and guns pointing out of the trucks .

As we walked past the grade seven block classroom; the empty classroom which was also used as a church on Saturdays; the big whitewashed wall of which had been used to show a bio-scope once; there was a whole bunch of African soldiers who had made themselves comfortable against the full length of the wall. They had arranged some of their guns in a line on the open ground opposite the wall. Some guns lay on the ground resting on tripods with belts of copper and gold coloured bullets neatly stacked on plastic sheets on the soft green grass. Some guns were lined up against the wall.

There were big guns; small guns; machine guns with banana shaped magazines and machine guns with straight magazines. Some guns were camouflaged; others were black with polished wooden hand guards and wooden butts. Some guns had metal frame butts and fancy looking camouflage belts. Everyone of those guns glistened in the sun; polished clean and shiny as if they were brand new.

Most impressive of all was a huge gun that lay resting on a tripod. It was painted in camouflage from the muzzle to the butt. It had all sorts of gears and levers; and a long chain of bullets coming out of an entrance on the top or side of the gun. There was a stack of other belts on a white plastic mat right next to it. At that moment I understood what death was; the gun looked like a living monster; whatever came out of that muzzle looked like it could punch through hell itself. As we walked past it I felt as if; if a bullet hit me it would take my leg off as if a lion had taken a bite out of it. Some of the bullets stacked on the white mats were as long or longer than a mans middle finger.

We walked slowly past the African soldiers, studying each and every gun we laid our eyes on. The guns were fascinating and we wanted to hang around them for as long as we could. The soldiers looked tired most of them were laying down or sat down on the ground or resting against the wall. All the African soldiers were tall and strong and immaculately dressed in their clean camouflages. By now I knew they were fighting on the wrong side. Somehow I didn't feel any animosity towards them. They looked exactly like us; spoke the same language and they looked quite smart and happy. I wondered what crazy circumstances had forced them to join up forces and fight and die for the white soldiers.

We lingered about near the guns; trying to take every detail in. The cute little funny shaped rough balls with a handle piled in a hip on a handkerchief; what were they. The soldiers could see; how curious we were about the guns and to get rid of us they started, shouting.

"Hey boys have you seen any terrorists - Magandanga arikupi?"; and burst out laughing raucously. That did the trick and we, hurried past and started making our way home, past the big pit towards the main road.

The main road was still busier than normal; but the long convoys had stopped. Now the odd truck or jeep heading in the direction of school and sometimes in the opposite direction drove past.

We discussed the events of the day.

"I can't believe they closed the school, a month early!", Christopher said.

We all agreed that they had closed the school because there was going to be a lot of fighting near the school and they didn't want the kids to be caught up in the fighting. But now they had closed the school what was going to happen to us. I imagined myself years from then; old, uneducated, stuck on the farm heading sheep whilst other men of my generation became doctors, pilots or teachers.

"What's going to happen to us Christopher; when can we get back to school?"; I asked.

He didn't reply because right then another convoy of trucks; raced past us. Amongst the trucks was a strange shaped truck with angular back that looked like a coffin. We were quite sure that's where they put all the dead soldiers before taking them back to town.

We reached my turn off point, I said farewell to the boys from the northern farms, Christopher, Simon, Frankie and a bunch of others and started what we called the lion walk back home. We called it the lion walk; because, if there was one place that lions would be found it was this part of the Chipembere farm. It was wild and untamed; with tall sand coloured elephant grass, wild umbrella thorn trees. I knew there were definitely hyenas about because at night this is where most of the hyena calls came from, so I moved quietly and kept my wits about me. To escape the soldiers and be killed by hyenas would have been a terrible shame.

My heart started beating faster the deeper the path meandered into the tall savannah grass and I walked quietly and fast; scanning the grass for any sign of movement and ready to run like the wind at any sign of danger. I didn't feel safe until I was back on my farm. I crossed the barbed wire fence onto our farm, and walked along the overgrown path along the edge of the old Northern fields which had only been cultivated once in my eleven years of existence. I crossed the dam wall, only then did I let my guard down. I was nearly home, a far cry from the turmoil at school. Here on the farm everything was calm and peaceful. You could not tell that there was a war going on all around us.

By the time I got home; the school closing was already old news. The other kids had already arrived home and let the adults know. Either; way there was not much for me to say and nobody ever really asked my opinion of anything.

I kicked my uniform off and changed into my every day shorts and tee shirt; ate some sadza; filled my belly with some water and stepped out to find the sheep and cattle. I listened for the mooing or bellowing.

The cattle were in the paddock. I got my catapult and headed out.

The life of a shepherd is an immensely boring one. All I had; was my catapult and my thoughts. That day I had a lot on my mind to think about. Thoughts were practically competing for space and time in my head. Hold on; had they really closed the school because Piye's lot had told the Boys about the soldiers who had gone and attacked them the previous night. Ah; that's why there were so many trucks; because they now knew the Boys were nearby. Oh; God there was going to be hell.

I laughed out loud until my stomach hurt; as I played back the images of the soldier beckoning Mr Big Head with his finger and slapping him in the face and then kicking him with his heavy boot. It was amazing how the lord sometimes answered our prayers. It sometimes took time for him to hear our prayers; but if his plan was to answer; he did so in the most amazing way.

Chapter 20 The Flight of the Eagle

I had just reached the paddock when the sun was blocked and a shadow hovered over me. Something touched my head for one second. I literally jumped right out of my skin and I looked up to see a brown eagle flying off in front. Its yellow and black talons as sharp as needles curled out as if it was ready to attack. I quickly raised my catapult loaded a stone and fired. This stone went right between its two talons, narrowly missing the eagle which continued flying away soaring higher and higher until it disappeared above the new house.

My heart was racing madly, I could feel it thumping against my chest. In all my years on the farm; I had never seen an eagle try to do anything like that. I wondered if it had tried to attack and pick me up as food; but I quickly discounted that idea. I had seen an eagle dive bomb a full size chicken once and a snake. The eagle had come down on the chicken flying so fast and had hit that chicken with its talons so hard that it had knocked the chicken out cold. The eagle had still managed to land on the ground and then hop up to try and grasp the dead chicken. Auntie Ruth had screamed so loud and shoed the eagle and it had flown off without its victim. When Auntie Ruth picked up the chicken its neck was broken and it was bleeding from the mouth. Everything had happened in the blink of an eye so close to me I could have jumped right onto the back of that eagle and taken off on it.

So; I knew that the eagle had not been trying to attack; because if it had; it would have done me some serious injury so I figured this was a sign. A sign of something good; or a sign of something terrible.

I looked down and realised that my foot was about to step on a small adder not much longer than a full length ruler. We called this adder 'mhakure', it was curled up in a tight 'S' shape ready to strike. I quickly jumped to one side placing one foot on the ground whilst the other was still up. The little adder switched direction and went for the foot on the ground; but I had already anticipated what it was going to do and I jumped onto the other foot.

This little dance happen one more time then I decided to jump forward; turning my head to look back at the snake as I flew through the air. I saw the little adder disappearing into the long sun bleached grass, it's body now straight as an arrow. That always amazed me, the faster a snake moved the straighter it's body was. How did it do it?; I wondered.

I couldn't believe what had just happened. Normally my six sense was so sharp that I was able to sense danger before anything happened. This had been close; my six sense had failed me twice in the space of a few minutes. Something was very wrong. I had long figured out that things happened for a reason, nothing was really as random as it seemed. If you looked hard enough the warning signs were always there.

I looked up at the spot above the house where the eagle had disappeared and asked; out loudly.

"What were you trying to tell me; Mr Eagle; what were you trying to tell me?

This sun beat down hard; there wasn't a single cloud in the sky and it was the hottest part of the day. At such times the cattle and sheep became lethargic and preferred to lay on the grass and rest, than to graze in the baking heat. Once I had located the animals and was sure that they were not moving much; I decided to go climb the old 'nzwire' tree where I had a good view of the entire surrounding paddock. Up there I sat on a thick branch, deep in my own thoughts, rocking myself gently on the long soft pliable branch. The nzwire was long out of season; its small lime tasting translucent fruit with a bright super bitter seed long gone. We loved it for the shear beauty of its flowers and fruits when it was in season.

For no apparent reason my thoughts turned to my favourite stories in the grade four English text book. The story of the lion and the mouse; which went something like this.

'Once upon a time great big old lion found himself trapped with a noose around its neck. The lion could not free himself; however hard he tried. Days went by and many animals walked past the lion and refused to help him. The lion was getting very hungry and very thirsty. Finally a little mouse walked past the lion.

Hey little mouse cried; the lion. Please help remove this trap from my neck. With your fine set of sharp teeth you can chew through this noose in seconds and set me free.

Nice try Lion; said the mouse. But no thanks. If I set you free you will; simply grab me and gobble me up.

No; no cried lion; weeping like a little baby. I would never do that to you; he said blowing his nose and tears streaming down his face. I would never do that; anyway you are too small for me to eat; you're barely a mouth full.

Satisfied with the answer and feeling sorry for the lion who was now sobbing quietly; the little mouse chewed through the noose and set the lion free.

No sooner was the lion free; than he pounced on that little mouse.

But lion; the mouse pleaded. You promised not to eat me.

But the Lions tummy was rumbling. He had not eaten in days.

You see mouse; I haven't eaten in days. I simply do not have enough strength to catch anything else. But; if I eat you; it will give me enough energy to catch a zebra; a warthog, hmm a bit smelly; may be an Impala; very tasty I like impalas, very delicious. My favourite, you know what my favourite is mouse.

Have a guess. Chocolate 'moose'. Ha ha. You see what I did there. The lion laughed.

Sorry old friend, a lion's go to do what a lion's got to do.

With that the lion opened his mouth and tossed the mouse in his mouth and that was the end of that little mouse.

Life; I thought to myself made; no sense at all. Why did the mouse survive all that time growing up; may be have a family living quite happily in his mouse hole; then one day while minding his own business come across a hungry lion and get eaten; without a chance to prepare and say goodbye to its family. What did Mrs Mouse think had happened to him when he didn't get back home, what did she tell their children. It really made no sense.

It made me think about the many events in my life. The many times I had come face-to-face with death and had been spared. What was all that suffering for. With the war raging on around us; would I simply one day soon just get shot and die and that would be the end of that; just like the mouse.

Sooner or later the animals started getting up and were on the move again. They headed up towards Fort Milton road that split the farms and ran all the way to Fort Milton School. I followed them to make sure that they did not cross the road and go over to the Sogwala farm. Even though the Sogwalas were really nice people; I didn't like going over neighbours farms on my own. I need not have worried as the cattle and sheep made no attempt to cross the road. The cattle and the sheep were grazing in tandem with each other. They seemed in no hurry to go anyway.

I stopped by the Muzeze tree which was one of my favourite trees; evergreen; its leaves untouched by the frost in the long winter months when not a single drop of rain fell. Its branches were flexible and virtually unbreakable. You could bend a thin branch all the way round and it would not break. A few branches hung nice and low so we could use them as seesaws or swings. I climbed up one and had a lot of fun bobbing up and down on it like a seesaw.

Being alone was sometimes quite a painful business that made time move so slow. Even as I enjoyed being lost in my own thoughts. Sometimes I wished I was one of those village reserve boys. I couldn't imagine they ever spent any time on their own. Their huts were so close together if they wanted to talk to someone they could probably just shout from an open window. They may have been poor; but at least they always had some company.

I climbed up to the top of the tree and popped my head above the very top of the tree line to get a clear view of my surroundings. I could see the new house it's grey asbestos roof gleaming white in the sun. The sun was was already getting low. But I could tell that there was still at least a couple of hours before sunset when the animals had to go and the curfew started. I remember the soldiers speech. Anyone found walking around in dark would be shot. I wondered that if they really would shoot a kid. I kind of wanted to test it. I wondered what it was like to be shot. Could I simply dodge the bullets; or be hit and just be lucky and not die from the shot. I had survived so many encounters with death; and I thought it my be worth a shot.

As I surveyed, the paddock; random thoughts raced through my head. I wondered what dinner was going to be; sadza and cabbage again; or sadza and potatoes. It definitely was not going to be meat; that much I knew. I couldn't remember the last time we had eaten meat. Even the dried meat was long gone. I recalled how once; Auntie Ruth had cooked some sadza and Chomolia vegetables and because there had been very little oil left to fry the onions and tomatoes for the vegetables, she had chopped up bits of the dried meat with a lot of fat on it. In the process of cooking the bits of fat had reabsorbed some of the moisture and swelled up into little fat globules.

Whilst eating the sadza and vegetables that night I had not noticed the piece of fat in the vegetables and casually chewed; regretting the day I was born because the Chomolia was so bad. The piece of fat had burst in my mouth going everywhere; to every corner of my mouth like a bazooka explosion. When the flavour of the beef fat; with a bit of salt and pepper hit my palate, I felt as if the back of my head had been blown away. I could feel my eyes dilate and my whole body right down to my toes tingle with sheer delight. That one mouthful was the most beautiful; delicious thing I had ever tasted in my entire life bar none. It was like being reborn; like something so pure and perfect. I had searched the rest of the vegetables for another globule of fat; but there was none more to be had.

I thought about the big new house. The previous night uncle Bill had discussed with Auntie that we should seriously consider moving up there; regardless of whether uncle Ben liked it or not. Auntie Ruth, had disagreed.

"We should just wait, because uncle Ben will not be very happy; if we just moved in without his permission".

Besides; she said "It's not finished yet; it still needs painting and there's no electricity yet".

Uncle Bill had back down.

Uncle Bill and his wife never argued. They seemed to me to be in total sync with each others thoughts and mind. When I thought about it; I realised I had never seen any of my uncles and Aunties argue. They all seemed to get along very well. It made me wonder; with all that love and harmony; what had happened to my parents that they decided to split and go separate ways. What had annoyed my own mother so much; she had decided to give up her own children; never returning to see us; never writing a letter to find out how we were. I lost my grip on the branch and nearly tumbled to the ground. It kicked me out of my sad stupid self pity and I scanned the horizon with my eyes.

From the top of the tree a figure appeared walking down the path that cut across our farm that the Shumba boys used as a shortcut to get to their farm to and from school. I watched as the figure grew bigger and bigger and became clearer as it approached. The figure was walking like a drunk; staggering every so often. When it was a few hundred yards away I recognised the blue uniform. It was the girls uniform for my school and I recognised the girl. I could tell she was in some sort of trouble; maybe she had been bitten by a snake I thought. I got down that tree as fast as I could; leaping from branch to branch and was on the ground in seconds and ran up to towards the girl.

"Sipho, Sipho!"; I called out her name.

"What happened; are you hurt. You're bleeding!". There was a streak of blood running down the side of her face; down her neck on the ripped sleeve of her uniform that she was holding together with one hand. I could tell that she was very upset.

"Go away!"; she hissed without looking at me and pushed past me. She was much bigger than me being about fifteen or sixteen years old. I turned around and watched her walk away. She now walked quickly and briskly and put a lot of distance between me and her in seconds. I look down at the ground; a small brown stripped lizard scampered across the path. It stopped when I moved; then I jumped to try and catch it; but it broke its tail off and the vanished into the long grass leaving its tail wriggling about like a worm.

I knew these little lizards were really very clever. In a little while the tail would grow back again; only to break off again; whenever the little lizard was in danger. Very clever.

By the time I looked up again Sipho was gone; so were the sheep. My shadow was now more than three times my height; which meant that the sun was quite low and it was time to get the cattle in. I wished I could grow that tall one day. The animals must have known that it was getting late and were heading towards the kraal.

In the distance I heard the cattle call whistle when everyone else at other farms was driving their cattle home for the night. I drove the cattle towards the kraal and quickly reached the gum trees near the kraal. My luck was in; because the sheep were happily grazing by the big pit; a crater of nearly fifty meters in diameter nestled around fine ever green wild lawn called 'shanje' and thorn trees.

As I approached the pit I instinctively looked out for Jezebel. Jezebel was the name John had given to a huge jet black snake that lived somewhere near the big pit. We had seen her a few times crossing the gap between the patch of gum trees and big pit on her way back to her home near the pit for the night. So many times we had found the skin that she had shed overnight. The translucent skin looked like a plastic mould of a huge snake, intricately woven along the ground into thorns; sticks and bushes. It was easy to see this was not a snake to mess with; one bite from her would be the end.

Satisfied Jezebel was not around; I briefly watched the lambs doing their usual pre lock up ritual; running in and around the big pit; leaping in and out; their pearly white coats gleaming in the orange sunlight.

I was content. It had been a strange day; but now I was going to lock up the animals and head home for dinner. I was very hungry.

When the sun got to a certain low point in the sky; it turned orange or red and swelled to an enormous size, then it started dropping down really fast; if you watched it closely you could see it literally slowly descend down and disappear beyond the horizon in the west.

I whistled loudly to drive the cattle and sheep to the kraal. Suddenly; there was the loudest of all bangs I had ever heard coming from the direction of the school. It sounded like it had come from inside the kraal a couple hundred yards away. It went right through me. This was followed by the rattle of machine guns.

I hurried the animals.

"Nkosi; Nkosi!"; I heard the voice of Steven the workman calling my name, in the middle of the deafening chatter of submachine guns and bazookas. He was running at full pelt. Something wheezed above my head and crushed into a gum tree in the middle the patch of gum trees. Since the start of the war; the fighting had never started that early in the evening; it was very odd.

"Come!' he shouted.

He was in a state of panic. His voice was high pitched like a girls; I thought I'd done something very wrong and I was in the big trouble.

"What's wrong; what have I done?". I asked him trying to stay calm.

Oh my god; a thought screamed in my head. Was it Sipho. Had she told them that I had attacked her. Would anyone even believe me; if I said I hadn't. My mind raced to search for an answer; before back came the unexpected answer.

"What's wrong with you?"; Steven asked. "Can you not hear the guns? The fighting is coming this way; come now; we have to leave right away!".

I was quite relieved that I wasn't in any trouble.

"What do you mean leave?"; I asked asked angrily wondering what the fuss was about. We had been hearing guns for months now so what was his problem.

"We have to leave the farm right away!"; he replied.

"I'm not living in the farm; what about the cattle; and the sheep?"; I retorted angrily.

"Leave them!"; he said. "We have to go right now; the fighting is coming this way. It will be here any minute now".

"I don't want to go; I'm not leaving!"; I said trying to hold back the tears. My mind was racing trying to find answers to so many questions. "Where were we going to go at such an hour; where were we going to sleep if we left the farm?".

In the distance we could hear the bullets hitting trees or smashing into the rocks.

"Nkosi this is serious; do you want to die here?"

"No!"; I replied.

"Then go now!", I will will stay and lock the animals up.

I could hear the drone of a helicopter in the distance coming from the direction of the school and the constant rattle of guns.

Steven stayed behind and I ran home as fast as I could. By the time I got to the homestead; everyone was standing in the middle of the yard; by the outside fireplace. Next to them were bags and blankets piled on the ground. I knew this was serious the moment I saw all the young children; John's four or five sisters; my sister; Auntie Ruth; uncle Bill and Gogo all standing together waiting for me. I ran into the house quickly folded my old blanket threw it into my old little brown suitcase and and carried it outside where everyone was waiting. It was quite easy to pack, I only had one other shirt and trousers, my school uniform and the old rags I lived in.

"That's everyone!"; Uncle Bill said.

"What about Steven?"; Gogo asked.

"No mama; he will catch us up!"; he retorted.

"Where are we going?;" I asked John in a whisper. He shrugged his shoulders.

"We will walk to the Shumba's; from there we will arrange for transport to take us to Mai Penduka's in the reserves".

My heart sank; when I heard those words and I cursed the war for doing this to us. The thought of spending a night in the reserves depressed me. I could not believe my ears.

"Rat tat tat" the machine guns went. The helicopter chopped the wind across the evening sky swooping low and making numerous turns round and round as if it was chasing a stray jackal.

"Let's go!"; Uncle Bill ordered. Everyone was carrying something; even the little ones except for the baby on Auntie Ruth's back. We walked up the hill all the way to the new house. By the time we got to the new house the sun had already dropped beyond the horizon and it was getting dark.

We stopped at the top of the hill and looked back down towards our old homestead and the school. Apart from the sound of guns and explosions in the the skyline looked like a giant roof over a giant black hut. In the limelight the dam looked like smudge of black ink spilled on the floor; or at a stretch a giant black snake with a giant head.

"Baba, I'm tired; couldn't we just use the tractor?"; John asked.

"Be quiet you!"; barked uncle Bill.

"Let's go!"; he ordered again. We descended downhill towards the Shumba's farm.

By the time we got to the Shumba's; the last of the twilight was quickly fading.

"Bhebhe; where are you going with the children at this time of night?; Mr Shumba asked in a booming authoritative voice the moment we arrived on his farm. He was a big man; as strong as an ox.

"The fighting is coming our way; Shumba"; we're heading to the reserves.

"You are walking!"; Mr Shumba asked incredulously; looking at the whole pathetic line of us; standing there like refugees.

"Yes", uncle Bill answered.

"What about your tractor!"; Mr Shumba observed.

"I'm worried about mines"; uncle Bill complained.

"Goddamnit man; no such thing; you will never reach the reserves with those children like that. Have they eaten.

Why don't you go back to the farm and get the tractor whilst my wives feed the children. You all get inside!"; he ordered.

"Bhebhe and I will got and get the tractor"; Mr Shumba said looking at Gogo.

The Shumba wives cooked us a very nice meal of sadza and roasted salted peanuts. I had never had this combination before; but it was incredibly satisfying. Sipho had gone round on her knees with a dish of warm water for us to wash our hands. She had changed into a clean yellow dress and looked really nice. When she got to where I was sitting I was about to ask her what had happened to her earlier; but she put a finger on her lips. She was medium complexion and very pretty; but even in the dim light I could see she looked sadder than usual.

Presently accompanied by Mr Shumba; and Jason; the other worker uncle Bill got back with the tractor and trailer hooked up to it. We were all loaded up onto the trailer; Jason drove the tractor. Uncle Bill sat on the stool on the side of one of the huge tractor wheel's mud guards. The trailer was bumpy and dusty; but we all sat in silence each one wrapped in their own thoughts. I had never felt so small; so sad and so lost in my entire life.

This is not how I had imagined that war would be like. I had never once imagined that it would end up with us fleeing our farm in the middle of the night abandoning everything that we owned and loved so much.

The tractor tractor passed the Maposa's store; the last farm before heading out towards the reserves seven or eight miles away. We huddled in the middle of the trailer whilst the tractor chugged along slowly kicking up dust that filled our eyes and lungs so much that I had the idea to cover my face with my blanket.

After what seemed like an eternity; we finally got where we were going. The tractor stopped outside a group of huts next to a couple of tall trees looming over the huts. Because of the bumpy trailer my bottom and back were aching like mad.

The noise of the tractor arriving brought everyone out of the huts in the dark. Mai Penduka (Penduka's mum) stood outside watching. She recognised us and welcomed us joyfully.

We all went into her hut. It was a big mud hut with a round fireplace in the middle just like our kitchen. But; instead of chairs; around the sides of the walls were ledges that went all the way round the hut and served as the chairs. I thought it was a very clever idea; except you could not really move a ledge closer to the fire on a really cold nights. The hut had two tiny triangular windows. Everywhere around the wall were ledges that served as shelves with pots; plates and pans stacked as high as the wall was tall. Lots of plates were arranged side by sided on the ledges; and their colourful patterns served as quite pretty decorations. It was a very novel and clever idea I thought.

Mai Penduka was Gogo's relative. She used to visit our farm every so often and spent days sometimes weeks with us. She was completely mad; and would spend all night talking all sorts of meaningless gibberish to herself in her own self invented language. But; every so often she would make a meaningful statement. Her favourite thing to say was. "When it comes; we are all gonna die quickly".

I had never understood what she meant by that phrase up until that night. I understand it clearly then. All those years we thought she was mad; she knew something we didn't. Our situation then was like dying. No different at all. I had lived all my life on that farm; it was the centre of the universe to me; everything went and everything came; but the farm was always there; an unshakable solid foundation that no-one could take away from us. Now we had left in the middle of the dark, and it appeared so far away; so fragile. I wanted to pick up my bag and walk back home right there and then.

How had she known all this, the crazy woman. Once when she had stayed with us; on the farm she had found a dead chicken that had been bitten by snake. Its skin had turned completely black. Even though everyone had told her she should not eat it; because the snake poison would kill her. She had simply plucked the dead chicken; cooked it and eaten it. How amazing that chicken had smelled; two or three days she had feasted on it whilst we ate cabbage and Chomolia and sadza.

Gogo; explained our situation to her, and she listened carefully. It was the calmest I had ever seen her. She did occasionally talk to the fairies; but someone shouted Mai Penduka please, and she went back to listening.

There was not a single item of furniture in the hut. It was the fireplace, the ledges and several cow skins on the flow. The man sat on the ledges and the women and children sat on the cow hides.

All the pots on the fireplace were made out of clay except for an old Mobil oil bucket used for boiling the water. In the fire itself she burned a mixture of small sticks and dried up cow dung. I had a good impression that we had now reached the end of the world and we were all going to die.

Somehow; all the people from all around the village had come to hear our story and brought food and blankets.

This was the longest night of my life. Sleeping arrangements were hashed out and in the end turned out to be quite simple. With so many little huts in the village, one hut was selected for boys; another for girls another hut for men and yet another for the women.

I only had my blanket and a cowhide to lie on. The night was unusually cold for early November. The mud floor of the huts; unlike the concrete floor of the main houses on the farm offered no protection from the cold whatsoever. The cold seeped from the ground, through the reed mats; or cowhides and into the skin and bones and drag you down like a dead corpse.

The next morning I went outside and was confronted with the most bleak sight I had ever set my eyes on. Everywhere I looked; was miles and miles of dust with nothing growing except for a a few trees on each homestead. The slightest gust of wind or breeze raised a fine dry dust that blew into my face. I had barely drunk any water since leaving the farm and already my skin was dry and chapped. My throat sore, my mouth was dry and I was desperate for a drink of water; but wasn't sure if I should ask for a drink until I find out where the water came from.

There were dozens of children from the village; none of whom I knew. We played football all morning on empty stomachs. When I thought it was time for breakfast; that time came and went; but there was no breakfast served. When I thought it was lunch time; that too came and went but there was no lunch served. In the end I had to make do with a cup of water from one of the clay pots. The water was surprisingly cool and refreshing. I felt every gulp, seep right to the very ends of my toes.

Eventually; some time in the mid afternoon; uncle Bill had got the message that there was not going to be any food until he had done something about it. He fired up the tractor and drove back to the farm where he and Jason picked up supplies. That night everyone ate well. The news was that there had been carnage at the school. Many soldiers had been killed. That the fighting was still going and that we could not go back to the farm. I could not believe my ears. We were stuck in this bleak wasteland forever.

John and I were bored with sitting around playing football all the time. We were used to working and doing interesting things on the farm all day long. John and I convinced some of the village boys to show us where the water came from. They took us to the river a couple of miles from the homestead. There; was a dry stream that suddenly dropped down into a wide dried up river bed. The point where the stream dropped down was surrounded by dried up thorn branches arranged round the stream like an enclosure to stop animals from getting in.

The enclosure protected a small natural spring that poured a gentle pool of water up from the ground. The sound of water welling up from the ground had a calming and inviting effect on me. We descended down into the enclosure through a well worn gap. The water was clear; clean and cool. All around the spring was fresh green grass. For a moment; I completely forgot where I was. We drank the cool water directly from this spring. It was cool and very refreshing and I completely filled my belly with so much water that when I shook my stomach by wiggling my hips a little; I could hear the water swishing about as if it was in a big plastic bag.

This little spring served the entire village. Besides the spring was also a big garden fenced with this same thick thorn branches. In the garden were fresh bright red tomatoes and lots green vegetables like Chomolia and cabbage.

It was strange to see such greenery in the desolate empty place; where the heavens touched the ground in a sea of emptiness.

We were stuck in that place for days eating just one meal a day. I missed the farm terribly. There; if I was hungry there were so many fruit trees; or berries like 'tsambatsi', or pods I could visit and eat. The worst that could happen was we could visit the old marula tree find some old kernels from the previous season on the ground; collect them and smash them between a large rock and a small one to get at the sweet nuts in the shells. This place was as devoid of trees and vegetation as far as the eye could see.

The fields were great big dust bowls; and the countryside was rolling hills of brown and black patches of grass; grazed so short it looked like a finely manicured lawn. Fortunately for us, we had found that spring and; and to stave off hunger and starvation at the worst of times; we filled our bellies with the water from that delicious spring.

Every day we relied on uncle Bill providing news about the farm and when we could go back. He said that Steven, had stayed back to look after the cattle and sheep; but we still could not go back up. The fighting was still very bad. To get away from the incessant crying and winging about being hungry of the miserable little children we roamed the villages aimlessly; avoiding aggressive looking adults as much as we could.

In the evening a fire was lit outside and all evening the women cooked food for the dozens of people who seemed to appear from nowhere for dinner. The women and pretty older girls darted back and forth carrying pots; pans and baskets and after a couple of hours of frantic activity; dinner was finally served. We were split into small groups of boys and girls. For each group there were two dishes. One bowl was full of sadza and the other was full of relish, either meat or expertly fried Chomolia. We sat around in a circle and the two bowls were placed in the middle. We ate like dogs. I had never seen anything like that in my entire life. Even before those bowls of food touched the floor; the local boys from the reserve had pounced on the plates and in a minute; when John and I had only managed a couple of mouthfuls the food was gone.

When there was meat; the idea of saving the best till last cost us dearly; because those boys went for the large pieces of meat first; devouring it fast, and going for another before even touching the sadza. They were like wild animals; I doubted whether they even chewed the food; because they ate so fast. By the third of fourth day, when hunger had driven us to desperation and experience had taught us a lesson; we had become ruthless around those dishes at meal times.

It was dog eat dog. It was a case of grab a piece of meat; swish it once in the delicious thick sauce; crush it once between the jaws and send it to the back of the throat and swallow it whole and as it went down pushing against oesophagus like an angry fish; go for another piece. If you were quick enough you managed two or three small pieces and then were able to turn to globules of sadza, dipped in the source and sent down the same way without even chewing.

Another day came and went. We played football in the dusty field until we were completely grey; covered in a layer of dust. I had not washed my face let alone brushed my teeth with a stick in days. You couldn't find a fresh stick to chew the end of and use to brush the teeth because there were no trees or bushes nearby. At least the dust came came off under blanket in the middle of the night; but there was not a lot I could do about the food stuck in my teeth.

The next day was the same as the previous until I had no notion of how long we had been in that desolate reserve. I was so sick of it I would have preferred to have stayed and died on our farm. On the farm; if I wanted to brush my teeth; I just broke of a fresh stick from a branch of a gum tree; chewed one end until it was nice and fluffy then gently and expertly worked the fluffy end over my teeth until they were squeaky clean; spat out any bits and tossed the stick away into a bush. I had never realised how wonderful life was on the farm until I had to stay at that god forsaken reserve.

Chapter 21 Salvation

Several days after we had left the farm uncle Bill returned early with Jason from his daily travel back to the farm to get provisions. He had the gravest of news. Steven had died. He been shot in the leg whilst running away from the soldiers; and bled to death. They had mistaken him for a terrorist. Gogo; Uncle Bill; Jason and a whole bunch of strangers got on the trailer and uncle Bill drove back to the farm despite the obvious dangers, to bury him.

The next day John told to me; that he had found out that we were not going back to the farm. Instead we were going to go to Gwelo, we were going to go Auntie Lizzy's in Selukwe first; then continue to Uncle Ben's in Gwelo. We were not going back to the farm just yet; maybe even until the war was over.

I could not believe it. Selukwe was OK; but Gwelo was like heaven to me. I had been there once to get my picture taken for the passport to travel to England. It had been the most beautiful place I had ever seen; with wide tarmac streets and large shops on every street. It was so built up that I hadn't even been able to find a bush to stand behind and do a wee. Everything I could remember about it was beautiful and given the choice of going back to the farm or Gwelo; I would have chosen Gwelo in a heartbeat.

I was ecstatic; but remembering what had happened with the failure to travel to England; I decided not to completely believe it; to lessen the impact of disappointment if it didn't happen. But; just in case there was some truth in it; we convinced some boys to take us to the river where they normally washed. This was a big mistake; because I later found out that I had contracted bilharzia from the place.

After washing I changed into my church clothes; a nice clean checkered shirt with a navy blue collar and my old beige bell bottom trousers; that made a wheeze; wheeze noise as I walked because it was made of one hundred percent Nylon; a material related more closely to plastic and really not suitable for clothes. I loved and hated that trousers so much; but it was the only trousers I had. When I walked from church in it; it got so hot and sticky; I could not wait to get out of it and into my normal dirty, filthy; but oh so comfortable khaki shorts. Both John and I were clean and all we could do was wait and see if uncle Ben or somebody was going to come for us.

Hour after hour went by; but no-one came. Lunch time came; the sun was directly overhead; the boys from the village got together and played football in the dusty field next to the huts. We could not join in as we didn't want to get dirty. My Nylon bell bottoms were already starting to get uncomfortable; but I stuck with them because I didn't want to look like a dirty country bumpkin when we got to Gwelo.

Hours more went by and I started wondering whether this was one of those false promises; I had experienced before. We were never going to get out of this place. The day went on and the sun was already starting to head west. Still there was no site of rescue.

Then we heard it; first before we could see it. The car that was coming to take us away. Soon it came into view trailing a cloud of dust behind it. When it arrived and stopped; I nearly jumped out of my skin. It was the same jeep; that I had seen so many times in my nightmares when when we were preparing to go to England and everything had gone wrong and we had ended up not going. In the nightmares the jeep wouldn't start so had to be pushed and in pushing it I always ended up getting left behind missing my flight to England. I could not believe it. It was even the same driver; a tall happy big man with the booming voice and arms as big as cattle kraal posts.

The man shook hands with Uncle Bill and after some discussion; he ordered those travelling to climb in the back of the jeep. There was no time to lose. The jeep had a canvas back which went over a thick wire cage. We loaded up our bags in the back of the jeep and climbed in the back and sat on the floor. My heart was thumping very hard. I was thinking; if the jeep failed to start; no-one was going to make me get out and push. There was no way I was going to be left behind in that place.

The big man was in a hurry; he didn't want to get caught up in all the fighting. His job was to collect us and take us to Selukwe and get back to whatever it is he did with his life. Everyone sat on the floor; in the back of the jeep; except uncle Bill who sat in the front with the big man and another man whom the big man had brought along with him.

Uncle Bill and the big man looked back through the grill and the big man mouthed; is everyone sitting comfortably. I was holding my breath. The big man tried to start the jeep; and it croaked weakly; but did not start. My heart was now in my mouth; and I could taste the blood on my tongue. He changed the gears; pulled a lever on the dashboard that made a sound as if someone was running a plastic ruler against a grill very quickly. He tried to start the jeep again. The jeep started.

I sighed and started breathing again. There was no need to push start the jeep. The driver pushed the gear forward and jeep started moving . The whole crowd of people gathered around the jeep started waving us goodbye. We waved back. The jeep didn't take long to find the main road. There was less dust and the road was less bumpy. We were on our away to Gwelo via Selukwe. We had been saved.

I had never experienced such a moment of pure joy as what I felt as that truck sped along the dusty road towards Selukwe; away from the pure hell; we had left behind us.

Soon we reached the small town of Chirashavana with its row two or three shops on one side of the road and beer hall on the other side. I peaked outside through the green canvas and the whole place was crawling with soldiers. These soldiers were not as smartly dressed in camouflage as the ones we had seen at school; some were wearing brown uniforms and others were wearing a dark blue uniform. They looked really disorganised; some of them were holding bottles of beer which they were sipping from every now and again.

I had not seen these kinds of soldier before; but at that point; I didn't care. I slumped back against the grill of the jeep and as it slowly passed through the small town. Once past the town; the jeep gathered speed again. No-one spoke. I knew that the next town would be Ndanga. I expected the whole town to be a broken and dilapidated wasteland because in my little head I thought it was close to the Shamba mountains where the fighting had started almost a year earlier.

I must have dropped off to sleep; because the next thing I remember was the jeep slowing down and the driver announcing that there was a roadblock ahead.

The jeep came to a stop. An aggressive voice barked.

"Hey you there; what have you got in the truck?".

"I just have some passengers officer; some women and children"; the driver replied; his voice much less authoritative than when he had picked us up earlier.

"You there have a look; the aggressive voice"; shouted. He was pointing at another soldier wearing a dark blue uniform and a very nice dark blue woollen jersey.

The corner flap of the canvas was lifted with the muzzle of a gun. A really dark face appeared on the mesh. Huge bloodshot bulging red eyes peered inside jeep through the mesh.

The man placed his hand over his nose and mouth and cussed loudly.

"Go damn it! Someone's crapped themselves in there man; it smells like the sewer!". The soldiers outside all laughed. It was the same brown and blue uniformed soldiers. John peered through a gap in the canvas.

"Madzakudzaku!", he said; describing the soldiers. I had no idea what that meant; by that word; but I was quite sure that it wasn't something nice.

"I had one of the soldiers say; just ten dollars old man to open the gate". The driver said I don't have any money.

"Five dollars; then shamwari - friend". The driver looked at uncle Ben; who fumbled in his pockets and handed the driver a whole bunch of coins.

The driver passed the money to the soldier. Then a soldier smiled very cheerful and said; "Sharp; Sharp old man!"; and waved his little finger at the soldier manning the barrier to lift the barrier up. The jeep took off slowly.

As the jeep drove past; I noticed the soldier stuffing the money into his pocket with a big grin on his face. Then he put his hands in his pocket; pulled out a cigarette and lit it; letting off a puff of blue smoke. I could smell the Shamrock; even though he was a hundred yards away.

Shortly afterwards we hit a bump; as the road surface changed from dust road to tarmac. "We're on tarmac Auntie announced; speaking for the first time since we had left".

Gogo breathed a big sigh of relief. We had left the wild; and were finally entering civilisation. For the first time in days; the atmosphere lifted; and the faces of the adults looked somewhat relaxed. We were truly on our way out of the hell that had started several days earlier.

The tarmac road was smooth and consistent; the gentle hum of the engine was calming and relaxing and before long all the children including myself were fast asleep.

How we had arrived at Auntie Lizzy's in Selukwe; I do not know; for I woke up in the morning to the unfamiliar sound of traffic and a bus engine ticking outside. Auntie Lizzy's house was near a national bus stop. It was busy with lots of passengers talking; shouting and whistling. Buses were coming and going all day long.

"Yesi; Daniel"; I greeted my cousin Daniel.

"Yesi; Nkosi"; Daniel replied.

We went round shaking everybody's hand and saying hello; how are you to the adults; and "Yesi", taken from the English word "Yes" to mean hello, to anyone of our age.

Daniels dad was the little man with the workshop on our farm and was Auntie Lizzy's husband. He had left the farm years back to live with his wife in Selukwe.

After a nice breakfast of bread and jam and a cup of tea; Daniel treated us to a nice tour of the town. I had been there once when I thought I'd nearly broken my wrist so the town was kind of familiar to me. The town was situated in valley right on top of the Selukwe mountains and was a small mining town. This soil was a deep red brownish in colour. The dust from the opencast mine hung over the city and covered everything. It was on cars and buses; it was on tree leaves; it was on the flower beds and it hung around in the air and choked you making it quite impossible to breathe.

Somehow; the locals didn't seem to mind it at all. I guessed that the people who lived there must have got used to it. Daniel complained that it had given him asthma.

We walked up to the the hospital where I had been treated for my sprained hand. I had such fond memories of it. The pretty nurse had made me feel like the most important person in the world; right before she had pushed an injection in my butt. I had even managed to not cry; as the sharp burning pain of the needle hit me really hard. When we got to the top of the hill; where the hospital was; I noticed a really nice house with a nice white gate on which there was a sign; that said "Basopo Lo Inja!"

We asked Daniel, what in God's name did "Basopo Lo Inja" mean.

Daniel laughed; and said that it meant "Beware of the dog".

John and I were in stitches. Daniel couldn't help joining in.

Then John said.

"What the hell does 'Beware of the dog' mean?".

We laughed until our sides hurt; then walked straight back down the hill; back to Daniels house.

As we were walking down; a bus with the 'Super Buses' logo; laden with bags on the roof carrier kicked up black smoke as it struggled to climb up the hill from the station. I had a sense of where Daniel's asthma was coming from. The whole valley was a mass of smaller rolling hills surrounded by steep mountains almost all round.

Daniels house stood right on top of one such small hill. There was a small electric stove on a small table and Auntie Lizzy had cooked a large pot of sadza on it. She served it with sour milk in individual bowls. We devoured it voraciously. It was the first proper meal we had eaten in days; and we were not fighting with anyone to eat it. It was so nice to get back to familiar habits. I did not like fighting for my food every time I sat down to eat.

After lunch uncle Bill instructed us all to get washed and ready to go to Gwelo. It wasn't until I tried to walk after sitting down that I wobbled and sat down again in pain. I hadn't realised that whilst walking barefoot on the tarmac, my feet had taken quite a beating. The soles of my feet were black and red from the tarmac; red soil and dried up blood. Auntie Lizzy took one look and said to Daniel.

"Daniel; don't you have some old pairs of shoes that don't fit you anymore that you can give to Nkosi and John?"

"Yes mama"; Daniel replied eagerly. He beckoned us to follow him, into the next room and rummaged through an old wooden box. He produced a pair of old black Tenderfoots and and an old pair of brown leather shoes. He asked me to try the Tenderfoots and John to try the shoes. The shoes fitted John perfectly and my Tenderfoots; were so snug they took away the pain in my feet immediately. I had not realised anything was missing; but somehow with the Tenderfoots on; I felt quite complete; I was ready for Gwelo.

Once again we found ourselves waiting; not really knowing what was going to happen next. My faith and trust in promises; had long been expunged out of my soul. However; I need not have worried. Quite early that afternoon; Uncle Ben arrived from Gwelo to pick us up. We were so happy to see him and all rushed down the hill to greet him and everyone was trying to tell him what had happened to us on the farm all at once. Uncle Ben could not fit everyone in the Peugeot 404; so they decided that Auntie Ruth; Gogo and the small kids should stay with Auntie Lizzy and the rest of us would go with him to Gwelo.

This one tiny little decision, one moment in a life time probably defined the rest of my life.

We were packed like sardines in the 404, even the boot was full of bags and kids packed tightly against one another. I don't how I managed to get a window sit;

pushed against the door next to John. Daniel and the rest of the family staying behind stood outside waving us good bye. I had the window right down and my head hanging outside to breath the fresh; but dusty Selukwe air. When the car was ready; to go Uncle Ben asked if everyone was sitting comfortable and a resounding yes was the answer and the car started.

Daniel who had been standing there the whole time with a big grin on his face; pointed at me and John and shouted.

"Basopo Lo Inja"; and burst out laughing.

John and laughed a little and I hung my head out of the window; pointed back at him and shouted back at him.

"Basopo Lo Inja; imperialist capitalist dog!"

For reasons; I couldn't explain the whole car was in stitches; laughing until there were tears coming out of their eyes.

Soon the car was rolling down the hill and onto the tarmac again. The hills were no match for the 404, it climbed up and down; quickly; meandering through the narrow streets of Selukwe; until it turned onto the main road to Gwelo, and picked up speed. We went past an electricity base station that carried the power the town we had just left behind. I wondered what kind of intellect and imagination could build such a thing; would I be able to build something like that one day?.

I looked out of the window the entire journey; trying to take everything in; in case I never saw such wonders again. Trees and telegraph posts raced past the car on the roadside; heading in the wrong direction. The edge of road was marked by a tree line which was so thick it looked like a solid impenetrable wall of trunks and interwoven branches. The engine of the 404 purred quietly as the car sped towards Gwelo. The excitement in the car was uncontainable. There were smiling faces all round. The experiences of the last few days already fading into a distant memory.

After a couple of hours or so speeding through completely uninhabited wild virgin country and barely seeing any sign of humanity; the car started slowing down as the road got busier. The car changed gears to slow down. I wiped the sweat from the side of my forehead with the back of my arm. We were now driving past grand houses with green; nicely manicured lawns. Some of them had sprinklers spraying water like fountains on the grass. Some had long swimming pools with sky blue water. The houses were are amazing. I finally saw where uncle Ben had got the idea of his grand house on the hill from. Each house was surrounded by a carefully manicured hedge or brick wall and the wall was painted a gleaming white so it looked like the gates of heaven; and any minute we might see angels flying out to bless the people.

Uncle Bill commented, that the whites lived like kings; so I understood those houses to belong to whites. From the road I had not see any whites; only two or three African workers trimming the hedge or cleaning the pool or cutting the grass.

"Look at the size of that house; and the pool!. How they live; how they live!".

The houses were very big and very nice; with large gleaming white windows and each house plastered outside and painted all sorts of pretty colours; with nice pools and pretty flower beds and green lawns; but I just worried about what they ate because I did not see a single maize field or garden inside the walls and hedges of any of the houses.

After slowing down even further and going round a big round about with pretty flowers lined all the way round; with long black and white blocks. We passed a truly magnificent white house to our left; nestled in the side of a hill. The house was two stories high and had a big balcony lined by grand looking statues all painted white. On one side it was draped by a green vine with pretty bright purple flowers. To me it looked like a giant throne; a place where God himself might sit. Everything about this part of Gwelo was so pretty; and so perfect. Even the trees on the side of the road grew straight up; were evenly spaced with bright orange blooms like balls of fire.

The car was changing gears often; slowing down; stopping at robots and starting forwards again. Soon we had reached the beautiful city of Gwelo. It was even prettier than I remembered from the first and last time I had been. Rows and rows of shops; rows of tall and short buildings. On the pavements; an endless stream of people walked up and down the streets; smartly dressed and carrying shopping bags; without a care in the world.

To my surprise; there were many white people walking up and down the streets as well; crossing the road; getting in or out of their cars all amongst the hundreds of Africans hurrying around with their shopping. I was surprised; here there wasn't the slightest hint of a war going on. I was confused; I thought we were at war with the white people. I had just abandoned my home in the middle of a firestorm with guns blazing all around me; but everyone here was going on with their business without a care in the world. They seemed completely unaware of the war raging on in the countryside.

I was mesmerised and confused by the leisurely atmosphere as we drove through the town. We stopped at a robot red light opposite the Midlands Hotel. A skinny young African man ran down the street at full speed; pursued by two African policeman; one of them holding his police cap against his chest whilst he ran. The policemen didn't seem to have the stamina of the young man who was literally flying on his legs.

"Tsotsi"; uncle Bill observed. Laughing out loudly.

The robot's light turned green and we drove past an underground toilet with the sign that said "Whites Only" on one side and on the other side it read "Blacks only". I pointed at the sign and asked John what the sign meant. Even though I had an idea what it meant, I wanted some confirmation.

What does it mean whites only. It means we are not allowed to use that toilet. That toilet is for white people only. We have to use the toilet that says "Blacks Only".

What happens if use the other toilet.

"You get arrested and thrown in jail"; came the answer from Uncle Ben.

Suddenly, just like that I understood what the war was about. All that time, all those years of fighting and I had no real idea what we were fighting for. I had just thought we didn't like them because they were white and because they had stolen our land. It had never occurred to me that it was because they held us in such contempt they thought themselves so much better than us; that we could not even use the same toilet as them. I knew enough to know that whites were not from Africa and as such were guests in our country, and guests don't tell you what to do or not do in your own house. It made the blood boil in my veins to think that there were places in my on country that I would not be allowed to go just because of the colour of my skin.

As we drove through the town I could see white people and African people walking along the same streets backwards and forwards without any problems. There was no one fighting anyone. There was no animosity of any kind; between them. I couldn't believe nor understand what was going on. We carried on west and past a green flower filled park which I later found out was sumptuous grave yard. The car reached another round about this time much smaller and no flowers; but a huge tall tree whose lowest branches touched and covered the entire floor.

The car passed through an Industrial park with lots of big factories and tall chimneys that seemed to touch the clouds; bellowing black and white smoke from the top. The smoke blew westwards in the direction we were heading.

Soon we passed the industrial part and were on a narrow straight tarmac road with no road markings and no black and white blocks as before. We were on that road for a few minutes then we reached our destination. The township called Mkoba. We turned off left on the very first turning on that main road onto a dirt road alongside which were small; but really nice houses. Most of the houses had a chicken wire fence around them with plenty of garden space. Some houses also had flower hedges behind the fence. We came to a house at the end of the street and the car turned into its drive.

The sign on the gate said; 17 Chiquaqua road.

Chapter 22 Every Dog Has His Day

The house was like a micro version of the houses we had seen on the drive into Gwelo. It had a tiny patch of pretty green lawn with a small pine apple tree in the middle. It had a gate and small drive to the side of the house. To the back of the house was a garden with a couple of tall papaya trees with ripe giant papayas on them.

Then a vegetable patch of Chomolia and tomatoes and a surprisingly large chicken coup. We went in the kitchen and were greeted by Mamomdala. Mamomdala was practically the queen mother of our entire clan. She gave all the children a hug and a kiss on the cheek. I was quite sure only; she ever gave kisses on the cheek like that. It was wonderful to feel so welcome.

The house had a floor of blue tiles and every wall was painted a pure brilliant white colour. Everything looked shiny clean and new. I literally had no idea such beautiful things existed. We went back in the kitchen and sat down on little chairs. In here there was not a single fly to be seen, there were gleaming white cupboards on the walls. There was no fireplace in the middle of the floor; instead there was a tall white electrical cooker with all sorts of knobs and dials on it and red and orange led lights; I wondered how anyone could ever know what to do with it. It looked more complicated than a radio. There was a big white box next to the cooker with a great shiny handle; that I later found out was called a fridge. It kept things cold.

I didn't know what to make of that house. I was experiencing an emotional overload. Everything about this place was so wonderful and beautiful it was like heaven to me. I knew that I had now reached my Nirvana and just thought to myself; God I love this place, and I hope I never ever go back to that farm again.

All my cousins that I called the town people were there; Lindiwe, Mandla and Jabulani and the baby called Zimazile. Lindiwe offered to take us round and show us the house. She and I had always been good friends for as long as I could remember.

She started with the dining room, then the toilet.

"This is a toilet!", I asked. It was a chair with a black plastic sit on it. How do you ..?

Noticing our complete consternation; she explained how to use it.

"You lift the lid and you sit and then you flash like this!".

The toilet made a terrible noise of gushing water. John and I smiled at each other. There must be a great big hole under the house I thought to myself; completely forgetting the explanation John had given me a year or so back. It seemed he too; had forgotten because he was just as impressed with the mechanism of the toilet as I was.

Next she showed us the the bathroom, with its great big gleaming white bath tub.

"Wow!"; we all went. Next she showed us the boys bedroom at the end of the corridor, then the main bedroom which she said we were not allowed to see, then the girls bedroom and last but not least she said. The sitting room.

The sitting room was the largest room and had three green sofas; a small table two display cabinets and was the only room with a carpet. Light streamed into the room from a large window facing the road to the west and a smaller window on the side of the drive to the north.

"And that there is the television!"; she said pointing at a brown cabinet.

John and I looked at each other.

"Television", we shook our heads.

"What does it do"; we asked.

"You watch TV on it"; Lindiwe explained patiently. It comes on at night at 6 o'clock at night.

"You watch films on it, like a bioscope"; Mandla shouted from the back of the house in his bedroom.

"Like a bioscope; no way"; I said.

"How often do the films come on?". I was expecting her to say once or twice a year.

"Every day"; she replied nonchalantly.

"Every day!", my jaw dropped down to the flow.

Everyone laughed.

Lindiwe and I had been friends since we were small. She was smiling as she showed us around. It literally was one of the happiest moments in my life. I had to pinch myself to make sure I wasn't in a dream and when I woke up; I would be back on the farm or worse; that place on the reserve we had a left a couple of days earlier. Yes, it had saved our lives; but still I prayed to God that I never found myself in such a place again.

Once done we were told to go and play outside.

The day kept getting better and better. When evening came, and dinner was prepared; we were served meat; potatoes and vegetables and followed with a pudding called jelly and custard.

It was cool and refreshing and tickled senses in my head that I didn't know I had. After dinner Lindiwe invited us to the sitting room and opened the doors of the cabinet in the corner of the room near the small window whereupon there was a great big wooden thing with a grey glass front and three huge knobs.

She expertly flicked the knobs on and after a few seconds the TV screen burst into life; gazillions of black and white shimmering lines appeared on the screen, then a big circle with numbers counting down; 9,8,7 and so on until zero, then one more flicker and there was an image on the screen; sound; music. A cartoon mouse and a dog was walking on the screen.

There are barely any words to describe what I felt that evening when I saw a television for the first time at the age of eleven.

In those few seconds; I new that my life had been transformed beyond recognition and I would never be the same person again. I could never return to the farm after tasting such sweet milk and honey. I had reached the promised land and would never leave.

Next a program called "Gun Smoke"; came on. There were cowboys fighting and shooting and killing each other. So much death; so much carnage. To me, everything happening was real, I had no idea there were just acting out and no-one was really being killed. I did not find this out till at least a couple of years later.

We sat there; glued to the TV until we were told to go to bed.

That night, we slept on a mattress on the floor with nice clean sheets and blankets. That night I said a little prayer before going to sleep. I said, thank you lord for everything. This was heaven. It couldn't be anything else.

Of everything that I had ever seen; the television amazed me the most. The first time that I had ever used a mirror and seen the room reflected in the mirror I had been amazed and had wondered how a whole room could fit in that tiny little mirror. Then I took the mirror outside then seeing a line of trees reflected in the mirror. The mirror only saw what it was looking at any one time. I wondered if only there was a way to take what the mirror was seeing and imprint on something then I would be able to see what I had already seen happen again. If I saw a snake in the bush I could simply point my mirror at it and instead of having to describe it, I would simply show them the mirror in the evening as we sat down for meals.

I had been sure it could be done; but just needed a way to imprint what was on the mirror on something. The I had got stuck and told myself I would figure it out when I was older. Seeing the television I realised my dream had already been realised. It reminded me of what uncle Bill always said.

"These white people are so clever!".

That always use to get my blood boiling whenever he said something like that; because it implied that we were not as clever and I hated him for it. I wanted to prove him wrong one-day. But now; as much as I liked the TV; I felt defeated because I couldn't imagine how such a fit as making images appear on a glass box could be surpassed by anyone. Maybe uncle had been right all along; these white people really were as clever as he had said.

There was only one other thing left in the world to discover as far as I was concerned and I thought may be I could do it before too long and uncle Bill would finally have some respect for me. I wanted to be the one that would build the first machine to beat gravity; and lift humanity from the dirt on the ground. Birds could easily fly; and I respected that because they had quite big brains compared to mosquitoes and dragon flies which I was sure didn't have a brain. All these completely undeserving creatures could perform this act with ease; whilst we were stack on the ground with snakes and scorpions.

I wasn't satisfied with flying in a plane or helicopter; I wanted the sort of flying that a dragon fly or a bird did. Just taking off from the ground from anywhere and going wherever I wanted.

The next day the town people went off for the day with their busy schedules. Mamomdala was a teacher at a local school and all my cousins were also still at school. My school had been closed a whole month earlier and felt like a distant memory; a million miles away.

We were pretty much left to our on devices all day long and John and I went around the township exploring our new neighbourhood. We stayed close to their house at first; venturing further away as we grew bolder.

Mkoba was a clean and beautiful township with row upon row of small; but pretty houses with green lawns; ample fruit trees; small green well-kept gardens. Everywhere we looked was greenery and colour. At the top of the road was a prison with a tall chicken wire fence around it. To the west side of the prison; was a huge park with a fine green lawn; well manicured trees; hedges and flowers. There was something for everyone there. There were all different types people there. Some played football; other sat around having picnics. Couples walked slowly hand in hand; stopping to admire the rose flowers in full bloom. It was hard to believe that life could be so amazing.

One afternoon we had just got back after a day of exploring when the kids got back from school. John and I stood by the gate watching everyone walk down the road when we saw Lindiwe. We we ran up the road to greet her. She was walking down with all the other kids from the same street who were all very eager to meet us.

Amongst them was a boy called Elliot who lived on the same street two three houses up from ours. It was the house with the hedge with pretty pink flowers. In the group were two sisters called Tsitsi and Anna who lived in a house opposite ours a couple of hundred yards across an open field with a great big tall Tower light in the middle. The tower lights were doted around the township and stood towering a hundred or two hundred feet above all the buildings and trees spewing out rays of light so bright that it turned the night into day.

It was very strange; because this Elliot was exactly the same complexion and looks like the Elliot from Fort Milton School back home. He even sounded the same. But instead of becoming enemies; this Elliot and John were instant friends.

Lindiwe introduced us to her friends; the two sisters Tsitsi and Anna. Tsitsi was a tall girl; slightly dark in complexion with large beautiful eyes. She was two or three years older than I was; but remarkably accommodating; very unlike the girls from the village back home.

She held out her hand, and I took it and shook it as she said.

"Pleased to meet you; Nkosi. Pleased to meet you John".

I had never heard those words before and I looked at her; and chuckled graciously

Then it was Anna's turn.

I nearly fainted and passed out when I looked at Anna and my eyes met hers.

"Pleased to meet you"; Anna said holding out her hand.

I barely managed to take her hand in mine; gently holding the fingers of her hand. They were soft and smooth as silk. I could barely breathe and I tried; to say hello but the words got stuck in my throat. My eyes never left her face as she spoke. I couldn't hear the words only beautiful sweet music was coming from her mouth. She was the most beautiful girl I had ever seen.

She tried to pull her hand away; but I was mesmerised and didn't let it go. Lindiwe must have been watching the whole thing, said.

"You can let go of her hand now; Nkosi"

Everyone was watching and laughed.

I let go of her hand and stepped back and said sorry; slightly embarrassed.

Elliot and John were shaking their heads and laughing pointing at me. I went over to join them.

After that encounter the only thing that I could think about was Anna. She had the same complexion as Diana; from Fort Milton School; but unlike Diana's porcelain perfect beauty Anna's beauty was both earthly and out of this world. Her face and eyes were friendly; as if she wasn't aware of or didn't care how beautiful she was.

Either way; I was gone; finished. My heart and soul belonged to Anna.

Every day that week after our explorations around the township; we would get back in time to see the school party get back home from school so I could get a chance to see and talk to Anna.

By the end of the week; as unbelievable and unlikely as it was; Anna and I had become really good friends. Even though I didn't know it at the time; they say that every dog has his day. This was to be my day, my moment of true happiness. One afternoon, after school Mandla jabbed me in the stomach and said.

"Hey, buddy your girlfriend is asking for you at the gate; outside".

"What!"; I retorted; embarrassed and thinking to myself, I don't have a girlfriend.

I was wondering who or what he might be talking about as I went outside, via the back door of the kitchen. Anna had already let herself through the gate and was walking past the 404 when she saw me and stopped. She leaned against the car smiling.

It was just the two of us alone for the first time. She looked at me and smiled and asked what I had been up to that day.

I tried to think of something really clever to say; but all I managed to blurt out was.

"You have really soft hands!"

I wanted to slap myself as soon as I said it. That wasn't the question you stupid; stupid donkey, I was literally kicking myself in my own head.

She smiled and giggled a little.

"Hey; would you like to try my watch on?"; she asked.

I looked at her hands; she had long delicate fingers and beautiful light brown skin.

She wore a pretty silver watch. I looked at her eyes; that were twinkling with life like shining stars.

"Yes of course; I want to"; I said eagerly; nodding my big Afro head.

She took off the watch from her hand and said.

"Hold your arm out".

I held out my right arm.

"Your left arm stupid!"; she said, smiling.

I held out my left arm and she slipped her watch on my left wrist.

I tossed my hand out and looked at the time; as I had seen people with watches do. It was the first time I had ever worn a watch.

"It's beautiful"; I said. My eyes genuinely mesmerised by the fineness of the dials and the numbers stamped with silver Roman numerals.

I took my eyes off the watch and looked straight into her eyes.

She laughed; gently and smiled. "There!"; she said. "You look so handsome with that watch on now".

Then she took both my hands standing; right in front of me.

She said, "I like you more than I like Elliot".

She leaned over and gave me a kiss on the cheek, and started walking away.

She stopped at the gate; turn around and said.

"Hold onto the watch for a little while so you can tell when I'm back from school. I finish at three o'clock".

I smiled and waved at her and stood there watching her walk away.

I was the happiest boy alive. I was standing on top of a mountain with an assegai in my hand; pointing it to the heavens and shouting.

"I am king of the world. I am Shaka Zulu; Nkosi yema Zulu. Nothing; Nothing will ever stop me now!"

The next day a yellow van arrived at the house. It was uncle Julius; one of my many uncles. He announced that he had come to take me and my sister to his farm in Lower Gwelo that day. He was in hurry as he had a few purchases to make in town before leaving for the long journey home.

Uncle Ben ordered my sister and I to go and pack up our things quickly. I didn't even have time to feel upset. Uncle Ben was not the kind of man you said no to or ask any questions; you just did as you were told. When he saw the look of total fear and consternation in my eyes; he said.

"Don't worry, the war is not so bad in Lower Gwelo. You and your sister will be fine with your uncle there!"

I removed the watch that Anna had given to me the day before and gave it to Lindiwe to give it back to Anna. Packed my little brown suitcase. My old blanket was gone; it had not left the reserve and I now I felt lost without it. But; I had a few more clothes; a pair of shoes even an old mini brief that Mandla had given me, my very first and only mini brief.

I sat with my sister in the back of the big yellow van wondering what had just happened. The van headed to the bus station in the town centre. There; we spent an hour or two whilst uncle Julius loaded the back of the van; full of people who only spoke Ndebele. It was my language; soft and beautiful. I barely spoke it; but I understood it perfectly. It was then that I realised, that even though I had never known my mother who was Ndebele herself; she had left me one gift when she went away; in those threes of our life together that I totally couldn't remember; she had given me the ability to understand and partially speak my language. When the van was full to the brim; somebody smacked the side of the van a couple of times and the van set off.

I searched for my sisters face in the myriad of faces sat in the van and found it. She sat there as usual, stoic, showing no emotion, except in her eyes where the story of our miserable existence was imprinted like the pages of a book. I wondered where this part of our lives was taking us now. I closed my eyes. Wherever it was taking us; I no longer cared. I had been kissed by Anna; the most beautiful girl in the world; and did you hear that old brain?. She liked me more than she liked Elliot. Me! A complete nobody; a poor farm boy; that's whom she liked. I managed a gentle smile.

There was still hope!

I closed my eyes. A voice rang out in my ears in the middle of the darkness. There you go my son, it said. This is who you are. You are made of the most beautiful things and the most ugly things, in equal measure. You have a long road ahead of you. Mind; how you go!

The End.

Printed in Great Britain
by Amazon